Guest Workers and Resistance
to U.S. Corporate Despotism

**THE WORKING CLASS
IN AMERICAN HISTORY**

Editorial Advisors
James R. Barrett
Alice Kessler-Harris
Nelson Lichtenstein
David Montgomery

*A list of books in the series
appears at the end of this book.*

Guest Workers and Resistance to U.S. Corporate Despotism

IMMANUEL NESS

UNIVERSITY OF ILLINOIS PRESS

Urbana, Chicago, and Springfield

© 2011 by the Board of Trustees
of the University of Illinois
All rights reserved
Manufactured in the United States of America
1 2 3 4 5 C P 5 4 3 2 1
∞ This book is printed on acid-free paper.

Library of Congress Cataloging-in-Publication Data
Ness, Immanuel.
Guest workers and resistance to U.S. corporate despotism /
Immanuel Ness.
p.   cm. — (The working class in American history)
Includes bibliographical references and index.
ISBN 978-0-252-03627-9 (cloth) — ISBN 978-0-252-07817-0 (pbk.)
1. Foreign workers—United States. 2. Labor market—United
States. 3. United States—Emigration and immigration—
Economic aspects. 4. United States—Emigration and
immigration—Government policy. I. Title.
HD8081.A5N47   2011
331.6'20973—dc22   2011004563

Contents

Preface and Acknowledgments

This book is the end result of five years of research on guest workers and transnational labor rooted fundamentally in my endeavor to understand the transformation of labor markets and worker representation from 2005 to 2010. In this historical era of neoliberal capitalism, individualism, and egoism, I was the beneficiary of the time and energy of so many people on four continents who always reserved precious time to guide my research in the field and writing and synthesizing the work. The assistance and advice renewed my awareness that this book is an endeavor that originates in people sharing narratives and knowledge.

The focus of this research has been to advance understanding the centrality of migrant labor in comprehending the nature and scope of the working-class transformation in the early twenty-first century. My strong interest to explore guest work and the restructuring of the U.S. labor market has inexorably directed my research, through which I came to recognize the inherent influence of the political economy of labor markets in countries of the Global South that are sources of temporary labor. Thus, this book examines how contemporary neoliberalism and guest worker policies reshape labor markets in two sending countries—India and Jamaica—and the United States, the dominant receiving country in the world for migrant labor. This research could not have been achieved without the support of workers, labor organizations, and academic institutions.

I was fortunate to have access to important archival documents, and learned a great deal from research conducted at the International Institute for Social History (IISG) in Amsterdam. Marcel van der Linden, research director of the

IISG, provided critical historical direction and guidance through explaining intricate history of U.S. and European trade unions and labor migration in the last two centuries. In New York, I also benefited from the use of the labor archives at the Tamiment Library and Robert F. Wagner Archives, headed by Michael Nash. I also am thankful for the use of research and archival materials at the University of the West Indies, in Mona, Jamaica; research at the Centre for Economic and Social Studies in Hyderabad, India; and the Institute for Social Development, Kolkata, at the University of Calcutta.

This book benefited immensely from the advice and critical comments of authorities on labor migration throughout the world. Numerous specialists have shared their time to explain the intricacies and trajectories of local, transnational, and global labor migration. I am most grateful to workers in India, Jamaica, and the United States who spoke with me and allowed me to write down their experiences. I would like to thank each worker individually for their time, but most have asked that I keep their names anonymous to protect their identities to ensure they are not discriminated against by government migration agencies and labor contractors. In addition, I would like to thank workers in the United States of all nationalities who also shared their experiences, from displaced employees to guest workers themselves. Thus, to ensure migrant guest workers' identities remain confidential, I have used pseudonyms to identify all the guest workers interviewed.

In India, I would like to especially thank Dr. Arun Kumar of the Centre for Economic and Social Studies in Hyderabad, who spent days interviewing low-wage workers in Telugu and translating the narratives into English. I also thank Kunal Chattopadhyay, professor of history at Jadavpur University in Kolkata, who carefully read and commented on the manuscript. I also thank Debdas Banerjee and Amiya Kumar Bagchi of the Institute for Social Development in Kolkata for sharing their exhaustive and detailed knowledge of labor and the Indian political economy.

My research on Jamaica notably was advanced by my conversations with Obika Gray of the University of Wisconsin, Eau Claire. In Kingston and New York City, I thank Kevin Gusscott for arranging incisive interviews with workers and students who traveled and were planning to embark on their journey in the United States. I particularly express gratitude to Olivia McDermott and Wynsome Eminike, present and past graduate students at City University of New York, who imparted indispensable knowledge of Jamaica's contemporary abusive system of labor recruitment and contracting for hospitality workers. Maderie Pam Miller, an astute observer of the

Jamaican political economy, labor market, and popular culture provided perceptive advice that advanced this project from beginning to end.

In other regions, I am grateful to Edson Urano of the University of Tsukuba, Japan, and Hirohiko Takasu, project director of the Research and Education Center for Fair Labor at Hitotsubashi University in Tokyo, who provided important comments on my research, advice, and guidance on labor migration policies in Japan and throughout the world.

I received important institutional support to conduct research from Brooklyn College and the City University of New York. A Tow Faculty Travel Grant that I received covered my travel expenses in India. In addition, I am grateful for travel funding from the PSC-CUNY Research Foundation for my research trips to Jamaica. I thank the University of Massachusetts Labor Center for a grant to commission my research among guest workers in the Cape Cod region, a major destination for guest workers from Jamaica, who are vital to servicing the region's tourist economy.

I especially thank Beverly Tomek, a historian of nineteenth-century U.S. migration, for relentlessly encouraging me to finish this manuscript, taking the time to read and have a second look at this book, and urging me to finish this work. I thank all others who have advised me on this project, especially Steve Bronner, Michael Goldfield, and Joseph Ness.

I am indebted to the two reviewers for the University of Illinois Press who helped focus this research and provided sage advice on my assessment of labor migration, which was indispensable in helping to transform the manuscript into a book. Also at the University of Illinois Press, I thank Laurie Matheson for her interest in this work and her dedication in shepherding this manuscript to publication, and I appreciate the guidance of senior editor Tad Ringo. Additionally, I would like to thank the copyeditor, Walt Evans. Last, I am most thankful to my family and friends, who tolerate frequent absences and detachment from customary activities of life to devote my attention on research and writing.

INTRODUCTION

Guest Workers of the World

Much of the present debate on immigration policy revolves around the failure and unintended consequences of utterly inconsistent U.S. government policies to establish and regulate the flow of authorized and unauthorized migrants. Ineffectual regulatory policies have bifurcated migrant workers into two groups—undocumented laborers and guest workers. Focusing on guest workers rather than on undocumented laborers foreshadows the potential prospects and pitfalls of the program for foreign workers as well as U.S. nationals, and the potential influence of such a program on the broader labor movement and working class. This book shows that if government and corporate efforts to replace undocumented laborers with an established guest worker labor force succeed, conditions for all workers will significantly diminish.

Focusing on the United States as the world's leading recipient of foreign workers, this book examines the intersection between labor, capital, and government policies in advancing corporate profits. As we have seen in past immigration bills, government programs are plagued with uncertainty and doubt. Can the federal government seriously address the status of more than twelve million undocumented migrants in the United States that most employers welcome in flagrant defiance of the 1986 Immigration Reform and Control Act (IRCA) law? Since 2000, the AFL-CIO and most major unions adopted a policy for repeal of Public Law 99-603 of IRCA, which sanctions "employers who knowingly hire undocumented workers" (USCIS 2010a). But if a new comprehensive bill is enacted repealing the most harmful provisions of existing law for undocumented immigrants, most proposals have called on a new guest worker law that will institutionally marginalize temporary workers. Furthermore, if the new legislation moves most undocumented workers into a guest worker program, many unions that have grown by organizing low-wage service workers conceivably could suffer significant loss in membership.

New Migration Policy Proposals

The U.S. government propaganda machine and the media greatly exaggerate and overstate foreigners' conviction that they will improve their living standard by working in the United States. To be sure, laboring in the hub of the *empire* might provide help to some workers, but only in the unlikely event that economic conditions improve soon; most migrants expect to return to their home countries. Why must global capitalists push, pull, shove, or force migrant workers to travel to the United States just for economic sustenance? The evidence in this book is that most unauthorized migrants do not enthusiastically go to the United States. Unlike some guest workers, the decision to migrate without authorization across the U.S. border does not represent a significant advance in wages but an economic necessity. Migrants risk life and limb in exchange for a job with low pay, low status, and lack of voice. It is not the job that degrades the worker but, rather, the powerless and poor conditions under which they labor.

Since 2004, government policymakers have sought to formulate a new migration policy that addresses the authentic reality of the dramatic growth of foreigners living and working in the United States in the neoliberal era. The failure to develop a consistent migration policy over the past twenty-five years in part is an extension of the enduring conflict between capital and labor. The weakening of the institutional and economic power of organized labor has contributed to growing nativist sentiment that ironically prevents capital from permitting unfettered migration. This development is eroding the base of the conservative movement and Republican Party that, since the early 1970s, has unified social conservatives and neoliberal capitalists. The resurgence and growth of nativism obstructs comprehensive immigration reform that would legalize undocumented immigrants and allow unfettered migration supported by capitalists.

In the absence of an enforceable immigration law to replace IRCA, as a result of growing poverty in the Caribbean and Latin America, migrant workers will continue to enter the United States with and without authorization, benefiting firms seeking low-wage workers and endangering the lives and human rights of newcomers through militarizing the border, labor contracting, and trafficking and creating a class of workers who can be arrested and deported at any time. Indeed, the intensification of enforcement since 2005 has set in motion a growing number of arrests, as object lessons to twelve to fourteen million undocumented immigrants in the United States from 1985 to 2010 (Cornelius & Lewis 2006; Kanstroom 2007; Sullivan). Figure 1.1 shows the dramatic increase in ICE enforcement arrest rates in worksites from 2002 to 2008.

But capital needs low-wage migrants, whether through legal measures or relaxed enforcement measures; if it cannot get cheap labor through a new migration law, undocumented immigrant workers will continue to work in the U.S. economy under constant threat of deportation. In view of the growth of working-class nativism, U.S. business has sought to advance a guest work program, without a path to citizenship, to reinforce control over a foreign labor force that will fear union organizing and is exposed to labor, workplace, and human rights violations. If a new policy is advanced that greatly enhances the guest work program, workers will cross the U.S. border legally; but under onerous and exploitative conditions that may become as abusive as indentured servitude, only *legal* guest workers will not have the opportunity to buy their freedom, as individuals had in the nineteenth century.

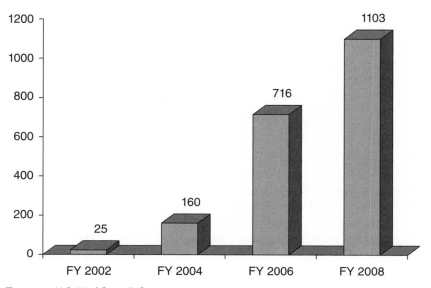

Figure 1.1. U.S. Workforce Enforcement Arrests: Fiscal Year 2002–2008. Source: U.S. Immigration and Customs Enforcement. April 30, 2009.

For the period 1852 to 1882, Terry Boswell demonstrates that employers and the state manipulated Chinese racial and ethnic differences as a means of lowering labor costs for all workers in the era, leading to the Chinese Exclusion Act (Boswell 1986, 352–53). Through use of "split labor markets" between white, black, and Asian labor, employers diminished the capacity of workers to move up the labor market to higher-paying jobs.[1]

A better policy toward immigration would recognize the need to increase wages in lower skilled jobs that once formed the base of the labor movement. Although some proponents of open migration argue that immigrants are a source of technological innovation and productivity, the fact remains that they are exploited at a higher rate than U.S.-born workers.

All new immigration proposals would almost certainly contribute to an enlarged guest work program that would further the erosion of decent-wage unionized jobs. I argue that it is not enough just to organize immigrants who may eventually gain green cards and citizenship through immigration reform for those who did not gain status under the 1986 reform; rather, the United States must also provide guest workers human rights, including the ability to organize and join unions. Because temporary workers are virtually power-less institutionally, business can easily resist mobilization attempts through sending militant workers back to their home countries.

Corporate Repression and Worker Resistance

This book will show how the expansion of guest worker programs is intended to increase profits for the capitalist class by further disciplining labor at home and abroad. Financial corporations benefit most from the restructuring of labor markets across gender, nationality, and race. I argue further that both U.S.-born and foreign-born workers will suffer from enacting a guest work program that fails to permit worker organizing. While undocumented work-ers face an endless fear of deportation, under current law they still can join unions to raise their wages and improve their conditions in the workplace. Guest workers, on the other hand, must go home upon completion of the job and have little or no recourse to join unions. Why establish a dichotomy among immigrants and divide one group against the other? The goal is to control all workers. The capitalist class learned from the massive and wide-spread May Day protests of hundreds of thousands of U.S. immigrants in 2006 in New York, Chicago, and especially Los Angeles that foreign workers will exercise democratic rights of expression to push for better conditions.

The mass actions also confirmed that undocumented immigrants opposed a plan that consigns all migrants to subordinate conditions in the process of legalization, and many oppose the guest work legislation that allows corporations and labor contractors to prevent worker mobilization and unionization through threats of deportation.[2]

Global Migration and the U.S. Working Class

But what of U.S.-born workers? How do they fit into this picture? Over the course of the past decade, a wave of mainstream scholarly and popular literature has appeared detailing the existence of a labor shortage in the United States. New research—by a wide ideological spectrum of scholars—concludes that U.S. workers are unqualified or unwilling to fill jobs in the *new economy,* a euphemism coined by business management to suggest that labor must engage in concessions to remain competitive on a global scale. In reality, the term *new economy* is a means for employers to justify undermining the power of workers through preventing worker self-activity to improve wages and working conditions through forming labor unions, striking, and other forms of direct action. Consequently, pundits maintain that the United States must enact policies that make possible the availability of foreign workers for positions that business is unable to fill (Friedman 2005; Levy & Murnane 2004).

Both liberal and conservative politicians whose districts benefit from foreign labor conveniently argue that globalization necessitates a free flow of migrant labor to fill needed positions. To appeal to nativist sentiment, conservative and Republican officials are vilifying undocumented migrant workers for taking away jobs. Yet these very same officials who seek the votes of working-class U.S. workers are actively advocating guest worker programs to promote business interests in their states and districts that would in some measure placate nativist xenophobic sentiment against permanent immigration. The corporate-dominated mass media in the United States and Europe do not consider inequality and immiseration caused by the imposition of neoliberal policies in poor countries as triggers for growing migration of impoverished workers and peasants (Dobbs 2004; Faux 2006; Ginsborg 2005).

While capital has always supported unregulated migration in the United States, Congress and the president must walk a thin line to create the impression they are tough on restricting unauthorized immigration while responding to business demands for cheap foreign labor through expanding guest worker programs. Less than one month after midterm elections in November 1990, Congress relaxed restrictions on immigration (USCIS 2010b).

Outline of the Book

The following chapters make the case that an expanded migrant labor force based on current guest worker programs is a means to maintain an orderly, steady, and continuous flow of compliant laborers in a larger range of labor markets. In chapter 1, we examine the new neoliberal phase of corporate restructuring that is producing a new foreign workforce that will have even less power than undocumented workers today. In this hostile environment, the working class and organized labor in the United States and throughout the world must search for a means to counter neoliberal reforms that only benefit corporations at the expense of workers everywhere. But unions must reject business as usual and new forms of labor organizations rooted in non-hierarchical structures must emerge to mobilize workers in the United States and throughout the world. As unions reach a breaking point, most are clueless about organizing new migrant workers and even protecting their own members from job loss. As globalized capitalist hegemony has expanded throughout the world, the need to organize transnationally is more pressing now than ever, especially among precarious, unemployed, and migrant workers who are most vulnerable to abuse. Concomitantly, the record of labor organizing in the United States and abroad demonstrates that most bureaucratic labor unions are indifferent toward precarious workers unless they are a source of substantial membership growth that poses no challenge to leaders.

The rise of guest worker programs is an integral component of a dramatic shift in the global division of labor, perpetuated through technological advances, which permits corporations to deskill many professional jobs and reduce the number of workers necessary to perform tasks, and relies increasingly on low-skilled labor. The shift toward neoliberal policies began in the 1980s and spread after the collapse of the Soviet Union in 1991. These changes have bolstered capitalist free-trade dogma just as they have imposed market policies on all countries.

Chapter 2 provides a historical comparative analysis of U.S. migration policy and examines why foreign migrant labor is growing at a rapid pace. In 1993, the Washington Consensus, the World Trade Organization (WTO), the International Monetary Fund (IMF), and the World Bank—multilateral financial institutions controlled by corporations in North America and western Europe—established a new policy that would impose harsh penalties on any country that closed its borders to foreign trade, thereby setting the stage for monetary crises and high unemployment. That labor has no control over these organizations more than suggests the dire predicament that workers and unions confront today.

Absent from the controversy over establishing comprehensive immigration reform are discussions of guest worker programs that, if enforced, will replace immigration with guest workers. Even more significant is the need to comprehend how capital is restructuring through the creation of a domestic low-wage temporary labor program that undermines the conditions of workers. The programs in place provide a model for the future that will extinguish a growing movement of migrant workers mobilizing and organizing into unions.

Nevertheless, if recent guest worker programs in skilled and less-skilled industries over the last decade provide any clue to what the future holds, one can expect that businesses will continue to sidestep federal laws that mandate the payment of wages equivalent to U.S. workers. As in the past, no means to monitor illegal corporate practices are likely to be implemented. Already, corporations and businesses make two fundamental arguments that restrain working-class consciousness: that U.S. laborers do not have the requisite skills for professional work or that they are not willing to "stoop so low" as to work in the hospitality sector of the economy. These arguments conceal the reality that labor conditions in occupations across the economy are threatened by corporate restructuring that is destabilizing the status of U.S. and migrant working-class jobs.

Chapter 3 examines the emergence of India as a labor-export economy through assessing the warped development of the country in its effort to create a mobile labor force in all segments of the economy. Though most observers have analyzed the dramatic growth of the high technology and business service guest workers on a world scale, India seeks to export workers in all skill and wage segments, from low-wage construction, trucking, and service laborers in the Arab gulf states to high technology and business services workers in advanced capitalist countries. The chapter examines two case studies of the outcome of new migration patterns in South Asia (India), examining the high-technology enclave of Hyderabad—viewed by many corporate leaders in the North as a model for the future workplace. However, the result of these policies is the training of a small number of privileged students from upper-class backgrounds, while the majority of the poor are ignored completely, many unable to obtain regular employment.

Workers and peasants in the informal sector are subsidizing the growth of high technology and business services as contractors, bonded labor, and day laborers—many displaced by the new corporate installations. Thomas Friedman and pundits in the media, leaders in academia, and corporate executives admire and express awe over India's technological progress without accounting for the mass displacement, environmental degradation, and human misery caused by the introduction of neoliberal policies. India's poor are worse off than before the initiation of privatization programs.[3]

India is by far the largest source of information technology (IT) consultants for U.S. high-tech companies because of its considerable cost advantages: programmers are paid a fraction of the typical wages of an American worker (International Organization for Migration, 2008; Kyōkai 2003, 76–79). Moreover, the Indian government seeks to extend low-wage labor exports to affluent countries but is stymied by legislative restrictions usually promoted by trade unions.

Chapter 4 examines how skilled and semiskilled guest worker programs contribute to the displacement of workers throughout the U.S. economy. In the future, as migrant labor programs are institutionalized through the World Trade Organization and are viewed as the latest formula for economic development, it is likely that this new commodification of labor will spread into a growing number of labor market sectors, including manufacturing and transportation. Corporations and contractors seek to create a spot labor market for all workers—from autoworkers to professors. It is conceivable that employers may artificially create spot shortages in goods and services to employ low-wage guest workers instead of skilled U.S. workers who demand higher wages. The chapter reveals that while corporate human resource executives view migrant laborers as docile and complacent, a growing number are resorting to collective action in the form of *micro organizing,* where small groups organize to address the specific problems they face. Indeed, U.S.-born workers must escape from their fear of challenging capital though collective action.

The account then turns to the failure of the new economy to benefit all workers as workers organize using these new technologies. Following the dot-com collapse, IT companies are implementing a new generation of migration policies—known as Stage 2—aimed at reducing wage costs through advancing technology and cutting labor expenses. Even after the start of the 2008 global economic crisis, the IT industry actively lobbied government leaders to increase the number of high-technology guest workers allowed to enter each year. U.S.-born workers contend that guest workers erode working conditions for all by speeding up the process of work and contributing to higher levels of unemployment. In response, we are seeing the rise of a variety of new forms of resistance outside formal unions.

Chapter 5 then examines the process and effects of low-wage migration in Jamaica to reveal the growing importance of hospitality and domestic services in the global economy and the specific effect of U.S. guest worker programs on guest workers and their families. Though multilateral agencies extol the benefit that migration has had on the Jamaican economy through remittances, the chapter will show that in reality the guest worker program does not appreciably improve living standards of most guest workers, their families, and communities. Since the 1940s, Jamaican workers have been forced to rely on working abroad to provide basic support for their families as the state withdraws from providing essential services to the country's working class. Consequently, while some development economists may argue that remittances from abroad are essential to support basic needs of Jamaica's poor, they neglect to demonstrate how poverty is generated by the IMF and other multilateral institutions that have applied onerous terms on the country's economy that contribute to the shortage of jobs, education, health care, and adequate housing. Rather, reliance on guest worker programs for remittances may provide funds for education for one or two children but does not put an end to poverty that pushes *more* Jamaicans into destitution and has increased violence and civil disorder.

In chapter 6, the concluding chapter, we investigate the policy and practice of established U.S. labor unions toward migrant labor and guest workers and provide alternative models for building worker power on a global basis. Organized labor operates at a disadvantage as it typically responds rather than acts as capital changes the nature of work to lower wages. Ideally, a proactive labor movement would shape the nature of work. Therefore, U.S. national labor unions and peak organizations have historically opposed all forms of migration. Most notably, in 1986, national unions were instrumental in shaping the employer-sanction provision in IRCA. However, because legal penalties for hiring undocumented workers are minimal, the law has not deterred employers from hiring them. Furthermore, because minimum wage and hour standards are often unenforced by state and federal government regulatory agencies, undocumented immigrants are frequently more desirable to employers than U.S.-born workers.

Paradoxically, from 1990 to 2010, in those instances when undocumented workers sought to organize unions, businesses have used employer sanctions as a means to fire immigrant organizers. As immigrants are now working in low-wage service positions where labor unions are attractive, several unions have sought to organize them. Subsequently, in February 2000, the AFL-CIO changed its position to support all immigrant-organizing drives and went on record to oppose employer sanctions. However, this historic shift ignores the despondent conditions of the growing ranks of guest workers, which business inevitably considers a reliable source of new compliant workers over whom to exercise absolute control, at lower labor costs, and of whom to dispose when no longer needed.

The chapter explores how the U.S. labor movement's historical stance toward migrant workers undermines the power of the working class. The expansion of guest worker programs may reduce permanent immigration but will also further undermine wages for all workers, as in the nineteenth and twentieth centuries. U.S. unions must forcefully seek to mitigate the decline in living conditions in sending countries and in the United States through opposing neoliberal globalization programs that generate poverty and prompt economic migration for those who are most poor. For those migrants who are in short supply and considered a necessary, the government—and not business—should enforce wage and workplace standards and allow workers to organize across national boundaries.

Organized labor is correct to oppose guest worker programs that interfere with recent strategies to organize undocumented workers. But some unions do not have the prescience to recognize the inevitability that, if enacted and enforced by government, the policy shift could replace undocumented immigrants with guest workers. Organized labor has supported an amnesty program that leads to full citizenship in the United States; yet it was not until 2009 that established unions joined in opposition to guest worker programs. However, no matter what the case, without a mass labor movement, guest worker programs are here to stay until labor develops a new strategic analysis to confront inexorable neoliberal globalization that infuses workers with a strong belief in their power (Piven & Cloward 2000). It is necessary to find a means to advance the rights of guest workers in all sectors of the economy, especially given migrant labor's penchant toward mobilization. Migrant workers have substantial power to disrupt capital and demonstrate a strong sense of solidarity. Because of their abysmal conditions, more are inclined to form and join labor unions. The majority of workers participating in the December 2008 Republic Window and Door sit-down strike in Chicago were immigrants, and as this book will show, guest workers are just as likely to engage in concerted action against managers and labor contractors.

Yet labor unions operate on the basis of opportunism. Though organized labor is correct to oppose temporary guest worker programs, it must also educate the U.S. working class to oppose nativism and xenophobia toward migrants, which only bolsters capitalist efforts to divide workers. Moreover, organized labor must challenge capital through risking friendly relations with employers and supporting direct action among U.S.-born as well as foreign-born workers. Trade unions must educate, mobilize, and encourage workers to challenge both union and nonunion firms.[4]

The only answer for building a strong labor movement is to consider workers in the global context rather than continuing to pursue a failed and unworkable strategy of concessionary bargaining, deserting unemployed and precarious workers, overlooking migrant labor, and continuing to pursue friendly relations with management. This suggests that unions must reach out to organize all migrant workers, irrespective of their status. Such a strategy would stipulate that all migrants have the right to organize unions and join existing working-class institutions to represent and advance their interests.

1

Migration and Class Struggle

For about twenty-five years, since passage of the Immigration Reform and Control Act (IRCA) in 1986, more and more U.S. businesses have been relying on a system of migrant labor that involves guest workers. A guest worker is a foreign laborer temporarily authorized to work in a host country with the knowledge and acquiescence of that country. In the United States, employers recruit guest workers to perform both skilled and unskilled labor in newly restructured industries. These workers sign contracts with specific companies before migrating temporarily to the United States to perform highly structured jobs for a fixed duration of time. Because of the nature of their contracts, these migrants face a number of unique challenges, including confinement to one employer, onerous work arrangements, withholding of wages, and lack of access to federal employment regulations governing minimum wage and hour standards. Why do so many migrant workers participate in such an exploitive system? Simply put, as economic conditions worsen, foreign workers desperately seek jobs in the United States as a means to provide for their families and communities through remittances for basic needs such as food, housing, and education. As the program expands, these new migrant guest workers inevitably form part of the subaltern underside of their respective labor markets in the United States and the Global North as labor markets are transformed through expanding use of foreign temporary workers.

While wages and conditions of work contrast significantly, highly skilled and unskilled guest workers occupy essential spaces in the labor market without the prospect of establishing a foundation of power and support, because they have no permanency and are almost always sent home upon completion of their assignments. In a range of occupations, from Internet technology, business services, and nursing, to welding, construction, and hospitality, the U.S. government is permitting private businesses to fill positions once held by U.S.-born and immigrant workers with guest workers. They require only that the employer "prove" that either, a) there are no U.S. citizens willing to fill the position or, b) there are no American workers trained and qualified to do the particular job. This situation transforms the labor market because there are no labor laws to protect these workers, who are paid less and work under exploitive conditions. Conveniently for the employer, guest workers are also in a position that leaves them generally afraid to protest because employers can send them home at any time.

A repositioning of finance capital and international pressure for greater business profitability is intensifying the spread of guest work that frequently offers even lower wages and less job security than most undocumented migrants in the United States. Guest work is not only filling a shortage of labor for substandard jobs or scarce skilled jobs, but it also is part of a calculated effort by U.S. business leaders in key sectors of the global economy to lower labor costs and expand profits by increasing profitability through reducing wages, speeding up the pace of work, and introducing labor-saving technology technological advances across a range of occupations through deteriorating wages and reducing standards.

This book examines the significance of this growing shift toward guest worker labor migration in place of formal immigration and settlement programs traditionally favored by capital, and the resulting growing financial and social pressure on U.S. and transnational migrant workers. In so doing, the book considers the competing social and political forces in the evolution of U.S. and global guest worker programs.

Essential to the growth of guest work under advanced capitalism is a dialectical relationship between capital and labor. Capital almost always requests open migration to enlarge the reserve army of labor and increase competition with native-born workers as a means to lower wages and job standards. In opposition, organized and unorganized labor has historically opposed new immigrants entering labor markets to compete for jobs at lower wages. As largely unregulated migration to the United States since the late 1980s to the first decade of the early twentieth century has expanded the immigrant working class, some labor unions have sought to restrict migration to shield the native-born workers most vulnerable to labor migration.

U.S. immigration policy plays an important role in this story. The country's policy toward migrant labor is a politically sensitive issue for policy makers. Since the passage of the 1965 Immigration Act, the political debate in the

United States has shifted from ensuring the rights of foreigners from formerly excluded regions of the Global South to training a U.S. workforce equipped for the neoliberal economy. Neoliberalism is set apart from preceding eras of capitalism, because it promotes free trade and deregulation as well as accentuates financialization and privatization at great cost to workers and the environment throughout the world (Duménil & Lévy 2004).[1] As more workers have migrated to the United States from 1986 to 2010 to compete with native-born workers, immigration policy has become a significant arena of political struggle between supporters and opponents of restricting the flow of foreign laborers.

The passage of IRCA in 1986 and the implementation of NAFTA (North American Free Trade Agreement) were decisive in greatly expanding the unauthorized entry of migrant workers in the United States. These workers were compelled by large and small employers to work for significantly lower than prevailing wages. As a result, by the late 1990s, a growing number of capitalist labor markets that once provided decent employment and wages had been eviscerated through outsourcing and insourcing of documented and undocumented labor. Central to the 1986 act are provisions that use employer sanctions to ban businesses from hiring immigrants deemed illegal, a stipulation that was requested by organized labor in the United States. However, federal and state authorities did not generally enforce these provisions from the time of the law's passage until the draconian Immigration and Customs Enforcement (ICE) raids began in 2005–2006. As a result, the pace of migration has accelerated even more rapidly in the ensuing two decades as undocumented workers have inundated old and new labor markets, creating an oversupply of low-wage labor in a growing number of manufacturing, service, and agricultural industries.

In 2000, responding to the dramatic growth of mostly undocumented workers in the United States in large labor markets, the AFL-CIO, spurred by service sector unions, initiated a dramatic policy shift. They began calling for repeal of the 1986 immigration law that uses "employer sanctions" to penalize employers who hire undocumented workers. This meant that the same labor unions that had supported the sanctions began requesting that the government not enforce the legislation. On balance, employers were rarely if ever penalized for hiring undocumented immigrants anyway, and employer sanctions had only served as a means for employers to evade unionization by threatening immigrant workers who sought to organize. Realizing this, unions reevaluated their stance and started undertaking efforts to facilitate the organization of immigrant workers. From 1995 to 2005, organizing campaigns contributed to increasing wages, and improved conditions in labor-market niches where immigrants were employed. In the late 1990s, more labor unions sought the reorganization of growing industries where membership nearly vanished, including building services, hotels and restaurants, food and retail trade, and security, along with the rapidly growing health care sector. Employers were not so enthusiastic. The unions were trying to find a way to circumvent corporate efforts to keep wages for undocumented workers in check through threats and coercion. Seeing their grip on immigrant workers loosening, employers responded by calling for expansion of guest worker programs.

Supporters of businesses engaged in contracting guest workers contend that a comprehensive program of legal migration is necessary to bolster the economy, filling a shortage of professional workers in modern industry and providing a pool of low-wage workers to fill menial jobs that U.S. workers do not want. Corporate advocates for formal guest work programs see new migrants as essential to expanding profitability through replacing higher-wage workers in the labor markets. Many of these occupations once provided decent wages to U.S. workers but were reorganized by business officials and transformed into low-wage migrant labor markets. Once migrant workers move into the jobs, they remain solidly working class—only as guest workers, their capacity to organize is severely compromised. When workers do engage in collective action, owners frequently dismiss and deport them. Although labor shortages have not directly compelled the U.S. government to allow more migrants, it is undeniable that a whole range of formerly "good" jobs in once solidly working-class industries that were organized by unions—such as hospitality, building services, retail services, food processing, and transportation—are now filled by guest workers and undocumented migrants at lower wages and drastically inferior working conditions. By organizing new immigrant workers who were part of the fabric of major communities throughout the United States, unions sought to improve wages and conditions in a range of labor markets. Organizing immigrant workers would reduce the incentive for employers to hire foreigners and, in so doing, raise standards for U.S.-born workers as well.

U.S. Policy and the International Labor Migration Movement

Over the past two decades, the insignificant penalties IRCA imposed on business did not deter them from hiring undocumented immigrants—primarily from Mexico, the Caribbean, and Central America. Corporate interests contend that the United States has a shortage of skilled workers while simultaneously arguing that new U.S.-born entrants into the labor force do not want to work in less-skilled jobs. Congress, taking as fact the corporate line of reasoning that the United States needs both skilled and unskilled labor—in high technology, nursing, education, services, hospitality, and even trucking—to fill a labor shortage, immediately responded to business interests by passing legislation raising the ceiling on visas for foreign skilled workers in locations where, purportedly, a deficit of American workers existed.

Beginning in the late 1980s, for the purpose of further expanding neoliberal trade in foreign workers, the U.S. government sharply increased approval of foreign immigrant guest worker and student visas in a range of high-skilled and low-skilled occupations, from housekeeping to medical professions to computer programming. Employers create labor shortages as a means of reducing labor standards and pushing wages down. By introducing guest workers in these occupations, business wants to create a surplus of workers, thereby turning well-paying jobs with benefits into low-paying dead-end jobs with no perks.

Through historical and ethnographic analysis, this book explores the erosion of labor conditions in both professional and working-class jobs that form the basis for the shortage and disinterest of U.S. workers in both the information technology and hospitality and tourism sectors. It argues that the shortage of high technology and hospitality workers is a condition created by business to allow them to contract foreign guest workers at a fraction of the prevailing wages paid in these industries, and thus lower labor costs.

NEW ORGANIZATION OF LABOR

A new configuration of industry has transformed the traditional institutional forms of labor organization that took shape through the industrial unions established from the 1920s through the 1950s. The institutional form of labor—management relations, based on recognition and collective bargaining—is inadequate for today's workers because it frequently does not facilitate new forms of labor activism leading to improved conditions. At the same time, corporate propaganda creates a great deal of anxiety and distress among U.S. workers by making them believe that they will lose even their poor jobs if they protest.

Further complicating this already bleak situation, over the past two decades the extraordinary growth of documented and undocumented migrant labor has transformed state and national labor regulatory systems, thereby creating new challenges for workers and their weakened unions in maintaining wages and labor standards. In some cases, migrant laborers have replaced unionized throughout entire labor markets. The demand to expand and institutionalize migrant labor systems will further erode the capacity of unions to organize workers typically employed for foreign contractors in professional and less-skilled labor markets. Simultaneously, efforts to enlarge the migrant labor programs leave immigrants themselves defenseless against corporate despotism. In the new global labor commodity chain, migrants in a growing number of service industries are considered factors of production to be dispensed with when no longer necessary (Gereffi & Korzeniewicz 1993).[2]

The research of this book provides a historical and comparative analysis of U.S. migration policy in the skilled (mainly IT) and less skilled (chiefly hospitality) industries and the reconstitution of class relations in these two sectors from the 1980s to 2010. Ethnographic interviews with workers, employers, activists, union leaders, and government officials in the United States, South Asia, Europe, and the Caribbean have helped to shape this investigation of migration, labor policy, and the constraints and limitations to building labor power in the neoliberal economy that the United States imposes on other nation-states. Focusing on the connections between employer political power, labor movements, and mostly submissive union organizations, the book reveals the structural constraints to developing power left by the residue of old labor, deep-rooted union traditions, and evolving migration law in the United States and throughout the global economy.

The United States had been hastily expanding low-wage and flexible labor migration even before completing negotiations aimed at ratifying an international agreement on migration by the World Trade Organization framework that regulates global trade. Prospects for a massive nonimmigrant labor force in the United States through the guest worker visa will surely further erode the power of organized labor as corporate America asserts its inability to find workers at home for more and more jobs—or maintains that U.S. workers are disinterested in working them. Such a policy will hurt traditional U.S.-born workers, undercut migrant workers, and intensify poverty in emerging capitalist countries in the less-developed world (henceforth designated the *Global South*).

DOES THE UNITED STATES NEED FOREIGN GUEST WORKERS?

The prevailing assertion on work shortages in labor policy and human resources literature is contradictory. On the one hand, advocates of expanding migrant labor say U.S. workers are at a competitive disadvantage as a greater number of students are graduating from higher-skilled professions in the Global South. For instance, India and the Philippines train significantly higher levels of Internet technology workers and nurses than the United States. In the Philippines, government provides training in skills specifically for those planning to work abroad, rather than those seeking to stay (Rodriguez 2010, 32–39). Conversely, other writers argue that the United States has a labor shortage of unskilled service and even manufacturing workers in a range of industries. Owing to the shortage in skilled and unskilled labor, the United States must reluctantly recruit skilled workers from abroad to meet the demands of high technology and business services on the one hand and hospitality workers on the other (Friedman 2005; Levy and Murnane 2004; National Research Council 2001; Papademetriou and Yale-Loehr 1996; Saxenian 2006). In some instances, advocates of expanded migration concurrently assert both opposing perspectives (Jacoby 2006). Since the world financial meltdown, academic discourse on labor shortages has declined dramatically, even if corporate business lobbies continue to argue that there is a pressing need for foreign labor, and contractors continue to press businesses to replace existing workers with foreign labor, especially in the hospitality and tourism industry (Chase 2009).

A large and growing concern among these academics and policy makers is that the American labor force may not be prepared to compete with equally skilled foreign workers willing to work at lower wages for longer hours. This book challenges the predominant view that an expanding global skilled labor market represents a threat to American dominance in new technological development but suggests, rather, that capital's search for profit directs government efforts to expand guest worker programs that will diminish wages in new labor markets.

This book asserts that finance capital and business have historically engaged in an open strategy to downgrade worker standards in a range of occupational labor markets. Large multinational corporations with no demonstrated interest in educating U.S. workers told Congress that America was facing a critical crisis of engineers, medical workers, and highly skilled professional workers. If the United States has too few high-technology workers, though, the primary cause is the nation's failure to promote education and training in new and emerging sectors. While professional training institutions have declined in the United States since the 1990s, over the past two decades, native-born skilled workers have been replaced by migrant workers to fill skilled positions at lower cost. As Grace Chang contends: " . . . immigration from the Third World into the United States doesn't just happen in response to a set of factors but is carefully orchestrated—that is, desired, planned, compelled, managed, accelerated, slowed, and periodically stopped—by the direct actions of U.S. interests, including the government as state and as employer, private employers, and corporations" (Chang 2000, 3–4). What has happened, then, is that the federal government has almost always allowed businesses to create artificial labor shortages to justify expanding guest worker programs in both skilled and less-skilled occupations (Gonzalez 2006; Mandel 1991; Vogel 2006).

With the backing of President George H. W. Bush, the United States Congress passed the Immigration Act of 1990, which authorized increases in the admission of foreign nationals seeking permanent resident status in the United States while creating a program to expand and expedite the admission of temporary foreign skilled workers and students pursuing careers in high technology. However, the act is in reality founded on the premise that the labor shortage was undermining American global preeminence in high technology and business services. But what Congress did not take into account is the restructuring of the industries and the downward pressure on wages. Founded on half-truths and speculation, the nonimmigrant guest worker program was significantly expanded, setting into motion a mass wave of migration that has almost completely transformed the economic geography of high technology, business services, and other professional occupations by assigning Indian, Chinese, and other guest workers who enter the United States for brief periods to fill the breach.

In the 1990s and 2000s, with attention drawn to the outsourcing of manufacturing jobs to the Global South, the growth of skilled guest workers in the IT sector went largely unnoticed, below the radar screen of public scrutiny. New skilled and unskilled immigrants, conventionally portrayed as assiduous and eager to work long hours at low pay, have entered an array of industries, which are often dominated by low-wage U.S.-born workers. In reality the plan is to further reduce wages and working conditions. Academic and popular discourse suggests that these foreign laborers are working in low-wage unskilled menial jobs in the service economy that have been vacated by U.S. workers without taking into consideration the fact that many workers have been forced out by the replacement of U.S.-born workers with foreign-born workers on local, regional, and national levels. For example, many unionized African Americans laboring in the public sector, building services, hospitality, and other industries were replaced by even lower-wage foreign labor.

Federal lawmakers have expanded guest worker programs in the United States in ways that allow them to control the flow and restrict the rights of these workers. Such government programs, if implemented widely, as conceived by congressional legislation and broadly supported by both the Democratic and Republican parties, could create an international contingent of temporary and seasonal migrant labor that will come and go as multinational corporations need them. This scheme could trigger a downward spiral in labor rights throughout the world.

THE NORTH–SOUTH POPULATION DISPARITY

Labor researchers have argued that the United States has a shortage of skilled and unskilled workers owing to the aging of the population (Dychtwald, Erickson, & Morrison 2006). The United Nations (UN) estimates that migrants account for some 3 percent of the world's population, or about 175 million persons. The numbers of immigrants in high-income countries increased at about 3 percent per year from 1980 to 2000, up from the 2.4 percent pace in the 1970s (see table 1.1 and table 1.2). At that rate of growth, the share of migrants in high-income countries' populations almost doubled during the thirty-year period, and population growth (excluding migration) fell from 0.7 percent per year in the 1970s to 0.5 percent in the 1990s. Immigration has contributed to population growth and increased revenues in several high-income countries. For example, without migration, Germany, Italy, and Sweden would have experienced a decline in population in the past few decades (United Nations 2005, 2006; World Migration 2005). Legal immigrants to Europe solve the welfare state budgetary problem. As Europe's population ages, immigrants work in essential tasks and increase government revenue through paying taxes.

This is not the case in the United States, where antiimmigrant sentiments prevalent from the foundation of the nation have mobilized nativist activism pushing Congress to restrict the influx of foreign-born workers from 2005 to 2010. In response to the growing xenophobia, since the enactment of IRCA in 1986, the federal government has passed laws to restrict low-

Table 1.1. Migrant Population, 2010

Geographic Area	Migrants (millions)	Percentage of Area's Population
Europe	69.8	9.5
Asia	61.3	1.5
North America	50.0	14.2
Africa	19.3	1.9
Latin America	7.5	1.3
Oceania	6.0	16.8

Source: United Nations, Trends in Migrant Stock: The 2008 Revision, data in digital form.

Table 1.2. Ten Leading International Migrant Hosting Countries, 2010

Country	International Migrants (millions)
United States	42.8
Russian Federation	12.3
Germany	10.8
Saudi Arabia	7.3
Canada	7.2
France	6.7
United Kingdom	6.5
Spain	6.4
India	5.4
Ukraine	5.3

Source: *Word Migration 2005: Costs and Benefits of International Migration.*

wage migration through increasing penalties on employers who knowingly hire undocumented immigrants and appropriating funds for policing the U.S. boundary with Mexico. Policy makers have also cracked down on immigrant students and tourists overstaying their visas. However, because of poor federal enforcement of illegal migration, primarily from the southern border with Mexico, policy changes aimed at restricting immigration to the United States during the 1990s have had little effect in stanching the flow of low-wage labor.

As the federal government places even greater restrictions on migration, demand for low-wage labor in the service and manufacturing sectors and the growth in the unregulated informal economy have stimulated regional and global migration from the Global South to the United States. The wide-ranging rise in migration flows from the demand for cheap unskilled workers in the Global North and a growing supply of workers in the Global South, owing to lack of jobs and growing poverty. Prior to 2004, the INS (Immigration and Naturalization Service)[3] guarded against *illegal* migration across the Mexican boundary—particularly during economic downturns (Massey 2003; Nevins 2002; Ngai 2005; Zolberg 2006). Of course, this nonenforcement is sporadic. Typically, U.S. border security ebbs and flows in response to unemployment levels, which lead to rising nativism and antiimmigrant sentiment. Even when demand for immigrant labor grows, at no time are newcomers embraced, as they frequently meet residential segregation, racism, and violence (Castles and Miller 2003, 220–52).

Roger Waldinger and other analysts of immigration consider the undocumented migration from the South to be a positive development. They argue new communities of immigrants provide necessary work while revitalizing neglected neighborhoods in and around major cities. However beneficial the new migrants are to the process of invigorating urban economies, though, the prevailing view fails to consider the fact that in previous decades, U.S.-born workers working for significantly higher wages and benefits had performed much of the same erstwhile unskilled work (Waldinger 1999).

Ruth Milkman argues that the increase of undocumented immigration to the United States has contributed to a resurgence of organizing among labor unions, particularly in low-wage service industries (Milkman 2006). Drawing on the rise of immigrant labor organizing initiated by the Service Employees International Union (SEIU) in Los Angeles, Milkman contends that the mobilization is occurring in the service jobs whose "location in expanding, nonmobile sectors of the economy" provides an advantage over industrial jobs that may relocate. However, Milkman and others who have advocated a revitalization of the union movement through immigrant mobilization fail to account for the fact that guest worker programs can eviscerate these same jobs. The contention that older former AFL service unions with an institutional legacy of representing craft unions are better positioned to organize wrongly asserts that a legacy founded in the late nineteenth century remains to this day under neoliberal capitalism.

The Supreme Court's Hoffman Plastics decision of 2002 allows employers to invoke IRCA's employer sanctions provisions against undocumented immigrants who organize unions regardless of whether they are in craft, service, or manufacturing unions (Supreme Court 2002). Thus the National Labor Relations Act, created in 1935 to protect against illegal dismissals, would have otherwise defended against employers firing activist undocumented immigrant workers. Upon abolition of a key NLRA provision, undocumented workers cannot seek remediation, irrespective of union, industrial sector, or locality. In addition, though the SEIU did not initially oppose the expansion of the guest worker program in 2007, many U.S.-born and immigrant service workers are prospectively exposed to permanent replacement by new guest work programs proposed by Presidents Bush and Obama and Congress. As neoliberal globalization erodes wages and conditions on the job, both U.S.-born workers and foreign-born immigrants are forced into jobs at lower wages and less job security in all sectors of the economy, in most cases without union protections, and under less-favorable conditions.

The restructuring of work has made low-wage jobs less attractive to native-born workers because of declining wages and working conditions. The argument that migrants are taking jobs that nobody else wants fails to consider the fact that the conditions of work and wages for those jobs have been downgraded significantly through closure of manufacturing facilities, globalization, and outsourcing of work (Faux 2006; Kalleberg, Reskin, & Hudson 2000; Uchitelle 2006).

Also missing from the debate is the even more dramatic growth in *skilled* worker migration to the United States. Following passage of the Immigration Act of 1990, the high-technology industry has augmented the skilled labor workforce in the United States through the Non-Immigrant Visa (NIV) system. NIV permits foreign skilled workers to work for six years in the United States in jobs deemed to have too few employees. As this study will show by highlighting the story of Indian IT workers, the consequences of bilateral migration policies are harmful for most workers. Though Indian IT professionals in the United States may benefit through higher wages, the oversupply of workers in the industry draws down wages for all workers. Even worse, India's labor-export program only benefits a small percentage of the population and contributes to a distorted economy that serves multinational corporations rather than the vast majority of the country's population who remain mired in abject poverty. Contrary to those who contend that the United States must recruit abroad to address labor shortages, the American working class is coping with a job shortage crisis of spectacular proportions. The crisis has two dimensions that encompass both class and race. The vast majority of job creation in the United States today consists of positions slated to be filled by workers from the Global South at significantly lower cost than once prevailed in previous decades, when employers were forced to rely upon U.S.-born workers who had some degree of protection through labor laws and unions. If we follow the evolution of the job market, it is undeniable that employers seeking to lower wages and conditions in unskilled sectors have degraded U.S. occupations by importing workers who have no such means of protection.

The federal government's stance toward skilled immigrant labor is widely divergent from its position on unskilled labor. As Congress enacts policy to restrict low-wage migration to the United States, it also is substantially increasing the quotas on skilled nonimmigrant workers. This policy divergence is consistent with the federal government's historical attitude toward immigrants since 1864, when the government hesitantly began regulating migration. Since the origins of the nation, the vast majority of immigrants to the United States came with few or no skills. Nonetheless, even as waves of unskilled migrants came to work in the manufacturing industries, the government has made special provisions for skilled migrants to enter the country (Zolberg 2006).

THE BOOM IN TRADING WORKERS

Since the proliferation of market reforms in the late 1970s, global barriers to trade liberalization have been systematically demolished. Finance capitalists and business support the deterritorialization of work but not the free movement of workers. In the meantime, the global market economy resembles a Lego building under construction to prevent the resurgence of social protections. The new wall of the building replacing government protections is a sturdy and essential component of market liberalization, one that expands trade in goods and services to promote the trade in workers between countries, without offering genuine worker mobility and rights. Resistance to the neoliberal program will build a wall around any country that seeks to moderate the market. The trade in labor—as opposed to the free movement of workers—is the next round of negotiations under a General Agreement on Trade and Services (GATS-4) that will from time to time fill spot shortages in skilled and unskilled labor that supporters believe are inevitable in the global trade regime. In contrast to the European Union, where workers in the region may migrate freely, GATS-4 will not mandate lifting restrictions on the mobility of workers in NAFTA and other regional trade blocs. Thus, rather than employing workers, GATS-4 will allow General Motors, for example, to contract workers from the Global South to fill spot shortages at significantly lower costs than full-time workers and without the obligation to pay for health care, unemployment insurance, pension benefits, or even workers' compensation.

A completely new perspective is emerging among corporate and government managers in the Global South. In the 1970s and 1980s, national leaders viewed relocating skilled labor from the South to the North as a *brain drain* that deprived developing nations of professional workers, a resource that would otherwise improve their standard of living. Now, China, India, the Philippines, and countries of the Caribbean basin view workers as profitable commodities for export to the Global North (see table 1.3). In the early 1970s, Arghiri Emmanuel saw workers as an international commodity only

Table 1.3. Three Leading Migrant Sending Countries

Country	Estimated Diaspora (millions)
China	35.0
India	20.0
The Philippines	7.0

Source: *Word Migration 2005: Costs and Benefits of International Migration.*

protected by the power vested in national unions in his conceptualization of *unequal exchange* (1972). Today, corporate and government leaders promote labor as an export component in the creation of capital through foreign remittances, and potentially a source of good will that will encourage multinationals to relocate subsidiaries to their countries.

We are observing that the economic standards of the majority of workers in the Global South are warping through exporting services to the North as new development policies direct disproportionate funding to IT, business services, and nursing, as well as infrastructure, construction, hospitality, and other services for global exports, ignoring other key components of their burgeoning economies. Ostensibly, in GATS mode 4 negotiations over the expansion of service guest work, the WTO is arguing that temporary labor migration is as vital to developing countries' economic growth as goods and services are to advanced economies. Explicitly, the Global South considers the expansion in the movement of people from poor to advanced countries to perform services an important source of exports and revenue (Mattoo & Carzaniga 2003, 1–19).

Guest Workers and Global Labor Solidarity

To respond effectively to a capitalist offensive against the laboring classes on a global scale, the workers and poor must win tangible organizing victories and must unify across borders by struggling for the right to join unions. Many foreign manufacturing jobs pay poverty wages even by the standards of the Global South (Elliott and Freeman 2003). Therefore, for an accurate understanding of the shortage of workers, we must follow the *job* and not the *worker* in order to assess the degree to which decent-paying jobs in the United States and Europe are transforming into poverty-wage jobs in the Global South. Because of restrictions imposed on guest workers, and employer efforts to circumvent laws that seek to equalize wages among Americans and foreigners, guest workers may be among the least-protected in the nation. This book thus maintains that organizing guest workers into labor unions would help to stanch the decline in the power of workers throughout the world.

To begin to stem the precipitous decline in the power of organized labor, in the 2007 debate over immigration, labor was divided on the guest worker question. The AFL-CIO firmly opposed the program, and the Change to Win federation (led by the Service Employees International Union) sought a policy to regularize undocumented workers, who they view as ripe for organizing. However, in 2009, even amid highly fractious disagreements, organized labor endorsed a common position that guest workers must have the same rights as U.S.-born workers. But if such efforts are to be sustained, this book argues that labor must oppose all policies that segregate immigrant workers into specific categories that reduce their bargaining power, especially in those industries that have minimal union density.

Nursing and education unions such as the SEIU (Service Employees International Union) and the AFT (American Federation of Teachers) frequently have the leverage to negotiate contract labor agreements with medical facilities and schools before temporary and seasonal workers arrive. Organized labor should not select only those workers who will become eligible for employment and citizenship in the imperialist center of power. Instead, unions should also support workers and organized labor suffering from the policies of international capitalists throughout the world.

Today the World Bank and international development agencies are turning away from the substandard and ecologically hazardous development policies from the 1960s to 1980s that invested in the economic infrastructure of the Global South, instead advocating policies that force workers to migrate abroad in order to survive, and to produce major sources of revenue. The World Bank considers remittances essential components of advancing national development: "Remittances reduce poverty. They finance education and health expenses and provide capital for small entrepreneurs. In Sri Lanka, the birth weight of children in remittance recipient households is higher than that of the children of other households. In countries such as Tajikistan, Tonga, Nepal, Honduras, and Moldova, they can be 40% of GDP or even higher. In countries affected by crisis or natural disasters, say in Somalia or Haiti, remittances provide a lifeline to the poor" (Ratha 2008).

Poverty in the Global South triggers migration to the Global North. Small segments of organized labor in the United States are only beginning to address poverty in the Global South through cross-border organizing.

To argue that guest workers are not to be permitted to stay in the United States like other immigrants, while at the same time embracing undocumented workers—as many unions have until August 2009—was a contradictory pathway to the further diminution of organized labor. While the AFL-CIO union federation has taken a clear position opposing guest worker programs that create a subordinate class of "indentured servants," some unions have not unambiguously opposed the plan (AFL-CIO 2009).[4] This book argues that organized labor and the working class must advance a policy that defends both undocumented laborers and guest workers to resist corporate exploitation through developing alliances with progressive unions and labor movements in poor countries.

The Farm Labor Organizing Committee (FLOC), an AFL-CIO affiliate, offers a good case study of a possible solution for transnational migrants. This union is negotiating with agribusiness in the United States to establish standards for guest workers who otherwise do not have the right to organize to defend their interests. In September 2004 FLOC reached a precedent-setting agreement with the North Carolina Growers Association to unionize eight thousand guest workers, ending a five-year boycott against Mt. Olive products. The success of FLOC in unionizing temporary agricultural contract workers in North Carolina in the early 2000s grows out of organizing workers both in the United States and Mexico. The initial victory of FLOC demonstrates that a more militant and antiracist labor movement is capable of resisting draconian capitalist labor-migration programs (Gordon 2007; Hill 2008; Smith-Nonini 2009).

Most migrant worker resistance on the job is sporadic and unsystematic, and frequently not publicized. Though hospitals and educational institutions in the United States resist unionization, some labor organizations are compelling foreign labor contractors to ensure that temporary workers join their unions with identical wages and benefits. But these superficial organizing victories must be expanded in order to address the needs of the broader working class in the Global North and South. Now that capital is increasingly integrating globally, U.S. unions must formalize a system of standardized wages, benefits, and conditions and engage in cross-border organizing to advance the standards of workers throughout the world (Gordon 2007).

But business is using prospects for guest worker programs to do away with decent—and in some cases prestigious—jobs and as a means of supplying a steady source of highly competent, skilled IT workers and low-wage laborers working in the U.S. hospitality industry. The corporate frenzy to restructure the workplace to reduce prevailing standards will not stop unless vigorously challenged by new labor organizing that transforms into a social movement capable of pushing government and business to advance the wages and human rights of working people in the United States and worldwide.

Although the International Trade Union Confederation (ITUC) has initiated more expansive efforts to defend migrant laborers, as an ossified organization representing general union federations, most of its proclamations are formalities. The human rights route through the International Labour Organization (ILO) has also fallen short of passing resolutions acceptable to the United States. ILO conventions on the rights of workers are a step forward, but without a base rooted in labor, they are unlikely to expand the rights of workers. Similarly, efforts by university students to eliminate sweatshops globally may represent a model for the treatment of guest workers. However earnest the efforts of activist organizations, for example Jobs with Justice and United Students against Sweatshops (USAS), little will become of their endeavors without sustained union support (Ansley 2008; Featherstone 2002; Kabeer 2004).

The expansion of a larger guest worker program, a fait accompli for international corporations, inauspiciously inaugurates a new era in U.S. labor policy that transforms workers into disposable commodities and disciplines them by establishing new laws to facilitate temporary migration. On a global basis, the United States is at the vanguard of advancing policies that greatly reduce barriers to importing labor. The WTO has yet to enact a global labor trade accord for workers, but the United States is the world's leader in importing foreign labor through formal guest worker programs.

This book asserts, contrary to prevailing scholarly approaches, that the effort to create a comprehensive guest worker program is activated by business imperatives to lower wage costs and degrade workers' jobs in a multitude of labor markets—from professional to unskilled jobs. The problem for employers is not that there are too few U.S.-born workers in the labor pool but that those workers are harder to exploit because of U.S. labor laws. IT and hospitality corporations have been especially adept at finding ways to import workers in both skilled and unskilled categories on a short-term basis for jobs that pay significantly lower wages than in the past. The guest worker program makes it virtually impossible to improve conditions through organizing unions because employers can use a range of punitive measures—such as extending hours of work, withholding wages, or reporting insolent or militant workers to the government for deportation. Because most guest workers are seasonal laborers, the majority do not have the time to mount an effective organizing drive against employers.

This book also addresses the issue of a labor shortage in the United States—maintaining that the advocates for expanding migration on this basis do not make known that the decline of education programs plays a part in the shortage of nurses, IT professionals, engineers, and even truckers. If we are witnessing a severe shortage in high-technology jobs, why are more and more employers cutting jobs that pay decent wages and reconstituting them as low-wage employment? Essentially, we are witnessing the comprehensive erosion of the employer-employee compromise that survived from the mid-1930s to the early 1980s providing for decent wages, unemployment insurance, social security, pensions, and social-welfare benefits. That relationship is rooted in the class compromise of the New Deal in the 1930s, which frequently obligated U.S. employers to continue to retain workers even if business slowed, and that also provides health and pension benefits to workers through the workplace (Faux 2006; Piven & Cloward 1993; Uchitelle 2006).

The erosion of wages and working conditions through guest work in the private sector is part of a much broader dynamic of the neoliberal era that extends beyond immigration and guest work. The new assault on workers' rights is an essential part of a corporate effort to expand surplus value through the process of production. An extensive examination of management and business publications by Boltanski and Chiapello (2007) show that U.S. and European employers have shifted emphasis from traditional forms of production to extraction of profits from independent workers, who have fewer ties to employers. These independent contract workers are essentially self-employed and thus responsible for their own health insurance and for paying their own taxes. Thus workers are technically independent, usually indicating they have fewer prospects to improve their wages and working conditions. Guest work is part of a broader strategy by capitalists to undermine wages and conditions on the job.

The United States is leading the way in hiring foreign contract workers en masse, even before the country negotiates a new General Agreement on Tariffs and Trade (GATT) treaty through the WTO, where widening the market for global service workers is negotiated and ratified. The insatiable urge of policy makers is to ease the way for corporations to create a new body of contract workers unprotected by U.S. labor laws and thus unable to organize into unions or to protest wages and conditions, an attitude punishable by deportation. The United States is at the forefront of negotiations with the WTO to do away with trade barriers that impede importing and exporting professional and unskilled labor through the General Agreement on Trade and Services Mode Four—GATS-4 (Bhagwati, Panagariya, & Srinivasan 2004; Maimbo & Ratha 2005; Mattoo & Carzaniga 2003).

Even while actively negotiating a global labor migration agreement, right-wing governments find that foreign workers are useful scapegoats that allow them to garner votes from workers fearing job loss. In 2006, President George W. Bush sent six thousand troops to the U.S. border with Mexico, followed by the building of a barrier between the two countries for the purpose of showing that he was tough on undocumented immigration and to deflect working-class attention from his 2007 plan to reform immigration through expanding guest work programs. The policies are a delusion intended to neutralize right-wing, populist, xenophobic policy makers who seek to gain traction and votes from workers who are dissuaded from countering avaricious multinational corporations through organizing resistance. Therefore, some U.S. workers are easily convinced that foreign-born workers and the relocation of industry are leading sources of declining job security, underemployment, and unemployment. Likewise, as we shall see, temporary migrant workers frequently view their position as victims of avaricious global contractors and often resist exploitation, sometimes with the solidarity of U.S.-born workers.

2

Political Economy of
Migrant Labor in U.S. History
Fabricating a Migration Policy for Business

In a sweeping analysis of U.S. history from the colonial era to the early twenty-first century, historian Aristides Zolberg challenges as "mythology" the prevalent view that the United States is an open and welcoming country. Contrary to the conventional historical narrative, Zolberg asserts, in *A Nation by Design,* that the United States has had long episodes of immigration restriction even as it has had phases of openness toward foreigners when the national economy required a larger supply of workers. Countering prevailing perspectives that migration policy is haphazard, Zolberg sees opposition from labor and nativist xenophobia as an invisible instrument that framed U.S. immigration policy. Focusing on competing institutional social forces of business, labor, emerging ethnic groups, and nativist sentiment, he does not see capitalists as occupying the commanding heights of immigration policies and practices (Zolberg 2006). He contends that from the Civil War to the civil rights era, nativist tendencies to restrict foreign migration have prevailed. Conveniently, the restrictionist era began at the close of the great wave of European migration in the post–World War I era and lasted until the civil rights era, when social exclusion of people of color came under attack. Despite the shortcomings in Zolberg's narrative, his effort to formulate a grand historical theory of migration grounded in the institutional history of the United States is a stimulating change from the monotonous academic discourse of the nation as a relatively generous and hospitable democracy for migrants and refugees who are willing to work hard. (Daniels 2005; Foner 2002, 2005; Maharidge 2005; Portes 1996; Sassen 2006; Smith

2006; Waldinger 1999). Of course, he is not the only one to offer a challenge to the traditional story. Other writers reveal the super-exploitation of migrant workers of color in the new country and their valiant efforts to gain dignity through forming labor unions and countering employer abuse (Bacon 2005, 2008; Delgado 1993; Fine 2006; Fink 2003; Hanson 2003; Hondagneu-Sotelo 2001; Jayaraman & Ness 2005; Kasinitz 1992; Kwong 1999; Milkman 2000; Ness 2005; Ngai 2005; Nevins 2001).

Both perspectives are sympathetic to migrant workers and see the influence of corporate power, but they both fall short of a wide-ranging explanation of the historical tension between state, citizens, and capital. For example, however compelling his narrative, Zolberg underplays the dominant power of capitalists in manipulating popular opinion to favor migration when it serves their interests. To gain the upper hand vis-à-vis the native-born working class, capital interests have always used migration to enlarge the reserve army of labor, to lower wage costs, and to dampen worker efforts to better their conditions.

Zolberg's perspective confuses xenophobic rhetoric for policy because even in the most restrictive era, from the 1920s to 1965, employers had their way, contracting guest workers from Mexico and the Caribbean. In this chapter I will highlight capital's use of migrant labor and guest workers in its constant search for the cheapest possible labor.

In recent years, unenforced federal immigration law has had crucial political implications for both parties. The Republicans, seeking to patch a coalition of social and religious conservatives and advocates of neoliberal market economic policies that benefit the upper class, have seen their coalition unravel over growing migration (Briggs 2004; Hayworth 2006; Tancredo 2006).[1] The conservative social base of the party, in place since the 1970s, could disintegrate over class politics as cultural conservatives view the ineluctable growth of migration to the United States as a threat to their working-class jobs. The *Wall Street Journal* editorial page uncovers the class division in the party, asserting "that these pseudo-conservatives have no alternative policy, other than to arrest and deport millions in a way that would cause far more social and economic disruption than we have now (2006)." Furthermore, the article warns that the GOP is alienating Hispanic voters with deep roots in the United States: "millions of Hispanics—both illegals and those who have been here for decades—will get the message that the Republican Party doesn't want them" (*Wall Street Journal* 2006).

The evolving Republican class fissure was not necessarily a boon for Democrats who see formal immigration as crucial to the party's political base. Across the ideological spectrum, Democrats, in the tradition of Franklin D. Roosevelt's "Bracero program," mainly support substituting a formal guest worker program to expanding labor migration, while restricting unauthorized migration leading to citizenship. In May 2006, Senator Edward Kennedy (D-Massachusetts), a leading advocate of expanding guest worker programs, joined forces with John McCain (R-Arizona) to support a bill allowing migrant guest workers to fill the void left by U.S. workers who unambiguously reject low-wage work (Fears 2005).

The political unanimity among Democrats and Republicans on core issues of immigration reform persisted into the Obama presidency, further exposing both parties' surrender to neoliberal guest worker policies. The national economic recession stood in the way of President Barack Obama's public support for reform of immigration law that would expand guest worker programs, while the socially conservative, nativist, white working class unified through the Tea Party movement pushed Republicans to vociferously oppose passage of a new law. The Democratic Party, which has maintained a more inclusive policy toward immigration, could not sustain a populist and nativist position on immigration and maintain the votes of new immigrants. Thomas Frank lays bare the seeming mystery of why Democrats have lost their erstwhile populist, working-class base to Republicans by failing to address their economic interests. Though the Republican Party has not attended to working-class economic concerns, it has gained voters through conservative xenophobic populism (Frank 2004, Mink 1990).

In the absence of government oversight, both U.S.-born and foreign migrant workers from the Global South suffer significant economic dislocation as employers seize on newcomers' vulnerability to undercut prevailing wages and erode labor standards. On the one hand, supporters of migration restrictions have been unable to persuade the federal government to put a ceiling on migration and enforce policies that might reduce competition for jobs that lower labor costs. On the other, migrant workers have been impaired by periodic upsurges in popular dissent against them. During those times of heightened nativism, historically linked with a faltering economy, migrant workers almost always lose what leverage they have managed to gain against employers in their efforts to form coherent labor unions, as evidenced by the U.S. Immigration and Customs Enforcement (ICE) raids against undocumented immigrants.

Historical Background of Migrant Labor in the United States

Since the late nineteenth century, employers' insatiable demands for low-wage labor have taken precedence over nativist efforts to control the flow of foreign labor. Populist fervor favoring restricting immigration has succeeded only temporarily and most often failed to suppress business demands for cheap foreign labor. For instance, in the U.S. Southwest, Mexican labor remained a mainstay even after legislation curbing migration. The Chinese Exclusion Act of 1882 also exemplifies the government's incongruous position on immigrants—and the challenges newcomers face as a result. Because the government defined them as illegal, the ability of Chinese immigrants to improve their wages and conditions as well as prevent nativist violence was compromised. Nonetheless, because of limited federal enforcement, labor contractors continued to transport Chinese workers to the United States, even under increasingly dangerous conditions.

Terry Boswell demonstrates that from 1852 to 1882, employers and the state manipulated Chinese racial and ethnic differences as a means of lowering labor costs for all workers in the era leading up to the Chinese Exclusion Act (Boswell 1986, 352–53). Through use of "split labor markets" between white, black, and Asian labor, employers diminished workers' capacity to move up the labor market to higher-paying jobs. As such, Boswell argues that employers have held down labor costs through segregating workers into discrete labor markets on the basis of race and ethnicity. This development of job segregation for Chinese workers in the late nineteenth century is comparable to the rapid growth of segregated labor markets for immigrants in the early twenty-first century, as demonstrated by labor historians Gregg Andrews (2002) and Mildred Allen Beik (1996/2006). It is also transparent in guest worker programs. In the late nineteenth century, labor market segregation was accompanied by anti-Chinese stereotypes and violence. In the California mining industry, Chinese workers who were present as contract laborers were considered "coolies," a derogatory term synonymous with slaves, despite the fact that Asian immigrants were employed as indentured servants. White anti-Asian racial hostility contributed to the dispersion of Chinese mine workers and other laborers from California to other western states and to violent resistance, especially when used by capitalists as strikebreakers. Following the 1876 recession, Chinese workers were subject to violent repression (Boswell 1986).

Since the federal government took responsibility for regulating foreign immigration in 1875, supporters and opponents of foreign settlement in the United States have waged an ongoing and often heated political debate on policies of opening or closing the borders to migrants. Federal government policies have substantially mirrored the debate in ad hoc form reflecting the general mood of the country, rather than forming a coherent foreign migration program. On the whole, employers have always demanded low-cost foreign labor to undercut the cost of U.S. labor. Leveraging native-born workers against immigrants is entrenched in corporate efforts to create a more compliant labor force. The federal government has been more open to foreign migration when employers and their allies could prove the need for migrants to fill a compelling national need for laborers. Conversely, during periods of economic recession and higher unemployment, rising resistance among labor organizations and native-born workers have turned the federal government to a more restrictionist stance.

Nonetheless, from the colonial era to the present, contract labor laws have required immigrants to repay their masters for the cost of transportation to North America—much like an indentured servant would. In fact, many guest workers of the early twenty-first century are less advantaged than the indentured workers of the mid-nineteenth century in that they are unable to purchase their freedom and are trapped by an insidious and self-righteous system that purports to offer training and experience but instead fails to offer education and restricts their mobility and freedom. Importantly, un-like indentured servants of the colonial era, modern guest workers have no hope of gaining citizenship in the United States. While populist nativism has prevented immigration on a temporary basis, through creating a patchwork of incoherent policies, ultimately business has successfully pressured federal elected officials to open migration to fill labor shortages and lower labor costs without opening the borders to permanent immigrants.

The perceived standing of the United States as a sanctuary for refugees fleeing tyranny or seeking economic opportunity is rooted in popular myth and reinforced by politicians comparing America's economy with more re-strictionist countries. Though rhetorically true, the country's openness to foreigners is more myth than reality. This assertion holds even if we take into account the postwar policy of permitting foreigners who could demonstrate persecution in their homeland to enter the United States. Since colonial times, the native-born have, for the most part, opposed migrants as interlopers and have discriminated against them on the basis of ethnicity, religion, and race (Zolberg 2006).

Although the federal government is empowered by the U.S. Constitution to regulate migration and determine citizenship, for nearly seventy-five years, the government was largely detached from migration policies. The passage of the Act to Encourage Immigration in 1864 permitted employers to compel foreigners to sign binding contracts before they traveled to the United States. Known as "pre-emigration contracts," contract laborers were legally required to repay their employers for transportation costs. The federal government assumed only limited oversight over immigration policy. In 1868, the law was repealed and authority over immigration reverted to the states for another seven years until passage of the Immigration Act of 1875, when the federal government began to recapture control amid a wave of nativist xenophobia (Calavita 1992).[2] It is no coincidence that federalizing U.S. migration policy coincided with greater employer demand for a labor pool to work in manufacturing. From the end of the Civil War in the 1860s to the 1920s, the United States opened the gates to European immigrants for them to work for low wages under sweatshop conditions in apparel and garment shops, steel mills, food processing, and other industries under the control of conglomerates and trusts that dominated the national infrastructure. Indeed, since assuming control over policy in the 1870s, the national government has never failed to provide cheap labor to corporations seeking to reduce labor costs. (Foner 2002; Sinclair 2004). The disjointed immigration system in the United States is a product of historical influences by business—faintly moderated by labor—and American nativism. Capital is most influential in the jumbled but determined immigrant labor system today in the United States and in efforts to shape a new comprehensive policy that applies to all foreign workers.

Forging a National Guest Worker Program

Growth in the foreign labor force is historically a function of employer demand for cheap labor and low wage rates in the United States. During times of rapid growth, employers seek to replace domestic workers with foreign workers willing to work at lower cost. As such, until the 1990s, the state of the economy was historically an important factor in federal migration policy. For example, during the Great Depression's high unemployment, employers could hire native workers at considerably low wages, reducing the necessity for immigrant workers (Calavita 1992).

Political imperatives shape the nature and intensity of the labor movement's desire to regulate foreign labor migration to the United States. Organized labor in the country has not built the capacity to control the flow of migrant workers—mainly because of the failure to create a national labor movement in the decentralized state. To be sure, the declining power of organized labor from the 1950s to the present, evinced through sharply lower union density rates and the decline in labor militancy, has consigned unions to a subordinate position in controlling migration.

Today, one facet of the attack against the 1930s labor regime established under the National Labor Relations Act (NLRA) is the hiring of migrants to fill jobs once held by white and native-born workers. A perpetual thorn in the side of the capitalist class, the NLRA allows workers to join unions freely, protects their rights of association, and negotiates wages and conditions with employers. Seen as the lynchpin of the New Deal plan to secure labor rights during the national labor insurgency of the 1930s, the NLRA transferred to workers a modicum of control over the workplace. It was watered down, however, through the Taft Hartley Act of 1947. The act came under further attack in 1981, when Ronald Reagan waged the first national assault against the law by firing thousands of air traffic controllers, leading the way for business to wage its own war on the NLRA. After that, to recapture absolute control over the economy, the capitalist class has waged a relentless attack against this law. Today the 1935 law is in shambles and effectively does not protect workers from business efforts to undermine unions through restructuring, reneging on collective bargaining agreements, and creating two-tier work forces (Brody 2005). Nevertheless, over the span of the twentieth century, regardless of union density rates, organized labor could mobilize opposition to foreign migration.

This opposition is best seen in the treatment of workers from Mexico. In 1917, the first Bracero program sought Mexican laborers to raise the number of available workers that had been depleted during World War I. However, during the Great Depression, vigorous efforts of the American Federation of Labor against migrants forced hundreds of thousands of Mexicans to leave the United States. During the height of the Depression, some historians estimate that the United States forcibly deported from 415,000 to one million Mexicans (Nevins 2001, 33). The labor shortage in the United States set off by World War II, however, prompted Congress to establish another Bracero program—a contract labor plan that became known popularly by the derogatory moniker "Operation Wetback"—to fill the business demand for low-wage service and agricultural labor. The Bracero program generated a dramatic influx of legal Mexican migration to work in jobs vacated by workers fighting in the war. Though Bracero was intended to promote only legal migration, a large number of undocumented migrants entered the United States to fill the demand for labor in the interwar years. From the 1930s to the 1990s, organized labor had been among the most outspoken institutional opponents of legal and undocumented migration to the United States.

The prevailing perception among unions was that foreigners competed with native-born workers, lowering wages and job security (Haus 2002; introduction, this volume). However, this trade union position that prevailed for more than a century disregarded the reality that working-class militancy and activism among the children of new immigrants who settled in the United States from the 1880s to 1924 were decisive in the mass growth of labor in the 1930s and 1940s. From 1935 to 1945, U.S. union membership expanded from 13.7 percent to 35.5 percent as a wave of labor struggles in manufacturing contributed to the passage of the NLRA and significant membership growth (Bureau of Labor Statistics 2010; Goldfield 1987). Moreover, the nativist perception that continues to prevail among most unions fails to account for alternative means that created transnational labor solidarity in the past.

The best example of transnational solidarity occurred in the late 1880s as the Knights of Labor fought for immigrant rights while also opposing employer efforts to break their bargaining power by enlarging new migration. Historian Marcel van der Linden explains that the Knights sought to prevent migration through advancing solidarity with workers in their home countries: "When, for instance, the window glass workers in the United States in the 1880s saw how their labor monopoly was threatened by the importation of English, French, and Belgian glassworkers, they responded, among other things, by going to the source, the countries of origin of the imported glassworkers, to convince their fellow tradesmen that their conduct was improper . . ." (van der Linden 1999, 1085). The work of the Knights, however, was unique, and the sustained position of unions in opposition to immigrants was typically upheld despite the fact that the lion's share of their members in manufacturing and services were recent newcomers or the children of immigrants.

Still, during labor shortages, the leading labor federations could not keep foreigners from migrating to the United States for work. The Bracero program was essential for the California agriculture industry, which, according to Kitty Calavita, an expert on foreign labor migration, depended on nearly 220,000 Mexican workers, particularly during the harvesting season. In addition, a large number of Mexicans admitted under the Bracero program were employed in service-sector jobs in the U.S. Southwest (1992, 20–28). The wartime Bracero program lasted from 1942 to 1947 but continued for another fifteen years until 1964, as the insatiable demand for low-wage Mexican agricultural workers continued. From 1942 through 1964, some five million Braceros worked in agricultural jobs in the United States. One generation earlier, from the 1880s through the 1920s, immigrants from eastern and southern Europe had gained legal status with relative ease. European workers formed the basis for the massive upsurge of the labor movement through militant strike activity in the 1930s and 1940s. However, Mexican workers were equally essential to the economy of the U.S. Southwest, and were treated as outcasts by the U.S. government, business, and labor. Nevertheless, Mexican workers, on the whole, remained in the United States and many have migrated without legal authorization.

Concomitantly, to address labor shortages in the southern and eastern United States, the British West Indies (BWI) Labor Program was formed in 1942 and officially continued through 1947. The BWI Labor Program was explicitly a guest worker plan designed to placate business' unease over a perceived shortage of labor in agricultural and rural jobs. Over the course of the program, 19,000 contract workers were imported from Barbados, Dominica, Jamaica, St. Lucia, St. Vincent and the Grenadines, and the Bahamas. Although the program ended in 1947, businesses continue to use Caribbean migrant laborers as seasonal workers up until the present, especially in the tourism and hospitality industries of the U.S. eastern seaboard. As the program has expanded, more low-wage women have worked in traditionally gender-based labor, such as housekeeping and cooking for the tourist industry.

Focusing on skilled workers, the United States established its first postwar legal immigration program in 1952. This program, for the first time since 1924, permitted new foreigners to enter the country permanently. The Immigration and Nationality Act (INA) of 1952 allowed workers with specialized skills from war-torn Europe admission into the United States. The immigration law expressly encouraged many leading foreign scientists, academics, and persons with specialized skills to settle permanently.

Unlike the Bracero or BWI guest worker programs and the subsequent guest worker programs established in the 1980s and 1990s, the INA provided for the immigration and naturalization of foreigners rather than solely authorizing temporary visas for employers ostensibly unable to find equivalent workers in the United States. With a maximum quota of 140,000 visas, to be issued to those recognized internationally as having "extraordinary ability" (U.S. Department of State 2008), the INA gave preference to migrants having national or international acclaim in the sciences, arts, education, business, and athletics. By encouraging renowned professors and researchers to seek tenured positions in U.S. higher-education institutions, or with private employers conducting research activities, the act set a precedent for providing visas for multinational executives and managers employed abroad by American firms or subsidiaries who seek to continue work in the United States. The INA set the basis for subsequent legislation providing priority status for the entry of foreigners with skills that were unavailable among U.S. workers (USCIS 2004b).

In the late 1990s, Congress revived efforts to establish a legal temporary migration policy. These new guest worker programs, modeled after the Bracero program of the 1940s, now form the basis for federal proposals for the creation of a mass temporary worker program to import hundreds of thousands of professional and unskilled guest workers to fill perceived labor shortages. The Bracero program is the foundation of U.S. government efforts to establish a legal guest worker program today and a global temporary labor force that spans skill levels and industries. The primary difference today is that the federal government seeks to create a temporary migration program that would closely monitor foreign workers and force all those whose permits expire to leave under penalty of law.

Guest Workers of the World

Migrant workers now form a large and rapidly growing share of the U.S. and global market for labor. In the coming decades, the number of migrants worldwide can be expected to increase even more rapidly as the population of the developed world (Global North) ages and the population of undeveloped countries (Global South) remains youthful. Over the past thirty years, as older industrial economies in the North have shed jobs to the low-wage economies in the South, the gap in wealth *between* developed and undeveloped countries has diminished, while the inequality of wealth *within* countries has expanded dramatically—a process that has transformed class relations across the world as income is redistributed from the poor and working classes to the upper class (Firebaugh 2003).[3] As job prospects diminish through economic stagnation and decline, the impetus for workers to migrate for gainful employment increases dramatically (Breman 1985).

The data produced by the United Nations is incontrovertible: its report states that transnational migration has more than doubled to nearly 200 million in the preceding fifty years. In 2006, the United Nations Population Division (UNPD) reported that "[s]ix out of every 10 international migrants live in developed countries . . . [t]hree quarters of migrants are concentrated in just 28 countries, and 1 in every 5 lives in the U.S." The report found that more than 80 percent of recent migrants to the United States and Canada originated in developing countries of the Global South (United Nations POP/844 2002; United Nations POP/943 2006).[4] The rise in international migration is startling, and would be even more striking if the 150 to 200 million internal migrants in China, India, and other countries of the urbanizing South were taken into account. Internal migration refers to relocation from one region to another within one country, in contrast to international migration across national and territorial boundaries. In China, internal migration from rural to urban areas is restricted by state law. Nonetheless, owing to growing rural poverty, many in the Global South are forced to migrate to central cities to survive economically.

In justifying their own existence, the multilateral agencies created by finance capitalists through trade agreements among states insist that the flow of migrant labor from the South to the North is vital to generating greater interdependence and cooperation between rich and poor countries. Of course, in the neoliberal era, all multilateral agencies are private enterprises that serve the interest of the ruling classes. Given their role as for-profit, private agencies, it should be no surprise that they fail to admit that this labor flow is also a direct outgrowth of declining economic opportunities for workers and the poor as the government and corporate representatives of the upper class expropriate labor and resources at a greater rate throughout the world. Migration has expanded even more dramatically with the collapse of the Soviet Union and the rise of the IMF, and multilateral financial institutions force national economies that once had greater economic sovereignty to conform to draconian demands of trade liberalization and opening markets in exchange for participation in the world capitalist market. The emergent bourgeoisie of the South are reluctant to drop out of the international system even as popular opposition grows.

To explain mass population movement today, this chapter maintains that neoliberal market demands of business give rise to economic crises, displacement, and political upheaval that activate migration for displaced workers and peasants who have no recourse but to pick up and move to urban cores in their home countries or abroad. Many who choose to migrate legally are forced to work in a new system of indentured servitude (Gonzalez 2006).[5] Under neoliberalism, migration is viewed by businesses as an effective policy to undercut established wage and work norms in the North while exploiting the labor power of workers from the South.

This chapter provides a historical and political backdrop to two rapidly expanding sectors of the global economy that are evaluated in this book: IT and hospitality. The chapters to follow segue to a historical and comparative examination of migration to the United States in the IT and hospitality industries. The brief historical sketch of U.S. national migration policy since the 1860s reveals the capitalist-dominated foundation of government policies that advance the interests of the wealthy at the expense of the poor. In turn, in an effort to establish a case that contemporary neoliberal globalization promotes free trade in labor that weakens the capacity of worker resistance in the North and South, this chapter covers the political and economic challenges that contemporary policies and laws place on both U.S. and migrant workers.

This chapter raises key questions that have important implications for labor on national and international levels, as the U.S. government deliberates on a new migration policy and the WTO negotiates new global agreements to deregulate the international flow of migration. To counter the newfound strength of capital, organized labor must find channels through which to recapture their influence on national labor laws and counterbalance corporate efforts to expand guest worker programs. Indisputably, to survive, labor movements must develop new agencies and forms of resistance. No matter what, workers will refuse to go along with new labor programs that exploit them more than ever. The puzzle for labor organizations is how to engage the working class in resisting the expanding international division of labor. In the post-9/11 era, labor is under a greater challenge more than ever in view of government efforts to link migration and guest worker policy with national security, while acknowledging that such types of migration policies also enhance corporate profit.

Trade liberalization through the expansion of guest worker programs will surely suppress U.S. workers' capacities to challenge the state as the terrain of struggle shifts to the international arena. The new labor regimes to be instituted by the United States and WTO will surely throttle national unions, but for the first time ever may offer an opening to building an international labor movement. Existing national and international labor organizations do not yet have the power to intercede and go to battle against what is plainly the formation of a large transnational workforce. But their efforts foreshadow the prospect of a new labor regime to resist state and international labor policies.

The matter of guest workers is of eminent importance on both the national and international fronts. On April 24, 2006, President George W. Bush called for what he termed "comprehensive immigrant reform," which would include "three critical elements: securing the border, strengthening enforcement in the U.S., and creating a temporary worker program" (The White House 2006.) To demonstrate that he was planning to get tough on undocumented immigrants, Bush said that, "a temporary worker program is vital to securing the border." To appeal to business, the president—in coded language—promised an expansive guest worker program: "a temporary worker program would make the system more rational, orderly, and secure by providing a legal way to match willing foreign workers with willing American employers to fill jobs that Americans are not willing to do" (The White House 2006). The theory expounded by the White House purported that the U.S. labor force is too educated and that most do not want to work in jobs that do not require expertise. Tamar Jacoby of the Manhattan Institute testified to the U.S. Senate Committee on the Judiciary: "Today's young people aspire to work inside, with their minds, not their muscles" (Jacoby 2005b). In a speech to the conservative American Enterprise Institute, Jacoby elaborated on the need for unskilled migrant workers: "[W]e no longer have much of a native-born working class that's willing to do manual labor and dirty, humiliating jobs. . . . Now of course, these changes are wrenching for some American workers, but by and large immigration is good for the U.S. economy. . . . Not only do immigrants fill jobs Americans don't want to do. But because of that—and because they're so flexible and willing to move at the drop of a hat to wherever the jobs are—they keep the economy growing at a pace that few comparable economies can match" (Jacoby 2005b). The White House and business' answer to a perceived labor shortage is to institutionalize a system by reinforcing and vastly increasing legal guest worker programs.

In the international arena, the United States is lobbying for a global migrant labor program through current WTO negotiations to expand free trade to skilled and unskilled workers. The U.S. government maintains that trade liberalization in labor provides a rare opportunity for young adults, the poor, and the dispossessed in the Global South to earn much-needed money that is sent back home as remittances, while filling the need for skilled labor. Most expedient, U.S. corporations and global financial institutions try to conceal the fact that migration supplies vast profits through fashioning a new peripatetic low-wage labor force. The government's U.S. Trade Representative (USTR) advocates for a massive expansion of guest worker programs, in spite of the domestic clamor against new migration.

The urgency of a WTO guest worker agreement for the United States derives from the importance of services to the balance of trade. From 1990 to 2004, service exports more than doubled, from $147.9 billion to $338.6 billion. Furthermore, the United States has a net trade imbalance of $666.2 billion, but exports $48.5 billion more than it imports in services (Office of Trade and Industry Information 2006).

The WTO, formed in Geneva in January 1995, is the newest multilateral agency that is the culmination of the Uruguay General Agreement on Tariffs and Trade (GATT) negotiations to eliminate national trade and tariff barriers. To detractors, the WTO constitutes one-third of the "unholy trinity" with the IMF and the World Bank, formed in 1944 to rebuild Europe and provide financing for developing countries. As a prerequisite to accession to the WTO, a country is required to change domestic policies that may interfere with free trade—which can mean eliminating subsidies for food or basic commodities for the poor that give one nation an unfair advantage. As of 2006, all three leading multilateral agencies support lifting global trade restrictions and are seeking to complete a labor and services agreement called the Doha Development Round (Key 2003; Peet 2003).[6] Eliminating barriers to free trade in labor is the culmination of the GATS-4 (General Agreement on Trade and Services, Round 4).

The World Bank views global migration as advantageous to impoverished countries in the Global South.[7] In its 2006 report *Global Economic Prospects,* the bank asserts that the remittances of money from migrant laborers to poor countries in the South are indispensable to economic survival and growth. The mantra it spins is that migration is a form of necessary trade liberalization offering opportunity to young adults willing to work hard in the North while sending remittances back home to support their families in the South. Paul Wolfowitz, former president of the World Bank, and deputy secretary of defense under George W. Bush from 2001 to 2005, viewed international migration as an important means to combat poverty in the South. As one might expect, Wolfowitz shared the same position on global migration as the Bush White House: "The prospects for migration flows are critical for development. Developing countries benefit through the money that migrants send home to their families (remittances) through reduced labor market pressures, and through contacts with international markets and access to technology. . . . Migration remains an important force for fighting poverty, the key mission of the World Bank" (The World Bank 2006).

But a monetary remittance from low-wage guest workers to their families in the South is scarcely a development plan for the new century. The fact that the World Bank under the leadership of Wolfowitz suggests that young adults go to the North for economic *opportunity* is also a prescription for social turmoil, as families are broken apart and children inevitably neglected. The guest worker program has no child care component for the young adults selected to travel and work in the United States. Child care in the South is almost always provided by immediate and extended families. Guest workers mainly leave their countries to pay for immediate needs and education for their children. In Jamaica and the entire underdeveloped Global South, however, IMF financial strictures have directly eroded public education through forcing governments to reduce public expenditures in social programs to bring national budgets into balance. Thus, guest workers' motivation to work in the United States—to earn money to support their families—is often futile, despite their best efforts to improve their standard of living.

Of course, most guest workers would prefer to make a living wage in their home countries. In interviews and meetings held from 2005 to 2006, the majority of thirty guest workers from Jamaica and Barbados stated that they would have preferred to stay in their home countries than go to the United States to work in menial jobs. But because no decent year-round jobs are available in the Caribbean basin, growing masses of poor and unemployed workers are enlisting in guest worker programs. Though U.S. Citizenship and Immigration Services (USCIS) depict hospitality work as unskilled, in fact, many guest workers selected by contractors to work in resorts throughout the United States are required to complete rigorous training programs in the hospitality industry. Almost all guest workers in the U.S. H-2B Program from Jamaica state that if they could earn decent wages in their home countries, they would never travel thousands of miles to the United States (interviews, February 2005 to June 2006).

Even workers who travel to the United States as part of their training program on J1 visas—ostensibly for the purpose of learning the hospitality business—come back sorely disappointed. Many students end up working for free through exchange programs that purport to provide extensive education over the course of a semester or two. One unemployed student from Jamaica said that the training program for which she had to pay included two hours of class work every week. The rest of the week, she was a waitress at an exclusive resort on Florida's east coast. For the most part, students are asked to clean rooms, wash dishes, wait tables, and clean swimming pools. Rarely, if ever, do they learn skills in managing hotels and resorts (interview, anonymous, February 2007).

Both the IMF and World Bank need to genuinely take an interest in economic development, school funding, preventive health care, adequate housing, and new infrastructure as priorities rather than supporting efforts by corporations to recruit workers to mop floors on Hilton Head Island, South Carolina. Undeniably, many of the social benefits—from public welfare to preventive health care—that are removed by multinational financial institutions in the Global South are also under attack and unraveling in the North.

To understand the distinctive importance of low-wage global migration, the origin and social class of guest workers, as well as their goals, must be taken into account. On the one hand, Indian migrants trained in the latest IT technology are treated differently than Jamaican housekeepers, who have few options once they return home. Those migrants in the IT and business service industries from India and China view working in the United States on an H-1B or L1 visa as a *means to a comfortable career* in the United States or in their home countries, while guest workers from Jamaica and Mexico see working in the hospitality industry as a *means of providing* for their families or saving for their children's education. For the most part, Jamaican H-2B workers and students in hospitality training in the United States are young adults between eighteen and thirty years of age.

North-South Demographics:
Finance Capital and Labor Migration

What social and economic forces are behind the expansion of migrant labor programs on the national and world stages? This book maintains that global capital—for the most part, multinational corporations in the United States and western Europe—see the cost of labor as a crucial component to increasing profits. Even medium- and small-sized businesses are prodded to lower costs by reducing wages in order to compete in the global marketplace for skilled and unskilled labor. Businesses that do not adapt by lowering wage costs are penalized by the financial institutions that maintain control over manufacturing and service businesses. The imposition of neoliberal programs can be traced back to the 1980s as governments in the Global North enacted market reform policies that have had the effect of redistributing income and assets from the working class and the poor to corporations and the upper class through privatization, removal of social welfare programs, and forcing trade liberalization policies on the entire world. French economists Gérard Duménil and Dominique Lévy lay bare incontrovertible quantitative and historical evidence through cross-national data showing a reassertion of upper-class power through a *regressive* process of freezing wages in sectors at low levels of technology and a *progressive* process of sponsoring new technology in sectors that have greater potential for profits without necessarily reducing labor costs (Duménil and Lévy 2004; Harvey 2006).[8] This book aims to show these processes in two sectors: hospitality, an industry with limited technological prospects, and the IT industry.

The formation of an international migrant labor force is the latest phase of the evolution of capital's efforts to reduce wages in all sectors of the global economy, from manufacturing to services. Capital is defined here as the constellation of international upper-class interests and their corporate institutions—from major private manufacturing and service industry to financial and banking interests, the latter now growing in importance as profitability writ large takes precedence over survival of firms and industries. As manufacturing—a mainstay of unions—declines, labor organizations are now seeking to organize workers in the growing U.S. service sector. But while organizing has made modest gains in services, industrial distinctions among jobs are now interchangeable. Housekeepers in the hotel industry can easily transfer to the health-care industry. Put more baldly, the restaurant, hotel, building service, and health-care industries no longer need exclusive skills from workers as labor is becoming more homogenized. Thus, job skills required for hospitality occupations are not appreciably different from landscaping and restaurant occupations. Therefore, homogenization of skill diminishes the importance of occupational boundaries within unions.

The expansion and institution of a permanent migrant labor force in the United States would impair the growth of union density in service jobs, where clear distinctions are delineated among health-care, food preparation, and building maintenance occupations, all of which are industries where unions are modestly growing as they become more important to the economy (U.S. Department of Labor 2006). To undermine modest wage growth and prospects to grow in power through unionization, corporations are substituting migrant workers for U.S. and European laborers in many professions. Therefore, corporate-sponsored think tanks advocate liberalizing the flow of labor trade between countries to ameliorate a perceived shortage of workers. In reality, these efforts are intended to cut labor costs and reduce the power of unions. Recent studies demonstrate that many—if not most—U.S. and foreign workers employed in hotels, restaurants, resorts, and hospitals (industries where pay is low and work is grueling and dangerous) are highly motivated to unionize (Milkman 2000; Ness 2005). The establishment and growth of guest worker programs throughout the world—and predominantly in the United States—is not a win-win proposition by which unwanted jobs are filled by desperate young migrant workers. Opponents challenge this view as jobs in professional and manual service occupations are marginalized by businesses intent on lowering labor costs, either through creating artificial crises and lowering wages or recruiting foreign workers below prevailing or minimum wages. Thus institutionalizing U.S. guest worker programs and the expansion of the WTO to permit labor imports and exports inevitably reduce wages and working conditions for U.S.-born laborers and migrant guest workers.

Political and demographic change is crucial to comprehending the demand for low-wage workers from the Global South. In many ways, Indian IT workers and Jamaican housekeepers are viewed as much the same by corporations seeking to increase profits through lowering wages. Both are seen by business as young laborers from the South willing to work hard and long hours for low pay in exchange for a remote chance to improve their life chances down the road. At the same time that business can be expected to seek out low-wage labor with no strings attached, U.S. and European policy makers are considering the aging of the population in the North and the opportunity to tap into the growing labor force of the South.

Unmistakably, the demand for unskilled labor considerably overshadows that for skilled labor today: 24.6 million unskilled workers versus only 3.1 million skilled workers are employed in the Global North. The World Bank projected that from 2001 to 2005, unskilled migration would grow by 9.8 million and skilled labor by 4.5 million. The aging of the Global North's population has placed younger guest workers from the Global South in high demand, even if they are considered social pariahs by national working classes.

There is abundant evidence to support the fact that big business pushes global migration as a method of lowering wage costs. The World Bank reports that "[a] key driver in the demand for international migrants over the next 20 years will be slowing growth, and then decline of the labor force in high-income countries." However, it is not so much a "decline of the labor force," but rather, worker demands for higher wages. Concurrently, the Bank projects that over the next thirty years, the Global South will grow by one billion workers—an important component in reducing the dependency on native-born workers in the Global North. Furthermore, migrant guest workers will not be provided social welfare benefits upon leaving the United States, as is the case with native-born workers (The World Bank 2006, 29–33). This sentiment—that migrants from the Global South will fill jobs left by older retired workers—is reinforced by U.S. national security agencies. In 2002, John L. Helgerson of the National Intelligence Council predicted that global migration will expand and attract younger workers that will "offset the retirement of older workers . . . and provide jobs for unemployed youth from developing countries" (Helgerson 2002).

Just as national and global agencies see the need for a larger number of guest workers in established positions, popular opposition has mounted against immigrants, both in the United States and western Europe. In the

1980s, in meat processing industries throughout the United States, jobs considered hard and grueling—but that paid enough to support a family—have been almost entirely relegated to migrant workers. These shifts have created great animosity toward migrant guest workers and unauthorized laborers from those Americans who have lost work to "imported" labor.

In view of the financial significance of low-wage guest service workers to the economy, U.S. trade negotiators seek rapid settlement in global service liberalization negotiations that would be open to all countries through the auspices of the WTO. To speed negotiations, the United States has agreed to take a leading position in proposing a plan for international trade in services. However, the country is working on two tracks: enlarging global labor trade through multilateral talks and establishing independent bilateral guest worker agreements. In May 2005, the United States submitted a revised offer on services to the WTO, in consultation with domestic business to expand the GATS Round 4 into telecommunications, computers, delivery services, higher education, transportation, energy, and temporary migrant labor. U.S. Trade Representative Rob Portman admits that the U.S. temporary migration program is the most expansive in the world: "Our existing temp entry commitments, so-called 'mode 4,' are among the most generous of all WTO members in terms of entry categories covered, and they apply to all services sectors where we have commitments. Only a handful of developed countries have comparable Mode 4 commitments. The U.S. report maintains that services accounted for a larger share of total output and GDP growth" (USTR 2005).

The raucous debates in Congress—and on American streets—reflect that the fundamental importance of guest workers extends far beyond national policies to expanding trade in services.

Labor Migration and the Matter of Skill

Those favoring expansion of the guest worker program say the United States is losing ground to India, China, and other countries where greater commitments to education and hard work are creating a highly skilled workforce that will outpace the United States in the future. Whether this is true or not, until U.S. companies can find workers with skills in engineering, sciences, and information technologies, foreign workers are essential to the service economy, which is vital to the balance of trade. Those against the establishment of a guest worker program say that it is fiction that U.S. laborers do not have the work ethic of workers abroad. Opponents of the expansion of a guest worker program argue that, while education of the U.S. labor force is essential, the skill-shortage argument is merely a pretext for importing low-wage foreign labor. In connection with the hospitality industry, most who support the expansion of guest worker programs claim that migrant labor is essential to U.S. business because citizens do not want to work in the industry (Jacoby 2005). However, a sizable and growing number of analysts controvert this argument, maintaining that a reduction of low-wage migration would benefit U.S. workers greatly by keeping labor markets tight. Their line of reasoning is that if service and manufacturing jobs paid decent wages in the United States, those who have left the labor market would return as gainfully employed workers (Briggs 2004).

Native-born workers only eschew hard manual labor because wages are so low. Still, most U.S. workers must pull together a living through disparate jobs that no longer provide an equivalent living standard as compared with a generation ago. Though the IT and hospitality industries are mandated by government law to pay prevailing wages to U.S. workers, as we shall see in chapters 2 and 3, there is abundant evidence that both high-technology and hospitality companies do not even try to seek U.S. workers nor encourage them to apply. In both IT and hospitality industries, we are finding the obliteration of the concept of a standard job that pays wages and offers benefits and vacation days.

To reduce labor costs, corporations eliminate full-time employees and seek to hire workers only when they are needed. Fashioning a flexible workforce is essential for human resource departments in U.S. corporations (Dychtwald, Erickson, & Morrison 2006).The conventional job of the postwar generation is being replaced by nonstandard contingent labor where work is unsteady, seasonal, part-time, and typically contracted by an employment agency. The expansion of the guest worker program is crucial to establishing a flexible labor model. The vast majority of guest workers are contract laborers for foreign companies providing workers to firms in the United States. No job is viewed as sacrosanct—anyone from a high-technology specialist to a day laborer is viewed as expendable.

Today, the U.S. Congress drives the transformation of the job market and in general has been supportive of guest workers or any program demanded by corporations. Congressional leaders and recent presidents have concurred that access to foreign low-wage temporary workers is vital to future business growth. In the 1990s, both branches of government promoted guest workers in high technology, even after domestic unemployment in the skilled job markets had expanded. Moreover, from 1990 to 2010, globalization expanded from the relocation of manufacturing to offshore countries to moving people to the United States for jobs as contractors in the high-technology and domestic services sectors (Briggs 2004; Jacoby 2006; Zolberg 2006). In some cases, women originally intending to work in manufacturing or services are trafficked into other jobs, particularly sex work.[9] In particular, a growing number of multinational high-technology and finance corporations demand increasing the cap on importing foreign IT and business service guest workers, and those from abroad earn a fraction of what comparable U.S. workers can command. Even when restrictions are placed on guest worker programs, U.S. companies move operations to India and other countries to take advantage of the enormous wage differentials. But hospitality work must be done by guest workers.

The United States is a leading actor in WTO efforts to broaden trade to include migrant labor and services. Workers and unions throughout the world are unable to resist through established channels, giving rise to mass demonstrations at virtually every major trade meeting and resistance on the job to outsourcing labor, whether through GATS or directly by the U.S. government.

Prospects for a Guest Worker Program

The projected expansion in migration grows out of the need for capital to extract greater profits through undercutting labor. On the one hand, jobs in the service and hospitality sectors that do not have the potential to advance technologically will be restructured and wages will be lowered so profits may expand. On the other hand, telecommunications, science, engineering, and financial service jobs with potential for financial growth through new technology will still make use of a trained workforce.

From 1990 to 2005, the restructuring of the American economy through the growth of the neoliberal free market and the expansion of the postindustrial service economy inexorably transformed the definition of labor and work in the United States. Perhaps the most prominent popular representation of this change is the dramatic growth of a new migrant labor force that is increasingly filling jobs once held by native-born workers across skill categories and industrial sectors. Immigrant workers, typically viewed as prepared to work long hours at lower wages than are U.S. workers, have entered an array of industries previously dominated by native-born workers. In the literature, new immigrant laborers have been stereotypically viewed in academic and popular discourse as working in low-wage unskilled menial jobs in the service economy (Waldinger 1999; Milkman 2002; Ness 2005).

No matter what policy is finally enacted, guest workers are the wave of the future—the only uncertainty is the number of guest workers authorized to work in the United States and the flexibility given to businesses to hire and dismiss them. In the IT industry, guest workers on three-year H-1B visas are deported when they are out of work for more than one month after completion of their assignment. In hospitality services, guest workers must leave the United States upon completion of their seasonal work and can be dismissed by their employer for any reason, after which they must return home. On an international basis, under current WTO rules, workers may only migrate to fulfill service contracts with one business. Efforts to expand the program over the past several years have failed. The trade negotiators did not reach agreement in Cancun in 2003 as global justice protesters disrupted the talks, known as the Doha Development Round. The WTO continues to negotiate for expansion of the plan to liberalize trade in people and services. The United States is far and away the world's leading recipient of foreign skilled IT guest workers, accounting for as much as 70 percent of all migrants from India.

The outsourcing and offshoring debate is charged with contradictory perspectives on the importance of expanding or limiting the number of foreign workers in the United States. Support for loosening restrictions on global migration and contracting foreign labor reflects domestic interests that stand to benefit from the expansion of visa caps for low-wage labor.[10] Although popular opposition to guest worker policies is growing in the United States, the government remains at the forefront of promoting a global migration system through its leadership in the WTO.

In March and April 2006, amid the debate in Congress to overhaul the migration system, millions of immigrant workers and their supporters engaged in mass demonstrations to oppose a guest worker program and stiff financial penalties for unauthorized immigrants working in the United States. On March 25, 2006, in Los Angeles, an estimated 500,000 to one million immigrants protested the Congressional proposals, which they saw as antiimmigrant. In the following weeks, a growing number of low-wage immigrants, supported by their unions, demanded that immigrants not be criminalized (Archibold 2006). Later protests against guest worker legislation expanded throughout the nation; in some cases, workers left jobs and students cut classes to join marches and demonstrations. The protests continued on May 1, 2006 ("May Day") as immigrant leaders called for a national strike. Immigrant and union demonstrators filled the streets of Los Angeles, Chicago, New York, and other major U.S. cities.

Immigrants protested a bill passed in the House of Representatives in December 2005 that would criminalize undocumented migrants and a less-harsh Senate proposal to regulate migration through creating a mass guest worker program. While nativist fervor abounds, serious proposals in the House and Senate call for an expanded guest worker program. Both proposals would severely damage the capacity of workers to mobilize into unions because migrant guest workers would compete for jobs with unionized U.S. laborers (Swarns 2006).

To participate actively in the highly competitive global environment, proponents argue that the U.S. immigration selection must shift its course from emphasizing issues of family reunification and asylum for refugees to encouraging economic migration. This "economic stream" view focuses on the reality that global economic integration requires the United States to promote the migration of skilled workers to remain competitive. If U.S. firms are to remain competitive, they must encourage foreign migration to retain a competitive position in the world economy (Papademetriou & Yale-Loehr 1996, 15).[11] From 2005 to the present, pushed by a perceived labor shortage, business lobbyists in Washington have proposed a dramatic expansion of a legal guest worker program to address the shortage of workers. Leading the way in support of an expanded guest worker program are the U.S. Chamber of Commerce, American Hotel and Lodging Association, American Nursery and Landscape Association, and the National Council of Agricultural Employers (American Hospitality, Travel, Tourism and Franchise Industries 2006; Phillips 2006).

Coopting the vernacular of those who oppose expanded migration, business has artfully crafted a position that the current law must be changed—but the question raised is precisely that of what kind of change. Randel K. Johnson of the U.S. Chamber of Commerce argues that, "it is crucial for our national and economic security to fix this broken immigration system," while simultaneously calling for legislation that "provides for a temporary worker program by creating an efficient program that allows employers to recruit immigrant workers when U.S. workers cannot be found" (Essential Worker Immigration Coalition 2006).

TEMPORARY FOREIGN LABOR
AND "SECURING THE HOMELAND"

The Bush migration proposals in 2005 and 2006 advocated a program for migrant laborers to work in jobs that corporations would rather see filled by lower-wage foreigners. Viewing immigration as essential, the Bush administration sought to provide labor to employers through a legal process. The plan attempted to fulfill two purposes: first, to "secure the border" (The White House 2006) to prevent those individuals who pose potential threats to national security from crossing the border; and second, to establish a stable temporary guest worker program that would benefit employers seeking skilled and unskilled laborers for a designated period of time.

This overhaul of immigration policy is couched in the language of defending the United States from potential foreign threats. However, the essence of the new program proposal is to create a temporary workforce across skill and industrial categories. Following a growing clamor among the increasing number of Latino and Hispanic voters seeking a comprehensive amnesty, the Bush administration's January 2004 immigration reform proposals, calculated to be promulgated before the November 2006 elections, were intended to mollify concerns that the plan was dead. Simultaneously, the proposals were calculated to heighten public fear that opening the borders to foreigners could compromise U.S. security. However, as noted, this political posture of promoting national security through importing foreign workers screened by the U.S. government allows corporations to increase access to "legal" low-wage workers. As President Bush stated in 2004: "We see millions of hard-working men and women condemned to fear and insecurity in a massive, undocumented economy. Illegal entry across our borders makes more difficult the urgent task of securing the homeland. The system is not working. Our nation needs an immigration system that serves the American economy, and reflects the American Dream" (Bush 2004). George W. Bush's guest worker proposals seemed intended to fulfill employer needs through foreign labor rather than provide training for U.S. workers to fill jobs that, as he maintained, "serve the economic needs of our country" (Bush 2004).

In effect, the guest worker program jettisons any hope of lifting low-wage U.S. workers out of poverty. If "American citizens are not willing to take" poverty-wage jobs, Bush asserted that, "we ought to welcome into our country a person who will fill that job" (2004). However, once the jobs are completed, Bush proposed that the program provide economic incentives to encourage guest workers to leave the United States, a policy of patent exploitation of migrants. Thus, rather than creating a wide-ranging program to grant immigrants legal status in the United States, the Bush plan sought to "match willing foreign workers when no Americans can be found to fill the jobs" (2004). The term "legal status" is a Trojan horse for all those migrant workers who seek permanent status in the United States. Instead of offering an avenue to immigration, however, it provides the basis for expelling undocumented workers from the United States upon completion of their work. In no uncertain terms, Bush argued: "This program will offer legal status, as temporary workers, to the millions of undocumented men and women now employed in the U.S., and to those in foreign countries who seek to participate in the program and have been offered employment here. This new system should be clear and efficient, so employers are able to find workers quickly and simply" (Bush 2004).

LABOR UNIONS AND GUEST WORKERS

In sharp contrast to the Bush administration and many Democrats and Republicans in Congress, the AFL-CIO and most national unions view the expansion of guest worker programs—not undocumented workers—to be the primary burden on the U.S. economy. Experience has taught the unions that undocumented workers can be organized to the benefit of all workers. Indeed in the early 1990s, a core of unions led by the Service Employees International Union (SEIU) and UNITE-HERE recognized that immigrants comprised a large share of workers in core services industries. At a time when manufacturing unions were losing members to offshoring, the unions and their predecessors put forward resolutions at AFL-CIO conventions to change immigration law to facilitate new organizing (AFL-CIO 2006; Bacon 2001, 2005; Milkman 2000; Ness 2005). In 2000, the AFL-CIO took a new position toward immigrant workers who are now filling many of the unskilled jobs in manufacturing and services that had been for more than a century considered a bastion of the labor movement. Above all, migrants—chiefly, undocumented workers from Central America—were filling jobs that were the mainstay of the labor movement for the last century: low-wage manufacturing and service work. The federation's new position of welcoming undocumented immigrants represents conclusive recognition by organized labor that it is simply impossible to control the nation's borders. Labor's shift from restriction to inclusion is an extension of "skepticism about the state's ability to completely control migration" (Haus 2002, 9).

At the same time, organized labor deems temporary foreign worker programs detrimental to both workers and the union movement because they undermine both migrant and native-born workers. Put simply, guest workers generally cannot be organized along traditional lines because of the temporary nature of their work without a broader transnational labor union representation (Gordon 2007). However, stimulating transnational unionization requires a mass upsurge of workers in their home countries as well as the United States demanding improved wages and conditions. Thus, the Bush administration's proposal to enlarge the temporary guest worker program is, in the AFL-CIO's view, a new means to create a "permanent underclass of workers" subject to employer "abuse and exploitation," and a means to reduce wage and labor standards (AFL-CIO 2006).

The federation contended that guest worker programs have "an egregious history" of reducing wages, benefits, and rights for immigrant and native-born workers. AFL-CIO president John Sweeney said that temporary labor programs "cast workers into a perennial second-class status, and unfairly put their fates into their employers' hands, creating a situation ripe for exploitation." In addition, the organization argued that the guest worker initiative would "encourage employers to turn good jobs into temporary jobs at reduced wages and diminished working condition and contribute to the growing class of workers laboring in poverty" (2006). Joined by SEIU-led Change to Win in April 2009, the federation argued that temporary workers are paid lower wages and have fewer benefits and job protections against dismissal (AFL-CIO 2009). Organized labor thus views Bush's plan and any plan by President Obama that greatly enlarges guest work programs as a method of establishing a new underclass of "second tier" workers that will chip away at the wages, conditions, and job security of "domestic" workers. Furthermore, in 2009, as the Obama administration developed legislation for a guest work program, the fragmented national unions could at least agree on a position in opposition to an expanded guest work program without worker protections (AFL-CIO 2009).

Given that undocumented workers in the United States are the foundation of new organizing for a growing number of service unions, the federation seeks a comprehensive amnesty program for migrants already employed in the country. A guest worker program would only reverse extensive new organizing among undocumented immigrants employed in unskilled low-wage service jobs. Instead, the AFL-CIO backs a plan of reform that would provide a legal means to permit migrants to work on an equal basis with U.S. workers. Under the plan, employers violating the law would be subject to rigorous penalties. Currently, sanctions for firms that hire the undocumented penalize workers rather than employers, while the temporary worker program neither strictly enforces prevailing wage laws nor demands that employers prove a lack of domestic workers for the same positions. In short, the AFL-CIO opposes expansion of temporary worker programs while seeking to create a pathway for the undocumented to gain legal status in the United States.

U.S. Guest Worker Program for IT Workers

The low-skilled jobs being filled by undocumented workers are not the only ones threatened by guest worker programs. In more recent years, skilled positions are increasingly being filled by guest workers, especially in the field of technology. In the late 1990s, high technology was considered by government, economists, and industry experts to be the primary engine of the U.S. economy and a requirement for maintaining the 1993–2000 economic bubble. Proponents of this view argued that sustaining an adequate supply of highly skilled workers was critical to the resilience of the high-technology industry.

This position, espoused by high-technology interests, became a mantra by the fall of 1997, spurring Congress to conduct hearings on the potentially deleterious effects on the economy that a shortage of skilled workers in the industry could cause, and the threat that it posed to the national economy. In 1997, a study by the Information Technology Association of America (ITAA), a high-technology industry interest group, estimated that there was a shortage of some 340,000 IT workers in the United States. The ITAA and other technology industry representatives argued that the shortage could only be remedied by recruiting an ample number of workers from abroad to fill growing needs in the high-technology industry.

Also in the 1990s, growing public hostility toward undocumented migration was largely ignored by American employers avidly seeking foreigners who would work at significantly lower wages than would U.S. workers. To demonstrate a resolve to control the borders from the growing numbers of undocumented Mexicans crossing into the United States in search of gainful employment, in 1994 the Clinton administration began a concentrated effort to guard the border through the Operation Gatekeeper program. Although the program endangered thousands of Mexicans, the effort was seen by most as a symbolic gesture to placate U.S. citizens who resented the failure of the government to control the borders. The program tangibly increased government resources to border security through vastly expanding physical impediments and increasing the number of patrol agents on the U.S.-Mexico border. To be sure, Operation Gatekeeper's reinforcement of the border through the construction of fences impaired unrestrained border crossings. However, the program did not stop the growing absorption of hundreds of thousands of Mexicans migrating to the United States.

Operation Gatekeeper's primary legacy has been to increase the risk of injury or death for those crossing the border, swelling the number of migrants dying from hypothermia, heat stroke, drowning, and other accidents. Nevins incisively documents the confrontational and resolute military nature of the Operation Gatekeeper program against Mexican migrants at a time of growing regional integration across the southern border (Nevins 2001). Expenditures on new fences and border patrol agents have not dissuaded desperate migrants from working in the United States, but have helped to mollify American antiimmigrant sentiment (Staudt & Coronado 2002). Concurrently, Nevins shows persuasively that although the program was aimed at appeasing opponents of unregulated migration, its relative failure stoked nativist sentiment against Latinos—U.S. citizens or not—as lawbreakers and a threat to national sovereignty (Nevins 2001, 95–122). In 2010, Arizona's state law requiring police officers to verify one's immigration status reveals that the unbroken white-nativist sentiment persists and presents a serious threat to all workers of color. Moreover, the law, pushed by a Republican governor, further exposes the contradictory factions in a party that is supported by business, which seeks to enlarge the pool of migrants, and antiimmigrant white workers who fear losing their jobs. Given that federal jurisdiction over immigration policy remains imprecise and nebulous, states are likely to continue to seek to legislate and apply policies in response to nativist demands for restrictions, or conversely, in response to business interests to ensure an ample supply reserve army of labor.

The failure to appease nativist sentiment was mainly a result of the contradictory policies of the U.S. government. Even as the government made a public show against undocumented immigrants through Operation Gatekeeper, corporations seeking guest workers pushed Congress to increase caps on guest worker visas for workers considered to be in short supply. Unlike the immigrants being shut out, these workers were highly skilled. Gradually, during the 1990s, the U.S. government responded by raising the cap on foreign guest workers to accommodate corporate demand for programmers and software workers. Ironically, in 2000, one year before the dot-com crash, proponents for raising the number of higher-skilled immigrants to the United States convinced Congress to drastically raise the caps on guest worker (nonimmigrant) visas for individuals to fill jobs that had to go unfilled because of the acute shortage of skilled U.S. high-technology workers at a time when the industry was perceived to be booming. The cap was raised from an annual level of 65,000 to 195,000. As the dot-com bubble burst and unemployment grew dramatically in the industry, U.S. companies took advantage of the expanded access to foreign guest workers. By 2004, estimates calculated that there were about one million highly skilled immigrant workers in the United States.

Even as joblessness remained high for skilled labor in information technology, engineering, and scientific professions, when the cap expired in October 2005, corporations vigorously lobbied Congress for an increase in the cap because of a so-called shortage of educated U.S. workers. On the other hand, organizations and societies representing domestic workers argued that the unemployment did not result from a shortage of labor, but rather from corporations' efforts to lower industry wages. However, the global economic crisis has lowered wages and reduced popular support for migrant labor that could compete with U.S.-born workers. If the Obama administration seeks to reform migration, which seems a priority for consolidating a strong base of immigrant voters, the government may generate populist working-class opposition to the Democratic Party. But, as we saw in this chapter, those who focus on deporting undocumented immigrants are recklessly misplacing their resentment against foreigners and imperiling their class interests. A greater danger to safeguarding jobs for all workers lies in the expansion of guest worker programs.

3

India's Global and Internal Labor Migration and Resistance

A Case Study of Hyderabad

On September 29, 2005, Indian unions waged a general strike to protest a national government plan to privatize airline, railroad, and banking industries. The strike was a blow to foreign and domestic investors who had been pushing the Congress Party–Left Front coalition government to privatize India's transportation network. The government, however, did not waver. In January 2006, despite several such mass industry strikes, the Indian government put forward a privatization plan for the Delhi and Bombay airports, demonstrating to international investors that they were serious about opening the country to foreign capital. The privatization plan did not include provisions for saving jobs and maintaining wages, so in early February 2006, most airport workers went on strike again. After a prolonged conflict and several unsuccessful strike actions, the Indian government moved forward with their plan and privatized the two airports in 2008.

The battle over airport privatization is but one chapter in what has become an ongoing conflict between Indian and international capital interests on the one side and Indian labor on the other. The liberalization of India's economy has become the grounds for unending political struggles between wealthier segments of Indian society, who stand to gain from opening up the county's economy, and growing numbers of workers who find themselves pushed into deeper poverty and destitution. The strikes are but one manifestation of the standoff between foreign and U.S.-national capitalists seeking to privatize all state infrastructure and an increasingly militant working class and peasantry fighting to maintain even a basic level of subsistence. In 2006, *Economic and Political Weekly* reported that 80 percent of India's nonagricultural economy consisted of informal (unorganized) employment. Meanwhile, from 2005 to 2010, persistent industrywide and nationwide strikes in the first decade of the new century by national unions in rival Indian labor federations have regularly shut down manufacturing, service, and public-sector industries. The strikes led to increased wages and slowed efforts to accelerate privatization of state infrastructure (Sakthivel & Joddar 2006, 2107–14).

Through neoliberal economic development, workers in India's formal economy—whether they choose to stay in the country and enter its expanding IT and/or business services sectors or instead travel to the United States or Europe as guest workers—face a number of challenges. First, either through outsourcing or guest worker programs, capital is striking down traditional labor-union accords by removing workers from established jobs in older organized labor markets and replacing them with lower-wage workers who are not subject to government labor laws and protections. Thus, Indian multinational proponents of using migration as a development strategy fail to account for the deployment of educated and trained workers in the United States and the shortage of Indian skilled workers in essential areas of human development at home. While U.S. and Indian capitalists and high-wage guest workers with multinational networks benefit from this system, the process renders U.S.-born workers jobless and neglects the needs of the poor, who comprise the vast majority of India's population.

Neoliberal global economic organizations falsely conclude that India is poised to become one of the world's leading economic powers—especially if internal and international migration were unleashed (World Bank 2008, 163), but in reality, most Indians are growing more restless as rural poverty, urban slums in the major metropolitan areas, and child labor dramatically grow. Finally, the increasing use of Indian guest workers by U.S. corporations in discrete labor markets where job shortages were deliberately created generates a need for new pliable and lower-cost labor and hurts both the U.S. and Indian workers in the long run.

In this chapter, I trace the background of neoliberal reform in India and the effects of global capitalism on India's class divide and economic development for the purpose of understanding the connection between the United States and India in the neoliberal global system that expanded dramatically in the 1990s. I look at two case studies: first, I focus on the fate of Indian guest workers who travel to the United States to find jobs in the low-wage industrial labor market sectors. I then contrast the guest worker situation with that of higher-skilled technology workers, many formerly guest workers who have returned from the United States to India, through a close examination of Hyderabad, a city that is modernizing yet facing growing levels of poverty.

Background of Neoliberal Reform in India

From the 1970s onward, the neoliberal economic order has directed the global economy—a trend accelerated by the breakup of the Soviet Union in 1991. This multilateral free market system, framed in the Washington Consensus of 1989, opens up markets for leading corporations and multilateral economic organizations and reduces the capacity of governments to regulate their own economies, forcing countries in the Global South, such as India, to shift from the import-substitution industrialization (ISI) promoted in the postwar era to export promotion advocated by neoliberal economists (Harvey 2006). The penalty for nonconformity is exclusion from participation in the international system of trade that generates revenues that are crucial for the national capitalist classes.[1] Indian political and labor economists such as Amiya Kumar Bagchi argue that these market reforms are devastating to the vast majority of the population, but Indian capitalists have been incubating a squad of propagandists known as "enthusiasts" to defend their neoliberal efforts (interview, Amiya Kumar Bagchi, Kolkata, December 18, 2008; Bagchi 2002; Das 2002; Sheshabalaya 2005). The information technology (IT) sector best illustrates the ways in which the neoliberal "partnership" between capitalists in India and the United States hurts workers in both countries.

When U.S. IT was flourishing and jobs were highly paid in the 1980s and 1990s, industry advocates argued that the shortage of skilled IT workers necessitated a large increase in the number of visas for foreigners to fill the labor gap. When the industry recession hit in 2000, thousands of workers were laid off. Yet companies extended their reliance on foreign guest workers, employing them and U.S. workers in nonstandard work arrangements.

Companies have historically introduced nonstandard work arrangements in response to intense competition created frequently in times of recession or slow growth. The term *nonstandard work* emerged in the mid-1990s to define the new flexible structure of the U.S. labor force, which, according to the Economic Policy Institute (EPI) in 1997, encompassed all forms of alternative employment: nonstandard workers include part-timers, independent contractors, contract workers, temporary workers, on-call workers, day laborers, and self-employed workers. By 1997, the nonstandard workforce encompassed an estimated 30 percent of all workers in the United States.

That same year, the EPI study found that approximately 13.7 percent of the total American workforce was employed in part-time subcontract work, encompassing 47 percent of all nonstandard workers (Kalleberg et al. 1997). The transformation from traditional employment to nonstandard work arrangements has permitted businesses to hire both U.S.-born workers and migrants as contractors.

In the IT sector, nonstandard work manifests itself in different and particular ways not widely seen in other labor markets. In the IT industry, the term *outsourcing* is commonly used to refer to a cost-cutting measure by which work is contracted out to an independent firm that hires its own workers to perform tasks. Often these workers hold H-1B nonimmigrant visas. From February 2000 to February 2004, Congress granted 165,000 H-1B visas. During the 2004 presidential campaign, the high levels of unemployment in the IT industry made the program a hot-button issue. Thus, no new visas were issued until Congress enacted a new program several weeks *after* George W. Bush was reelected in 2004. Over 2005 alone, the number of new H-1B workers on immigrant visas has climbed to nearly 125,000. In addition, many workers are now performing the same tasks for contractors to U.S. firms while in their home countries, hence the emergence of the term *offshoring*.

Outsourcing and offshoring are typically not conducted by small businesses seeking to lower costs. The World Bank and the OECD (Organization of Economic Development and Cooperation) are leading proponents of the export of guest work programs for economic development in the Global South. The OECD, which represents thirty-two developed countries that are primary destinations for skilled to highly skilled migrants from the Global South, seeks to reinforce and expand temporary labor programs that they view as a crucial to the economies of developed and developing countries. The leading U.S. clients for outsourcing firms are multinational technology corporations seeking to lower costs and increase profits by strategically shifting lower-cost temporary labor on a global scale. Outsourcing can be vital to advancing global economic growth, particularly in China, India, and other developing countries in East Asia. Aaditya Mattoo, an economist at the World Bank, asserts:

> Indeed, there is good reason to believe that reduced barriers to the temporary movement of service providers will produce substantial global benefits. Significant gains already are being realized, for example, in the software industry—some 60% of India's burgeoning exports are provided through the movement of software engineers to the site of the consumer. And with greater

liberalization of barriers to the movement of people, many more developing countries could "export" at least the significant labor component of services such as construction, distribution, environmental services, and transport. Furthermore, a major benefit of the fact that such movement is temporary is the presumption that both the host country and the home country would gain (Mattoo and Carzaniga 2003).

The general trend in the United States high-tech workplace is the growth of temporary help and outsourcing through staffing firms to replace permanent full-time positions that once paid decent wages and provided health benefits (Aneesh 2006; LeMay 2003; Samuelson 2004). In 2006, as a U.S. senator, Barack Obama called the guest worker program " . . . essentially a sop to big business," seeking that any immigration reform bill include language that "employers not undercut American wages by paying guest workers less than they would pay U.S. workers" (314).

In many instances, nonstandard workers are contracted for a short time and discharged when the job is completed. IT professionals find themselves without a contract job or frequently, even if they do have a contract, they do not receive benefits, pensions, health care, and severance fees that would have accompanied such a position in the past. Recent survey research of Indian IT workers in the United States H-1B program found that employers hire skilled foreign workers on a temporary basis to allow for labor flexibility that creates an exploitative subcontracting system. In a study of forty workers, Payal Banerjee found that U.S. firms created a dependent relationship between Indian contractors and visa-sponsoring employers to maintain legal immigration status and continue payment of wages. Banerjee reports that: "The compulsion to remain *employed and legal* drives H-1B employees to accept severely exploitative work conditions, including wage cuts, deduction of commissions from hourly wages, lack of benefits, and frequent relocations" (2006).

Further, under traditional arrangements, wages paid to workers were sufficient to pay for basic survival needs. Under the new restructured work arrangements, this tacit bargain in high technology is undermined, as every worker may potentially become an owner through hard work and greater risk-taking—at first blush, a noble aspiration (and a way of life that has been promoted by the second Bush administration through its ownership society rhetoric). But in reality, members of the IT workforce end up with *all* of the responsibility of meeting their own basic needs—such as health insurance— yet control *none* of the resources or wealth within the industry.

To invent nonstandard jobs where workers engage in *risk-taking* while corporations are *guaranteed* profits, employers offer the possibility of riches that are almost never realized by workers. More important, the nonstandard job arrangement reduces employer commitment to the worker. This arrangement is now the dominant trend in high-technology industries. Furthermore, employees' ownership options (employees owning stock in their employer), even if realized, offer limited upward mobility for workers, as they are even more closely dependent on their employer's success than they would be in traditional jobs.

Data from the Bureau of Labor Statistics (BLS) shows the failure of the IT industry to recover from the dot-com collapse and the lack of job growth in the industry. For the first time since the emergence of the IT industry, a large segment of the labor force remains unemployed. Recent research shows that the IT industry is highly vulnerable to economic downturns. From 2000 to 2003, IT unemployment among U.S. workers more than doubled, from 3.2 percent (in 2000) to 6.8 percent (in 2003). From 2007 to 2008, unemployment in the industry expanded again, from 4.4 percent to 7.0 percent, the second-highest rate among IT sectors.[2] The number of total extended mass layoffs in information technology soared more than 44 percent, from 5,363 in 2007 (965,935 workers) to 8,259 (1,516,978) in 2008. In the first three months of 2009, more than 1.6 million workers in the industry were subject to mass layoffs. From 2007 to 2009, more than four million workers in the IT industry have experienced layoffs, and the number of mass layoffs has nearly tripled, from 48 in 2006 to 139 in 2009.[3] At the same time, outsourcing and offshoring have expanded.

By shifting skilled work to offshore contractors in India and elsewhere in the Global South, multinational IT firms primarily based in the United States avoid national social welfare mandates and extract greater surplus value from the labor exchange process (Banerjee 2006). From 1998 to 2009, the United States was the primary destination country for Indian nationals migrating to OECD countries, with nearly 520,000 mostly skilled workers entering the country, far outpacing any other in the twenty-two-nation bloc. Nearly 90 percent of Indian migrants to the United States were employed in the professional sector (OECD 2009). According to Binod Khadria, a leading Indian migration expert: "The strong profile of Indian immigrants in the U.S. supports the proposition that the mobility of human capital through migration of Indians has been the backbone of India's high-skill diaspora formation there. No other diaspora in the U.S. preceding the Indian numerical rank acquired its position predominantly because of an American demand for its labour skills, which has been the main factor for admitting the Indian high skill workers on a large scale" (Khadria 2009, 12). Global outsourcing consultants calculate that businesses save between 35 and 65 percent of their IT and telecommunications labor costs (Morstead & Blount 2003).

Instead of hiring full-time workers subject to prevailing standards, the IT and business services industries have formed a global labor market of temporary workers hired only on demand. The expansion of India's IT and business service capacity coincided with the initiation of market reforms in 1985. Government-sponsored high technology, business, and engineering education expanded substantially at Indian universities and polytechnic institutions. Consequently, the domestic software industry has soared from 6,800 workers in 1986 to 650,000 in 2003. The Indian National Association of Software and Service Companies (NASSCOM) attributes this growth to expanding global demand for Indian software services and actively promotes such services to IT industry leaders in the United States, the United Kingdom, and elsewhere in western Europe.[4]

Sensing a synergy between U.S. corporate goals and Indian labor capacities, some American business interests sought to boost profits in the industry by convincing government officials that the shortage in IT and software workers in the United States placed the nation at risk of losing global sales. Indian business leaders echoed this sentiment, and since the initiation of the U.S. H1-B visa in 1982, India has provided a preponderate proportion of guest workers in the IT sector, in effect forming a wholly new contract labor market. From 1982 to 2007, India has sent some five million H1-B skilled guest workers to the United States, primarily because of a greater commitment to investing in higher education in India, as well as China (Freeman 2007, 132–40). The vast majority return to India, while others go back and forth directly or through third countries.

India is by far the largest source of migrant IT consultants for U.S. high-tech companies, owing to its considerable cost advantages. First, H1-B computer programmers in the United States are not paid comparable wages as equivalently trained U.S. programmers. Moreover, Indian programmers do not receive Social Security benefits while working in the United States, because they are foreign guest workers. IT companies, by some estimates, pay their guest workers as little as $200 a month plus living expenses, and profit from renting company housing to contract laborers. Indian IT professionals may work six-day weeks and sometimes sixteen hours per day. India also provides a large pool of high-skilled workers who are fluent in English. By 2004, the Indian Institute of Technology, for example, produced 215,000 sub-baccalaureate and baccalaureate graduates in the IT and engineering fields, the most worldwide after China and the United States. (See Arora & Athreye 2002; Friedman 2005; Gereffi & Wadhwa 2005; Zakaria 2008).

There is evidence that the U.S. presence in the Indian market is growing, as more U.S. multinational IT firms relocate corporate facilities to Bangalore, Hyderabad, Mumbai, and other Indian high-tech centers. Since 2002, Adobe, Computer Associates, Intel, Microsoft, Oracle, and Sun Microsystems have established presences in India, and in response to growing opposition from U.S. migration opponents. Since 2007, the USCIS issued fewer H1-B visas to foreign skilled laborers, leading to increased relocation of IT and business services to India.[5]

Global Capitalism and the Class Divide

India's high-technology boom exemplifies a pattern of new industry replacing old, stable communities by introducing new technology and securing low-wage labor. To undermine the power of labor unions, the government assists businesses in closing older factories that once provided living wages and in opening new enterprises that receive financial, technical, and logistical support from the state, while paying workers lower wages and repressing labor unions. A consensus among political economists in India is that new installations do not pay competitive wages and thus undermine the economic stability of entire communities (Bagchi 2002, 2005; Banerjee 2006; Bhatt 2005; Joshi 2005; Nayyar & Sharma 2005). Thus, although the "outside world" (or free-market economists in the Global North) views India as a first-rate model for economic development, only a small segment—the nation's capitalist class—profits from these technological advances.

As India opens its economy to the world, the country possesses the advantage of a democratic tradition, but the failure of India to advance at China's pace is palpable. Some argue that the Chinese Communist Party's one-party rule has fueled its economic advance, a contention that contradicts the neoliberal relationship between democracy and free markets as a means to prosperity and growth (Garnaut & Ligang Song 2005; Preston & Haacke 2003). Outside the leading high-technology centers, dependable electric power is the exception rather than the rule. Thus, the technological boom in India has not set in motion broad access to the Internet. Even the World Bank reluctantly concedes that the unreliability of electricity and frequent blackouts stymie economic growth (World Bank 2009a). To compensate for the routine power outages, most small- and medium-sized companies must run their own power generators because energy shortages are endemic to businesses and civilians (Baldauf 2005).

At the same time, India has become a site of innovation in several key skilled service sectors of the economy, each relatively new and interconnected: IT, software, business services, and call centers. But while experts argue that India's national economy has grown through the expansion of high technology and skilled guest worker programs (Das 2002; Thatchenkery & Stough 2005), the development of the Indian economy is even more warped because more skilled professionals enter industries that do not improve and/ or ameliorate grinding poverty or produce tangible human development to the vast majority of the poor. Multinational contractors invest in nonunion new, high-technology facilities, unlike garment, steel, and other basic industries. In the Indian state of West Bengal, organized labor—in partnership with the Communist Party of India-Marxist (CPIM)—have opposed the installation of new factories, which undermined wage and workplace standards in established industries. In 2009 and 2010, the CPIM that supported these policies lost state and municipal elections in West Bengal, which weakens its veto power over the introduction of neoliberal policies (Hobsbawm 2010; Thakurta 2010). However, trade unions who control the major industries continue to sanction new corporate investments that destabilize wages. Consequently, Indian multinationals and global corporations are opting to invest in capital-friendly states outside West Bengal and in new labor market sectors that have limited union organization, such as Internet technology, call centers, and business services (Bagchi 2002).

Meanwhile, since the 1990s, federal government agencies in India have reduced services and funding programs beneficial to the poor and working class while targeting resources to private interests in core high-technology hubs with concentrations of workers. In turn, the Indian federal social programs and initiatives that are crucial for the rural and urban poor in poverty-stricken regions are starving for resources. The resulting internal migration from India's rural regions has become crucial to building, maintaining, and serving new technology corporations. Most internal migrants work as construction workers, landscapers, security guards, and hospitality workers in the new IT complexes in Hyderabad and beyond. Though the Indian state prohibits discrimination on the basis of one's caste, informally the system continues to operate, as those of higher castes are also likely to have greater wealth than members of lower castes. Approximately 65 percent of Indians are people of lower caste status—Dalit, Other Backward Classes (OBCs), and

Scheduled Tribes. The Indian caste system reinforces the contracting of low-wage labor, creating a food chain where those from more privileged castes are only permitted to interact with those immediately below them. The Indian caste system shapes exploitation by, in many cases, preventing members of higher castes from networking with lower castes, creating a condition that contributes to the tendency to contract labor. Thus, the convergence of Hindu fundamentalism and capitalism consigns those at the bottom of the caste system (the Dalit, OBCs, and Scheduled Tribes) to work for privileged-caste contractors, who take a cut out of their salaries depending on their place in the caste system (Bagchi 2002; Bagchi 2005; Srinivas 2008; interview, Arun Patnaik, Hyderabad, December 17, 2008).[6]

Even by the inflated World Bank statistics, from 1981 to 2005, the number of people in India living under $1.25 a day increased from 421 million to 456 million (World Bank 2009b). Still, as the majority of Indians are mired in abject poverty, even if the middle-class constitutes only 3 percent of India's inhabitants, the country is so large that this population constitutes thirty million residents, a considerable number of people for domestic and foreign corporations seeking to invest in the national economy. Beyond the middle-income bracket is a growing low-wage working class in urban and rural areas that fails to benefit from economic reform, but works longer hours for low pay.

INDIAN SKILLED MIGRANT LABORERS IN THE UNITED STATES

The growth of Indian skilled guest workers in the United States reflects the rise in corporate demand for flexible contract laborers, used to reduce labor costs for multinational corporations through providing on-demand services. After their contracts expire, migrant laborers must find new jobs in host countries or are unceremoniously deported. In the first decade of the twenty-first century, the United States imported more IT workers than any other country (OECD 2001).

From 1995 to 2010, more and more Indians of all social classes regarded a temporary stint as a guest worker abroad as a route to economic prosperity. Landing a job in the United States is considered particularly beneficial to skilled and semiskilled Indians. Even for those with skills, jobs that pay wages corresponding to those in the United States, Europe, Japan, or Persian Gulf states are extremely difficult to find. Even though wages are higher in the United States, Indian high technology workers are shamefully exploited as guest workers, laboring as many as sixteen to eighteen hours a day on the job with almost no down time. It is true that there is an emerging "IT elite" nexus among Indians in the United States and South Asia. While the industry is growing, those entering its top end already come from the middle and upper classes that, as noted, comprise a small fraction of India's population (interview, Sona Shah, New York, March 18, 2005).

Even if Indian contractors charge high hourly rates for skilled guest workers, U.S. firms profit immensely by making use of unrestricted discretionary labor services rather than hiring full-time workers. As nonemployees, guest workers provide a distinct advantage for corporations, who do not have to contribute government-mandated social security, unemployment, and disability benefits nor prevailing pensions and other benefits. For U.S. companies in IT and business services, Indian guest workers provide a clear advantage over U.S.-born workers, because the government does not monitor working conditions and wage and hour standards.

Labor contractors in India also profit. Corporations and labor contractors in the United States and India draw closer to one another by the capacity to establish reciprocal facilities in each country where workers are interchangeable. Indian contractors expand corporate flexibility and profits by providing the equivalent of global temporary agencies selling skilled laborers for IT and business services jobs. In addition, Indian contractors are seeking to expand trade in unskilled migrant jobs in production, transportation, and material moving beyond the Persian Gulf to the United States and other OECD countries (Khadria 2009, 14).

Even with this expansion of U.S. guest-worker programs, it would be inaccurate to conclude that massive waves of Indian and other workers in the Global South procure "good jobs" at the expense of U.S. workers; rather, corporations willingly pay Indian contractors to provide low-wage labor to take responsibility for ensuring that work is completed according to specifications. U.S. capital is indifferent to the abysmal wages and conditions of foreign guest workers. The widening use of Indian guest workers among U.S. corporations in discrete industries illustrates how capital deliberately creates job shortages through undermining established labor market relations, generating a need for new pliable and lower-cost labor. In turn, by introducing guest workers, U.S. labor markets slacken, wage rates decline, and corporate profitability grows. The result is a direct correlation between corporate downsizing and Indian guest worker programs in several labor markets, turning erstwhile good jobs into bad ones. One important example is the trucking industry.

INDIAN LABOR EXPORTATION:
MANUFACTURING AND SUPPORT SERVICES

Since 1980, when U.S. President Jimmy Carter deregulated trucking, the industry has eroded the labor power of long-haul drivers. Deregulation in U.S. trucking gradually reduced worker power through allowing companies to operate in all states without consent from the Interstate Commerce Commission (ICC). The NAFTA regional accords that became law in 1994 further reduced the labor power of truck drivers by permitting Mexican and Canadian haulers to enter the United States without prior authorization. Consequently, long-distance trucking companies have sharply reduced wage rates to drivers by hiring workers in states and countries that pay lower wages. In the 1980s, deregulation of trucking permitted employers with higher wage rates to reduce costs by encouraging competition from workers in states where prevailing wages were significantly lower. NAFTA has allowed Mexican drivers to compete with U.S. workers, and efforts to import Indian truckers trained in Andhra Pradesh has set in motion a process of lowering wage costs even further.

In May 2005, the American Trucking Association (ATA) issued a report prepared by Global Insight, a research organization that forecasts a shortage of 114,000 long-haul drivers in the United States if current trends continue. The report, "US Truck Driver Shortage Analysis and Forecasts," concludes that the decline in drivers is a result of high turnover, the arduous work of long-haul trucking, the long hours away from home, and expectations that the number of male workers, who predominate in the industry, will drastically decline. The report notes that " . . . demographic trends will turn against the industry over the next 10 years" as "white male" truck drivers between thirty-five and fifty-four years of age leave the industry and wage rates in the industry continue to decline (Global Insight 2005). To ameliorate the dearth of drivers, the industry is advocating introduction of the H-2B guest worker program.

In June 2007, two years after issuance of the ATA report, *The Hindu*, a nationwide newspaper of record in India, reported that 217 truck drivers were undergoing training by the Overseas Manpower Company/Andhra Pradesh, Ltd. (OMCAP) in Hyderabad to secure positions as guest workers in the U.S. long-haul trucking industry on H-2B visas. The article continued: "Of these, 79 had been cleared by the trainers of the United States as eligible for obtaining Commercial Driving License in the U.S." (Rajeev 2007). OMCAP is a government-sponsored organization that refers to itself as a "Recruitment Services to all business and industries in Middle East, US, Cananda [*sic*]" that "Placed hundreds of various skilled workers, experts, specialized construction, mechanical, electrical, engineering teams, etc." The firm also claims that it "provides visa processing, air-ticketing, and emigration services "for the Candidates selected by you (OMCAP 2010)." Within a year, Indian contractors began establishing a broader presence in the United States to channel truckers through the H-2B visa. In the spring of 2007 they signed a memorandum of understanding with USCIS to recruit two hundred drivers of heavy trucks to the United States.

The effort to extend guest worker visas to low-wage Indian laborers reveals the corporate economic interests behind political efforts to establish comprehensive immigration reform. The Teamsters are actively seeking to restrict what they consider the importation of foreign truckers into the United States, while the trucking industry lobbies the government to increase visas for foreigners as a new means to lower labor costs. The initial opening of opportunities for Indian labor contractors to export labor from Hyderabad into the U.S. trucking labor market in 2006 by Gagan Global LLC, which sought to contract low-wage Indian drivers, reveals that in all locations, capitalists seek to expand profitability through the use of temporary labor. The contractor, Gagan Global LLC, advertises that it processes training visas for Indian workers who are seeking certification as "diesel mechanics for USA." After eighteen months of training as diesel mechanics in the United States, Indian workers who complete the program are "guaranteed placement in Canada and Europe" (Corsi 2006; Gagan Global LLC 2010; Hoffa 2006).[7] Failing in its effort to implement the plan to send Indian temporary drivers and mechanics to the United States in 2007, one year later Gagan then turned to "dental tourism" through providing one hundred patients a month from the United States who were in need of dental treatment and surgery services at lower cost (*The Hindu* 2008).

As we will now see, the growing effort to use temporary guest workers to fill labor demands is harmful to most Indians in India as well as in the United States, as our case study of high-tech workers in Hyderabad reveals that rural migrant workers from that metropolitan region and the state of Andhra Pradesh are exploited through commodification of agriculture in the region and the displacement of farming with new high-technology sectors that pay exceedingly low wages. As our case study will show, this is just one more example of how the developed world's unquenchable thirst for low-wage labor is wreaking havoc on the social and economic structure of labor-exporting nations like India.

A Case Study of Hyderabad:
Modernization, Migration, and Poverty

Geography, religion, class, and caste divide Hyderabad, a sprawling city in the heart of the state of Andhra Pradesh on the southeastern coast of India, a separation exaggerated by the investment and growth of high technology industries. Hyderabad is the core urban center of Telangana, the northwestern region of Andhra Pradesh that was incorporated into the state in the aftermath of independence and since the late 1960s has sought autonomy as an independent state, partly on account of its distinctive Telegu language and culture. The Telangana independence movement, which would make Hyderabad the capital, has strengthened with the support of Congress Party leaders in 2004, but is opposed by Andhra and Rayalseema, the coastal regions of Andhra Pradesh, leading to growing political tensions. Independence for Telangana could erode revenue that the region produces for the economy of the two other regions of Andhra Pradesh, further undermining living standards.

In Hyderabad, IT complexes exploit migrant workers in surrounding Andhra Pradesh with promises of riches. Yet as Hyderabad grows geographically, an increasing number of peasant villages surrounding the city are concurrently displaced by high-tech establishments, forcing vulnerable construction and service workers from their homes. An increasing number of workers in rural regions of the Indian state of Andhra Pradesh are forced to migrate to Hyderabad because of economic necessity, as the growth in market-based corporate farming is driving down living standards. Once in Hyderabad, the typical rural migrant is employed as a construction worker or in a similarly unsafe job, is paid low wages, and lives in a tent without access to potable water. Their fate, and the fate of their region, illustrates the ways in which labor exportation is deleterious to the exporting nations.

SLUM GROWTH

There are roughly 1,607 slum dwellers throughout Hyderabad and the twin-city Secunderabad, with slightly more than 2.8 million people residing there. The majority of residents fall below the poverty line and have no access to medical or eye care services. In the absence of developed land and clear policies to address their problems, the poor suffer from many inadequacies in terms of access to basic services.

The numbers of slums and the squatter population in the Municipal Corporation of Hyderabad (MCH), the urban center, has been increasing at a faster pace over recent decades. In addition, in the municipalities around the city constituting the Hyderabad Urban Agglomeration (HUA), there are around five hundred slums. Because these municipalities were constituted only in the late 1980s, the slum population is high. In Quthbullahpur, Alwal, and Rajendranagar, slums constitute about 60 percent of the total population, highlighting the enormity of the problem. The slum population in HUA is heterogeneous in character—with Hindus, Muslims, and Christians having migrated from different neighboring districts. The languages predominantly spoken in slums in Hyderabad and Secunderabad are Telugu and Urdu, followed by a smattering of Marathi and Kannada. A similar pattern exists in surrounding municipalities.

Slums in HUA are controlled by municipal, state, and central authorities on quasi-government-owned, private, and unclaimed lands. The state government of Andhra Pradesh classified all the slums on its land as either "objectionable" or "unobjectionable" in 1985. Categorization as "objectionable" was based on location and land use—location on riverbeds, low-lying areas, drains, road margins, and so forth. Only a few slums were deemed "unobjectionable." In the case of surrounding municipalities, they were the small and scattered villages inhabited by the poor, particularly laborers from the industrial areas, where the absence of physical and social amenities contribute to lower living standards and even greater economic deprivation (Greater Hyderabad Development Plan 2010).

HYDERABAD'S CORPORATE HIGH TECHNOLOGY AND MANAGEMENT CONTROL

As India modernizes its economic base, the state privileges firms that are nonunion, leading to the growing marginalization of organized labor. As a consequence, the most modern industries are likely to be free of union representation. Hyderabad's unions are struggling to organize new industries, including engineering, IT, and business service, but each of these seek to avoid union organizing campaigns.[8]

Internal disagreements over the role of unions are exacerbated by international pressures. Basically, outside forces would prefer that Indian workers accept jobs that benefit multinational corporations rather than focusing on building up Indian industry. Business, multilateral agencies, and the U.S. government, for example, see India as an attractive source of workers as the baby boom generation ages. Likewise, the World Bank guest worker development agenda views migrant labor as the primary development policy. In all of these cases, Indian workers are employed in jobs that focus on the needs of foreign corporations.

New Indian and multinational firms have been created to coordinate India's role in the global labor community. High-technology workers earning middle-income wages are employed in new corporate complexes that are now swallowing up land in Hyderabad. These new buildings are constructed by low-wage Indian temporary laborers, and though the new Indian and multinational firms are primed to enter the global economy, working conditions for the white-collar IT workers are arduous and despotic. College-educated workers employed in high-technology development as programmers, business service specialists, and call center operators work long hours in facilities that resemble prison blocs rather than corporate offices. At the Centre for Economic and Social Studies, political economists note that IT companies segregate employees with different tasks in separate buildings and prohibit interacting or mingling with fellow workers in the same complexes (interview, Arun Patnaik, December 17, 2008).

Indian proponents saw market reforms as a means of reducing communal divisions and directing the country to the international market, according to Prakash C. Sarangi, professor of political science at the University of Hyderabad. Instead, Sarangi argues, over the two decades from 1985 to 2005, neoliberalism has only reinforced caste, communal, and gender divisions in Indian society, which in turn has obscured class divisions. He observes that only those at the very top of the class and caste system go on to careers in the IT sector, while the rest work in low-skilled precarious jobs such as building cleaners, security, and landscaping (interview, October 6, 2005). All of the workers involved in this situation earn low salaries that would be considered quite exploitive in the United States. The process continues, however, because when converted into the Indian rupee, it is a substantial amount of money. Therefore, capital interests are able to justify this offshoring by saying they are giving Indian workers opportunities they would never have otherwise. Of course, this ignores the fact that they have found a way around paying a fair wage, not only to Indian workers but also to workers in their own countries. In the end, both sets of workers lose.

Another loser in what some still consider as the "brain drain" is India itself. For one, as Sarangi suggests, training IT workers to the exclusion of other skills is not in India's best interest. He contends that India needs workers with a full range of skills to promote development at home, but most workers are stuck in exclusively IT positions at multinational companies. To enter the upper–middle class in India, many have a family member working in the United States. He adds that many IT guest workers return to India with the intention of enjoying what many would consider an upper-class lifestyle in the United States: employing servants, owning a large home, and several automobiles (interview, Prakash C. Sarangi, Hyderabad, October 6, 2005). For working-class Indians in steel, apparel, and other manufacturing industries, however, the neoliberal reforms are leading to the closure of older factories and the building of modern factories that employ fewer workers at far lower wages (Bagchi 2002).

At the same time, the perception that India is a technological giant is misleading, and the country bears the genuine cost of an ongoing brain drain of necessary expertise. When IT, software, and business service workers return to India, they are not equipped with the diverse skills needed to serve the vital needs of the population. Also, despite the naïve argument that India is poised to compete worldwide in business service professions, the 2001 government census reports that 35 percent of its population, including more than 54 percent of women, is illiterate. Pankaj Mishra, an Indian writer and essayist living in the West, argues that the official literacy rate "includes many who can barely write their names" (Mishra 2006). Although India is poised to compete worldwide in business service professions, only a small proportion of its overall population stands to gain from the growth in IT professions from 1990–2010, which account for 1.3 million of the national population. Moreover, a growing share of Indian IT workers wind up employed for multinational corporations in the web of labor migration system between North America, Europe, and India.

Those who stay to work in the new corporate complexes in place like Hyderabad end up in dead-end jobs that contribute little to Indian development. Many will stay in India in call centers to service Western consumers—jobs that require twelve to sixteen hours of work each shift—usually starting at night and ending in the late morning of the next day. Intel, Microsoft, IBM, Siemens, and other leading multinationals prime workers to travel to the United States and Europe as guest workers in the IT sector. Upon returning from the United States, Europe, or Japan, Indian IT workers often end up in these call centers, gravely disappointed. Many recall disturbing stories of lives that revolve around work and the promise for a better life (interviews, anonymous workers, November 2006–February 2007, Hyderabad). One IT worker returned to India from the United States after paying most of his salary to a contractor who promised a green card. When the green card failed to materialize, he was forced to return to India and find a job there.

The political economy of Hyderabad, like the IT center of Bangalore, is differentiated among upper-class corporate officers, contractors, IT professionals, actuaries, business owners, a growing working class laboring as food-service workers, car service drivers, security guards, building cleaners, and day laborers in the construction industry, and the majority in the informal sector who are unable to find regular employment. The informal sector marginalizes workers into jobs with little prospect of earning enough to survive. In Hyderabad, many construction workers are displaced former peasants who live in ramshackle slums surrounding the city. As the cities grow more prosperous for those employed in the IT and business services sectors, attention has been deflected away from the needs of the poor in the rural areas. Workers and peasant farmers in the countryside are left without adequate housing, education, and public services (interviews, Arun Patnaik, October 7, 2005, and December 17, 2008).

Hyderabad is divided into what amounts to two different cities: one high tech, and the other the old established core. In this respect, Hyderabad bears a remarkable resemblance to Bangalore. In addition to a booming IT sector, Hyderabad is home to garment manufacture and the production of precious goods deriving from the region's abundance of pearls and precious stones. The city is also a leading producer of pharmaceuticals and medicine and is emerging as a banking center. Bangalore's economy relies on the presence of leading corporations and the aeronautics industry. Both cities have large working classes and displaced peasants, but Hyderabad's economy is considerably more diverse. In Hyderabad, the expansion of an urban underclass of precarious laborers creates a severe housing crisis. The villages of peasant laborers are displaced by high-technology complexes in the Genome Valley technology cluster, and there is a concurrent dramatic rise in contract and bonded labor who must work in debt peonage to pay off loans. Between 1995 and 2008, Hyderabad and Bangalore have been experiencing vast and dramatic expansion in high-technology sectors, spreading the construction of new complexes to the hinterland of the cities.

Contractors frequently hire these same displaced laborers to build and maintain the new high-technology centers on formerly agricultural land expropriated by Indian technology firms. The vast majority of those working as contract labor now live in tent communities near the high-technology centers. Upon completion of their work, most workers must move on to new construction sites, continuing the process of dispossession and labor exploitation. In interviews with thirty-eight workers living in makeshift housing and tents laboring in Hyderabad construction sites from November 2006 to February 2007, the vast majority indicated that they had no choice but to work as contractors and subcontractors building and maintaining the buildings and grounds of high-technology complexes and residences for those working in the industry (interviews, anonymous workers, November 2006–February 2007).

The Yagar family is a prototype of the tens of thousands of rural workers forced to toil in Hyderabad who can no longer survive as agricultural workers, attributable to growing inequality. In an interview, Yagar, a Dalit, one of Hinduism's lowest castes, said he was forced to migrate to Hyderabad from the city's hinterland with his wife and daughter because of their inability to survive as agricultural laborers. The family accumulated a huge debt to landowners in rural areas of the state. As tenant farmers, the family incurred significant debt cultivating chili. Owing to their accumulated debt and anxiety, they could not afford the dowry for their daughter's marriage, and therefore the family moved to Hyderabad.

The husband and wife landed jobs as joint-temporary laborers in the garden of Larsen & Toubro Limited, a Mumbai-based technology, engineering, construction, and manufacturing firm, among India's largest companies. Because the couple belongs to a "backward caste," contractors filter payments through a contractor and two subcontractors to the couple, reducing the money allocated by the company.[9] Though typical wages for couples working in similar jobs are 200 to 230 rupees a week, Yagar and his wife earned only 150 rupees combined (eighty rupees for Yagar and seventy for his wife). The Hindu hierarchical system prohibits privileged-caste Indians at the construction company to interact with Yagar. The hierarchy in the caste system serves to marginalize Yagar through the capitalist system of subcontractors, who each take a commission of the original wages.[10]

Yagar and his family live in makeshift tents made of plastic covers, for which they are charged 150 rupees per month. The family lives in an area with no sanitation and no sewage system. The construction company provides the couple with a meager supply of water for drinking and cooking. Although all of the family members work in Hyderabad, the higher cost of shelter and food in the city offsets their gains in income, and their lot is only marginally improved. Yagar said that because of the strenuous nature of the work and little hope of improving the family's standard of living, most of the remaining income is used to pay for alcoholic beverages.

As Yagar's story shows, the rise of high technology in Hyderabad provides an unqualified example of Bagchi's contention that the capitalist class and multinationals make use of caste, communal, and gender divisions to diminish the living standards and suppress the expression of workers and peasants (Bagchi 2002, 263–91). Because workers will not transcend caste and class divisions and join together to better their conditions, the divisions are an expedient means to contain working-class dissent and protest against super-exploitation and economic destitution. However, while the Indian working class have few organizational options in major urban areas, the stark divisions that are emerging between rich and poor will eventually lead to social upheaval. Political economist Debdas Banerjee provides the following allegorical account of the consequences of a society beginning to generate greater revenue without allocating the resources equitably: "A traffic accident causes all vehicles on a two-lane road to screech to a halt. Suddenly the traffic begins to move in the right lane—the traffic in the left lane remains at a standstill. People in the left lane will veer to the right lane or will become highly irritated and angry. In India, poor conditions are widespread but if the general level of inequality changes dramatically, a relative peace can turn into mass conflict as people move out of their social station" (Banerjee, October, 10, 2005). The question remains how an organized workers' movement can emerge to capture the imagination of India's urban poor who have lost hope and feel consigned to the rapacious neoliberal order.

INDIAN CORPORATE UNION AVOIDANCE SCHEMES

One way equitable allocation of India's still-too-scarce resources could be attained is through new forms of independent worker unionization. As we saw before, the Indian government privileges nonunion firms, and the firms work hard to keep workers apart. On the other hand, though unions frequently resist the implementation of neoliberal capitalist reforms, they are too centralized, which diminishes their capacity to mobilize rank-and-file workers and the vast majority of unorganized workers. Thus, without an organized workers' movement, even those privileged few who may find full-time work in India's IT firms remain subject to oppressive conditions by employers who have maintained rigid control over the new workplaces. Paradoxically, unions are seeking to organize security workers in India's new urban high-technology installations (G4Solidarity 2010).[11]

The effort by corporations to maintain security and avoid unionization is fundamental to ensuring absolute control over the workplace, a practice that is highly evident among India's leading corporations. For example, Hyderabad is a major business hub for a number of IT firms. One of the main ones is Infosys, one of India's leading high-technology firms. The company has a huge facility of six separate buildings, which employ about three thousand high-technology workers and some four hundred security, maintenance, and support personnel. The support staffs at the complex, dormitories, cafeteria, and health club are all contractors working an average of fifteen to sixteen hours a day.

Satyam, one of India's four largest high-technology firms, also has extensive operations in the Hyderabad/Telangana region, in compounds where workers are segregated in buildings reserved for specialized IT operations and employees are prohibited from interacting or mingling at the conclusion of their shifts. Situated within the Hyderabad Information Technology Engineering Consultancy, a gated business, residential, and hotel zone in the city, Satyam prohibits workers from entering buildings other than those designated or communicating with one another, ostensibly for security purposes (interview, Arun Kumar, Hyderabad, December 18, 2008). Workers in each structure are in different segments of the company. The operation reflects the caste system itself, as some buildings house workers with specialized skills who earn higher wages and working conditions, while other blocks employ workers in other segments of the company that may pay lower wages. Recognizing the hierarchy in skill and wages, to keep workers apart, Satyam uses a sophisticated security system, staggers the hours of workers, and prevents access through use of security and barriers between parking lots.

The fate of workers who remain in India is different in some ways than the fate of those who join the ranks of guest workers seeking jobs in other countries. Though exploitation is endemic in both systems of labor relations, variant regional conditions lead to differing outcomes. The best example is the growing sector of guest Indian service workers seeking employment in the United States.

Conclusion: Mobile Workers and Resistance

The most important factor in U.S. high-technology and service jobs moving offshore to India is the capacity to recruit foreign workers to perform services identical to those done by U.S. workers. The fact that companies in India pay workers significantly lower wages than those that U.S. workers earn is the most important factor in business decisions to move jobs to overseas branches or contractors. Forrester, a technology research company based in Cambridge, Massachusetts, argues that the job loss will continue unabated. This research company, influential in the IT industry, released a study in May 2004 projecting that by the year 2015 about 3.3 million jobs in the industry will move to low-wage foreign competitors or guest workers in the United States. According to the Forrester survey, firms are moving offshore to take advantage of lower-cost labor (McCarthy 2004).

U.S. corporate executives persistently demand more global guest workers while ignoring India's public health disaster, illiteracy, and the rigid caste system that consigns nearly three hundred million Dalit (formerly known as untouchables) and OBC (Other Backward Classes) to wretched and persistent poverty. In June 2008, the Indo-Asian News Service reported that contrary to propaganda depicting a wealthy and prosperous country, nine hundred million Indians live on less than $2 (Rs 85) a day (De Sarkar 2008). True enough, IT services in Hyderabad, Mumbai, and Bangalore can compete with those in the United States, but it is amid the human tragedy that is growing ever more rapidly as open markets and the ending of hard-won government benefits challenge both Americans and Indians. The endemic poverty in India, China, and most of the Global South is ravaging stable communities by exposing workers and peasants to market forces without even minimal safeguards.

From 2000 to 2010, leading U.S. academics, investors, and media pundits have portrayed India as the site of the next wave of technological growth and economic prosperity (Friedman 2005; Rajan 2009). This logic hinges on the belief that as a democratic society, India will permit greater innovation through unfettered capitalism. The reality is that India's market reforms have solidified the power of the upper classes while further marginalizing workers and peasants. According to most Indian economists, the imposition of neoliberalism in 1985 has dispossessed the working poor and peasants of their jobs and property (Bagchi 2002, 2005; Banerjee 2006; Deshpande, Sharma, Sarkar, & Karan 2006; Joshi 2005; Lieten and Sharma 2007).

While India "enthusiasts" including Gurcharan Das, Thomas Friedman, Nandan Nilekani (2009), and Fareed Zakaria boast that the model Indian is an IT worker earning enough to own a large house and fancy cars, they conceal the fact that this model Indian depends on several low-wage servants to cook, clean, and care for children. Many more are displaced by economic crises in old industries and agriculture and are working in low-wage sectors in poverty conditions. Development economists willingly admit that such conditions exist during what they describe as an economic transition. They insist that during a short period of economic crisis the poor majority will suffer as the economy transforms (Srinivasulu, Kumar, & Sekhar 2004). Contrary to what they predict, however, the vast majority of Indians are not joining the middle class and, according to authoritative U.N. sources, more are falling into poverty.

In July 2010, the Oxford Poverty and Human Development Initiative (OPHI) developed a new index for measuring poverty for developing countries, identified as Acute Multidimensional Poverty. Under the new scale, poverty is an aggregate weighted measure of 30 percent of the following deprivations of health, education, and standard of living. A family is poor if any child has died in a family; an adult or child is malnourished; no household member has completed five years of schooling or any child is out of school in years one to eight; a home has no electricity, no toilet/shared toilet, and a floor of dirt, sand, or dung; drinking water is not available within a thirty-minute walk; the family has no cooking fuel; and the family lacks assets, owning no more than one of the following: radio, television, telephone, bike, or motorbike (Alkirei & Santos 2010).

The report found the number of poor in eight states in India, comprising 421 million residents. This exceeded that of the twenty-six poorest countries in Sub-Saharan Africa, with a population of 410 million living in poverty. The study found that the poor in Bihar, India's poorest state, with ninety-five million residents, exceeded nine of Africa's ten poorest countries (Alkirei & Santos 2010). Based on the MPI composite measure of ten markers of poverty, 645 million Indians, or 55 percent of the population, is poor, not even remotely attaining the status of working class (Shrinivasan 2010).

The notion that the country's enduring democratic institutions provide an advantage over other countries persuades some to assert that the nation's economy will adapt to neoliberal capitalism more swiftly than China's erstwhile socialist economy (Das 2002). India is not superseding China economically, however. Unlike India, a working class is emerging in China. In 2005, India's GDP per capita was estimated at $3,300—less than half that of China's $6,800 (CIA 2006).

Political economists are challenging the prevailing consensus among Indian enthusiasts who view the country as an emerging global power. The core empirical evidence is that market reform creates homogenization of labor in specific labor markets in India and a drive to the bottom. Indian migration is not exclusively comprised of high-wage educated workers going to the United States and Europe, despite the media's focus on H-1B high technology laborers. The majority are low-wage internal migrants from poverty-stricken rural areas and manual-labor migration to the Arab states of the Persian Gulf states, and, increasingly, the Global North.

Whether living in the United States, western Europe, or India, Indians must work long hours at a low wage even if employed in the high-technology or business services sector. According to Banerjee, India is now experiencing the onerous conditions of work found in early capitalism. IT and call center workers are employed twelve-hour days and are monitored and subject to constant surveillance. We are seeing the return of sweatshop conditions, only now in high technology and business services (interview, Debdas Banerjee, Kolkata, October 5, 2005, and December 18, 2008). Similarly, standards in U.S. IT facilities are also requiring employees to work long hours and force laborers into onerous working conditions (Benner 2002; Pellow & Park 2002).

India's IT and business service workers in Hyderabad are unlikely to be union members, because the industries are new and stable workforces have yet to develop. Business, multilateral agencies, and the U.S. government see India as an attractive source of workers as the baby boom generation ages. Meanwhile, the World Bank guest worker development policy replaces the brain drain concept in India and elsewhere with a "ready and willing" attitude among the multitude of young workers coming of age and entering the workforce. In the 1960s-1990s, the term "brain drain" was used ubiquitously to refer to the outflow of skilled workers from third-world countries to the developed countries, therefore stunting development in countries like India. Today, economists refer to the brain gain, denoting that skilled workers send remittances back home, which helps fund development. But because many of the most highly skilled workers leave, India and other poor countries lack the capability to reduce poverty that stunts most of the population (Hunger 2002).

Proponents of expanding the supply of guest workers fail to recognize the poverty that an export-promotion policy creates in India and the Global South. As shown in this chapter, it is more likely that Indians will work in menial jobs, whether in India or as guest workers in the United States. Although only a small share of India's huge labor force includes skilled laborers primed to go abroad to work in the IT and business service industries, they are now generating an unprecedentedly large share of foreign revenue for the country. India does not have an infinite number of knowledge industry workers. This false idea is promoted by experts like Thomas Friedman of the *New York Times* and Nandan Nilekani, who point to exclusively IT hubs while neglecting to evaluate the nation as a whole. The radically disparate narratives outlined in this chapter and the hard evidence of growing poverty in the Global South prove false the fiction generated by multinational corporations and India's capitalist class. Capitalists in India and the United States ignore stultifying poverty and focus on their own economic gains, the modernization of two or three economic sectors, and growing foreign interest in India as beneficial to the country overall, when that is simply not the case. New roads and infrastructure are linking India's rapidly expanding IT centers, airports, hotels, and affluent communities, while urban and rural transport and intercity railways rust away. Meanwhile, the market-based economy neglects basic needs such as sanitation, clean water, electricity, medicine, and food for the majority of the population. Considering that migration is not producing palpable economic development through remittances to solve the problem of poverty, in the next chapter, we examine how the ideology of remittances as development is producing labor resistance among Indian workers.

4

Temporary Labor Migration and U.S. and Foreign-Born Worker Resistance

As the Internet is used more and more as a medium of communication in the United States, we are entering a new era of collective action at "the point of production" that is growing in significance to workers as a form of resistance. The practice of organizing at the "point of production" is what socialist labor unionists consider the "purest form of unionism." In contrast, traditional unions habitually organize through bargaining with management to achieve a contract stipulating the wages and conditions of employment. This strategy ultimately benefits capital that mostly fears worker direct action at the workplace. To reinforce employer power over workers, the contemporary workplace consolidates management dominance through electronic surveillance that prevents any form of democracy on the job. Since the origin of capitalism, employers have continuously sought to reduce worker power derived through skills or collectivities through restructuring labor markets by means of introducing new technology and lower-wage workers. Since the eighteenth century, workers have engaged in various forms of direct action at the "point of production" as the most effective means of controlling employer abuses in the absence of militant trade unions.

In 1905, the Industrial Workers of the World was founded as a means to resist the abuse of the capitalist class through new technology and low-wage labor. The Industrial Union Manifesto is applicable to workers more than a century later: "The great facts of present industry are the displacement of human skill by machines and the increase of capitalist power through concentration in the possession of the tools with which wealth is produced and distributed. . . . New machines, ever replacing less productive ones, wipe out whole trades and plunge new bodies of workers into the ever-growing army of trade-less, hopeless unemployed. As human beings and human skill are displaced by mechanical progress, the capitalists need use the workers only during that brief period when muscles and nerve respond most intensely" (IWW 1905).

Just as in the early twentieth century, workers remain under assault through the introduction of new technology and low-wage replacements, which contributes to rising labor competition and working-class conflict—today as a century ago, through the rise of nativism and xenophobia toward migrant laborers. The I.W.W. Manifesto declares that: "These divisions, far from representing differences in skill or interests among the laborers, are imposed by the employer that workers may be pitted against one another and spurred to greater exertion in the shop, and that all resistance to capitalist tyranny may be weakened by artificial distinctions" (IWW 1905).

As this chapter will demonstrate, instead of relying on large union bureaucracies, more workers in and out of labor unions are opposing employer domination through electronic communication—a form of electronic direct action—as opposed to relying on traditional grievance systems and other forms of employer and trade union–based dispute resolution, which are less effective than at any time since the 1930s (Lynd 1992). Though success is not certain, it is crucial to develop new forms of democratic unionism grounded in class solidarity to break the absolute power of the capitalist class over workers ever more divided by immigrant status.

In this chapter, we will see how this syndicalist form of activism and *micro-organizing,* which is common among anarchist unions, is currently growing among U.S.- and foreign-born workers. As Staughton Lynd claims in *Solidarity Unionism,* it is not yet apparent whether numerous yet discontinuous forms of worker self-activity will lead to a mass working-class movement— but a labor movement in the United States and beyond will only grow if it is founded by direct action by workers in shops, offices, factories, and beyond. As Andrej Grubacic asserts: "We should rely not on a fantasy that salvation will come from above, but on our own self-activity expressed through organizations at the base that we ourselves create and control" (Grubacic & Lynd 2010). However, in the capitalist-controlled workplace, with or without traditional unions, we must recognize the value of new forms of worker control that occur spontaneously through rank-and-file direct action, often leading to profound transformations in the class-consciousness of workers.

One cannot just identify forms of democratically controlled work in a prism. This chapter will examine how U.S. and migrant laborers engage in direct action to resist employer domination.

These new organizing forms are typically spontaneous actions. Information technology (IT) and new media workers in the United States have engaged in direct action on the job to defend their job stability and to challenge the prevailing wisdom that the U.S. technology workforce is somehow inferior to that of India, China, and newly developing countries in the Global South. Syndicalist direct action, generally with no union support, has emerged through use of the Internet and IT as organizing tools, as means of mobilizing supporters, and as methods to influence public opinion.

Worker direction transcends skill level and national status. Skilled IT workers—the very people who once were expected to benefit the most from the Internet and the new economy—are using these technologies to improve working conditions. As we saw before, in the wake of the dot-com collapse, companies have intentionally used political and economic labor-market tactics and strategy to erode wages and working conditions for IT and skilled workers in the United States and throughout the world. In response, from 2000 to 2010, there has been a steady rise in micro-organizing among workers outside unions, both among displaced U.S. workers and migrant laborers working in the United States as guest workers (Amman, Carpenter, & Neff 2006). Indeed, the very concepts of the workplace as a *place* and of employment as involving an *employer* are becoming outdated. As a result, wages and employment prospects of U.S. IT workers have eroded significantly. One consequence of this transformation is that it is necessary to rethink the nature of employment regulation at a fundamental level. Furthermore, it is not only the regulatory regime that is out of alignment; private organizations, public institutions, social programs, and activist strategies that have constituted progressive politics in the social welfare state also need to be rethought in light of the kinds of changes brought about by globalization that we explored in the previous chapter.

The economic turmoil that affected most workers employed in the IT industry following the bursting of the dot-com bubble in 2000 was created as a means to restructure and reduce wages in the labor markets once considered a source of secure high-wage employment. Subsequently, as we saw in our case study, nonstandard part-time and temporary work expanded in the IT industry, along with the growth in demand of skilled and professional guest workers in the high-technology sector. To facilitate the entry of guest workers, foreign-owned labor contractors are used as intermediaries between migrants and U.S. firms. Foreign IT workers are recruited to work in U.S. firms on the assumption that no American citizens can be found to fill the job tasks.

As we saw in our case study, the reality is that IT work does not create quick wealth for most people working in the industry. Some IT programmers earn high wages and steady incomes at large firms where high-technology is core to operations, but most do not become millionaires or even break into middle class jobs that can provide long-term employment stability. Among U.S. laborers, until the dot-com bubble burst, this trade-off was represented to workers as hard work now in exchange for the promise of substantial compensation or stock ownership later. Foreign nonimmigrant visa holders working in the United States are working under a similar assumption, namely, that short-term contract employment will bring about long-term wealth and income stability. But the reality is that U.S. firms are exploiting foreign workers and domestic workers alike. And, perhaps even worse, they are playing foreign-born and U.S.-born workers against each other to keep workers divided.

Playing the India Card

The divide and conquer tactic is working, as a growing number of academics, pundits, and journalists are now using India as the scapegoat for moving IT jobs abroad and replacing U.S. workers with lower-paid workers. They argue that if U.S. workers do not gain competitive skills and work for lower wages, jobs will go offshore. Conveniently, the literature on labor training is dominated by business school professors preaching that if the United States is to compete in the global economy, the country must promote education and training to catch up with foreign workers that have one way or another left Americans in the dust (Friedman 2005; Levy & Murnane 2004; National Research Council 2000; Papademetriou & Yale-Loehr 1996).

Thomas Friedman, a columnist for the *New York Times,* is one of the most recognized figures to put forward the argument that new technology has allowed skilled foreigners to replace U.S. workers. In his bestseller, *The World is Flat: A Brief History of the Twenty-First Century* (2005), Friedman equates the challenge the United States faces from India and China "practicing extreme capitalism" with the challenge for global hegemony with the Soviet Union at the height of the cold war in the late 1950s (Friedman 2005, 375). Friedman's conclusions are drawn from a trip to Infosys, a leading IT corporation in Bangalore, the high-technology center in India. Friedman claims that India has gained a technological and manufacturing edge to compete with and surpass the United States. His book does not consider what our case study revealed—the fact that while India's IT sector may be growing, the rest of its economy is in shambles. (Friedman does admit, however, that while being escorted throughout India, his travels were never far from the modern five-star hotels, and he was lavishly welcomed by corporate officials at leading IT complexes). The author posits that because of India's focus on education and rapid technological advances, the United States has lost its competitive edge as Internet technology has facilitated the instantaneous capacity to perform functions from anywhere in the world. It is this so-called convergence of technology that Friedman sees as "flattening" the world's economy (Friedman 2005, 51, 202).

Friedman does little more than popularize what most U.S. corporations already know—that labor cost savings can be achieved through shifting technology and manufacturing to Indian high-technology centers in Bangalore (recently renamed Bengalūru), Mumbai (formerly named Bombay), and Hyderabad. Global migration diminishes wage rates even further for skilled and unskilled workers as well as U.S. businesses, with the purposeful support of elected officials, facilitating additional erosion of wages and working conditions through expanding guest worker programs. The way Freidman and others frame the narrative, intentionally or not, plays into growing nativist xenophobia among American workers. This growing resentment of foreign workers only plays into the hands of corporate interests and conceals from most U.S.-born workers the multidimensional exploitation that keeps them and the guest workers in check.

Of course, U.S.-born workers lose out in the outsourcing and offshoring of labor. The elimination of labor markets for U.S.-born workers and their replacement with lower-wage foreign-born workers has led to a job shortage in the United States for professional and, more recently, less-skilled workers. According to Rob Sanchez, founder and administrator of Zazona.com, a right-wing, antiimmigrant Web site that monitors the U.S. government's guest worker program, native-born workers employed at large established companies in Silicon Valley or Washington state expect to stay for their entire careers (interview, Rob Sanchez, June 9, 2005). However, younger workers at start-up companies in the new media industry frequently considered the jobs to be a way station to a better position or career. But the majority never reach their goal. In the 1990s, a growing number of workers in the IT industry continued to sacrifice current wages for potential earnings as owners in the future. While many take this risk, only a few were lucky enough to become independent owners—or to gain enough wealth that they no longer had to work. As corporate demand has expanded for lower-wage workers in highly skilled occupation, unemployment has grown and is expected to increase in the IT industry to unprecedented levels, and many more become involuntarily out of work rather than retiring rich at a young age, as they had hoped. Thus, despite the rhetoric of success and the confidence that so many in the industry espouse, many became marginal nonstandard workers performing perfunctory tasks (see table 4.1). The great deception in contemporary neoliberal society rhetoric, also espoused in the guest work programs, is that each person is an independent agent, responsible only for his or her own life. The reality is that U.S.-born workers are losing benefits like health insurance and pensions by becoming "independent contractors." Foreign-born workers lose out in this situation as well.

According to the Bureau of Labor Statistics (BLS), employers are expected to accelerate offshore outsourcing of jobs between 2010 and 2018, a process that is facilitated by the growing capacity to shift operations to foreign countries with lower wages and educated workers. The BLS estimates that employment of computer programmers is projected to decline by 3 percent from 2008 to 2018: "Advances in programming languages and tools, the growing ability of users to write and implement their own programs, and the offshore outsourcing of programming jobs will contribute to this decline." If guest worker programs are restricted further in the United States, the likelihood that employers will transmit programs digitally will increase, as the job functions can be conducted anywhere in the world. As such, the BLS views computer programmers at higher risk of having their jobs offshored than software developers and workers employed in functions that require higher levels of

Table 4.1. Number of U.S. Jobs Moving Offshore, 2000–2015

Job Category	2000	2005	2010	2015
Management	0	37,477	117,835	288,281
Business	10,787	61,252	161,722	348,028
Computer	27,171	108,991	276,954	472,632
Architecture	3,498	32,302	83,237	184,347
Life sciences	0	3,677	14,478	36,770
Legal	1,793	14,220	34,673	74,642
Art, design	818	5,576	13,846	29,639
Sales	4,619	29,064	97,321	226,564
Office	53,987	295,034	791,034	1,659,310
Total	102,674	587,592	1,591,101	3,320,213

Source: U.S. Department of Labor and Forrester Research, Inc. Note: All numbers have been rounded.

sophistication. Thus, the expansion of guest worker programs that U.S. IT firms are demanding is likely to diminish as the process is further deskilled and the need for local knowledge lessens (Bureau of Labor Statistics 2010–11).

Most migrant laborers across skill categories find themselves in situations that amount to bonded labor. In addition to close supervision at work, they are confined to workplaces and housing complexes controlled by labor contractors. This chapter will complicate the standard narrative by documenting Indian guest workers whose lives revolve around work and the typically thwarted promise for a better life. Contrary to the prevailing image, after a stint in the United States, most Indian IT business services guest workers I interviewed in 2005 considered life and labor in India to be a form of liberation from the demanding jobs they filled in the United States. Other workers who had been promised U.S. green cards returned to India disillusioned, in some cases after paying enormous sums of money, and most of their salaries, to contractors. In effect, workers like these are paying contractors for the "privilege" of working long hours and the *chance* at a future job in the United States. For the most part, even those who still want this chance after spending time in the United States will not get it.

For upper- and middle-class graduates of the Indian Institute of Technology, a large university system with locations in seven cities, the opportunity to obtain a visa to work in the United States is promoted by the posteducational institution as a guarantee of a lifetime of wealth and prosperity.[1] Just as U.S. high-tech workers in the 1990s were willing to risk exchanging traditional jobs and salaries for the promise of potential of riches by dot-com businesses, Indians and other workers on nonimmigrant visas are also risk takers (Amman, Carpenter, & Neff, 2006). From 2000 to 2010, Indian technology and business services workers are offered the possibility of making long-term connections with leading American corporations, compelling many Indian technology workers to work twelve to sixteen hours a day, six or seven days a week. Upon completion of their stay in the United States, most take for granted that they can return to India and live comfortably working for Indian IT companies and subsidiaries of multinational corporations.

The Prevailing Wage Sham?

The only ones who win in this labor sham are employers, and they have worked hard to expand the system during the past couple of decades. A growing number of companies are taking advantage of immigration laws to pay lower wages because, in recent years, the U.S. Department of Labor—which is responsible for overseeing the H-1B process—has not monitored information technology firms for such violations. Documents from the U.S. Department of Labor released to Zazona.com through a freedom of information request revealed that high-technology companies including Cisco Systems, Intel, and Motorola offered positions through contractors and independent firms to foreign H-1B holders, even when U.S. citizens were seeking jobs in the industry. The primary motivation for high-technology and business services firms to hire foreign workers is to reduce wage rates, even though the U.S. government forbids issuing nonimmigrant visas to lower-wage workers. The law allows that the H-1B worker can be paid as much as 10 percent below the prevailing salary in the industry. If year after year foreign skilled workers are paid 10 percent less, wages for everybody in the industry, both citizens and immigrants, will get lower and lower (interview, Rob Sanchez, June 9, 2005).

Hiring nonimmigrant visa holders has the allure for corporations of reducing prevailing wages for foreign and U.S. workers alike—further eroding wage rates in an industry that already tends to replace their middle-aged workers earning higher salaries with younger workers entering the industry who are willing to work longer hours for less pay. Many workers such as Sanchez say that since the dot-com collapse, labor in the IT industry has been in a constant state of churning, searching for younger workers and forcing older workers out. Nevertheless, though some IT workers worry about job security, the majority usually consider themselves immune to the outsourcing of their own work. Sanchez said that only after IT workers lose their job to a foreigner do they start complaining, contact political officials, or join high-technology and labor organizations that oppose U.S. guest worker policy (interview, Rob Sanchez, June 9, 2005).

Business groups such as the Arizona Chamber of Commerce, and national industry interest groups like the Information Technology Association of America (ITAA) and the National Association of Software and Service Companies (NASSCOM), complain that there is a shortage of every kind of worker. The number of U.S. nativist opponents and activists has expanded between 2000 and 2010 throughout the country, with members seeking to reduce outsourcing of work to nonimmigrant foreign visitors because they think that the purported shortage of skilled labor is largely a fiction to cover the loss of domestic jobs and the underpayment of wages for foreign workers.[2] Sanchez and other proponents of limiting nonimmigrant visas argue that foreign subcontractors should be restricted because they encourage U.S. employers to dismiss high-wage U.S. skilled workers and provide ready and willing replacements to work as contractors. Moreover, foreign labor contractors like Infosys, Tata, and Wipro benefit from a system that typically prevents foreign workers from being promoted to higher-wage jobs, driving down labor standards for both U.S. *and* foreign workers.

On-the-Job Resistance

Resistance to globalization has taken a spontaneous form, as U.S. IT workers take direct action against their employers through on-the-job resistance. Typically, this type of spontaneous militant activism or micro-organizing never gains organizational traction, because workers are quickly dismissed from their jobs before they can organize themselves into associations. Evidence of worker militancy both within their companies and through Internet organizing indicates that the direct experience of employer victimization on the job produces worker resistance. The terms *militant* or *radical* are not conventionally proffered by IT industry leaders to describe the common programmer or skilled specialist.

Frequently, H-1B replacement workers depend on U.S. colleagues to train and coach them. To smooth the transition, retaining experienced workers diminishes the possibility of major mistakes and, according to one anonymous human resources recruiter, establishes a sense of continuity. As the remainder of this chapter will show, experienced high-technology workers have resisted the outsourcing of their jobs in ever-increasing numbers. This resistance has taken many forms, from campaigns against individual companies or government representatives to the formation of organizations to promote jobs for Americans. For the most part, resentment is directed against corporations that engage in outsourcing and offshoring and the government policies that sanction them. However, the anger sometimes takes antiimmigrant, xenophobic, and nativist form.

HIGH-TECH BODYSHOPS

One of the earliest and most well-publicized disputes concerning unfair job competition between foreign nonimmigrant and U.S. high-technology workers is the Sona Shah legal dispute that gained widespread attention from 2003 to 2007 and continues to influence debates on immigrant workers. Sona Shah, an American citizen of Indian descent, lost her programming job at the New York corporate headquarters of the investment bank Goldman Sachs in April 1998, when the firm decided to subcontract the entire department to ADP Wilco, a London-based global outsourcing firm. According to their Web site, ADP Wilco casts itself as a cost-efficient way to reduce labor costs by replacing higher-paid permanent staff with lower-paid temporary workers: "Users of ADP Wilco's outsourcing solutions can benefit from lower operating costs. Processing expenses become a variable cost based on transactional volumes, rather than a fixed overhead requiring a significant up-front investment. This results in a more predictable profit stream and a fast-track return on investment."[3]

In 1998, before her dismissal, Shah found herself working in New York City's financial district alongside foreign programmers whom Goldman Sachs had outsourced through ADP Wilco. The majority of the workers were then earning a fraction of the going wages for programmers of $200 to $250 per hour. Still, according to Shah, ADP Wilco billed Goldman Sachs $275 per hour. While the subcontracting is a common practice, U.S. workers command significantly higher wages than foreign guest workers, who do not earn prevailing wages in IT (interview, Sona Shah, March 18, 2005). Though government researchers have not reached a consensus on the contention that the individual experiences at specific firms reflect a general pattern where highly skilled migrant workers undermine wages for corresponding U.S-born workers, a consensus has emerged that the growth of H-1B workers has increased the reserve army of the unemployed. While insufficient data is available for conclusive evidence of their general wage effect on the United States as a whole, according to the Federal Reserve Bank in Atlanta, "As skilled immigrants assimilate over time, they may become more substitutable for native workers and may create adverse wage effects in the longer run" (Zavodny 2003).

High-technology businesses always envisage labor shortages of information technology workers while at the same time laying off tens of thousands of employees every year. Biao Xiang reports that the industry is in constant search for flexibility in a global neoliberal system where cutting costs and job security will lead to higher profits. Xiang views India as a principal source of workers who are readily deployed at will by multinational businesses seeking long-term cost advantages and emergent Indian firms seeking penetration into new markets.

Shah confirms the widespread evidence that Indians are employed under highly onerous working conditions. ADP Wilco, according to Shah, is a *bodyshop,* a term that suggests an automotive body repair shop, which objectifies human workers as disposable entities and returns them to their home countries once their labor is completed.[4] The majority of the workers, though, believe that they stand a chance at permanent green card–status employment. Shah noted in an interview that H-1Bs must work diligently without complaining in return, if they are to obtain a job in their home country or return to the United States on L-1 visas as essential company employees (interview, Sona Shah, March 18, 2005).[5] Though most H-1B workers are obedient and earn enough to establish a business back home, they are willing to work at significantly lower wages in the United States and Europe, according to the *India Migration Report* (Khadria 2009).

While most H-1B workers employed in large multinationals are primed for lucrative careers, smaller firms follow ADP Wilco's lead in misleading workers by promising they will prosper in the United States, only to subject them to living insecurely, barely covering living expenses or not paying them at all. Workers who complain can always be fired, subject to deportation by government authorities. According to Shah and a number of visa holders who worked for the company, this is exactly what happened at ADP Wilco.

When H-1B workers at Goldman Sachs discovered the disparity in salary and benefits, a large number wanted greater parity. In 1998, Shah and H-1B employees who complained about their conditions were dismissed. Shah claims she was discriminated against as a U.S. national, and dismissed because she was a regular staff employee. Since her dismissal, Shah pursued a long employment discrimination case in New York state and a media crusade against ADP Wilco as well as the practice of outsourcing in general. Though federal law stipulates that U.S. workers may not be displaced by foreigners if they have equivalent skills, Shah claims she is a victim of illegal outsourcing by ADP Wilco. For Shah, the lawsuit, which was settled in June 2008, has metamorphosed into a crusade against outsourcing. Claiming that she cannot find work elsewhere in the industry, Shah has publicized her plight and has initiated a campaign to change the law by advocating directly to members of Congress.

This campaign supported a bill (HR 2702), sponsored by Connecticut Democrat Rosa DeLauro, that would place restrictions on outsourcing through subcontractors and impose limits on both H-1B and L-1 visas. Among the growing number of bills directed at outsourcing, DeLauro's proposed legislation is seen as the toughest and most serious in curbing the abuse of H-1B and L-1 visas by foreign subcontractors operating in the United States. Several bills have been initiated by Republicans—notably HR 2154, which amends the Immigration and Naturalization Act to prevent employers from transferring H-1B guest workers to another employer. This bill, introduced in May 2003, sponsored by Representative John Mica of Florida, among others, is viewed by activists like Shah as a sham that does little to prevent employers from outsourcing. Rather, Shah supported the DeLauro bill because it caps L-1 visas—which currently have no limit—at 35,000 per year.[6] The bill also requires companies to pay comparable wages to U.S. workers and nonimmigrant visa holders, and would force businesses to wait one hundred days after laying off U.S. workers before hiring foreign L-1 guest workers.

Shah has put together a packet of information that high-technology workers can use to lobby their representatives to support HR 2702, which is gaining momentum in Congress. She pressed Democratic Representative Bill Pascrell of New Jersey to sign on to DeLauro's bill. In January 2004, after two meetings with local IT workers, Pascrell came out in support of the proposed legislation.[7] Shah has traveled to regional meetings of IT workers to promote De-Lauro's bill and is active in the Programmers Guild, an organization founded in the late 1990s by New Jersey IT workers with a reach throughout the metropolitan area. The group has successfully lobbied the New Jersey state legislature to pass a law that prohibits the outsourcing of state jobs. Currently the guild is active in pressing members of Congress to support the DeLauro bill. Shah is emphatic in her support for both U.S. workers displaced by nonimmigrant workers and foreign workers who are exploited by corporations and outsourcing firms that pay them a fraction of what domestic workers earn and that treat them like indentured servants.

DIRECT ACTION IN THE "BODYSHOPS"

One of the best-recognized worker struggles in the IT industry was between Siemens Information and Communication Networks (ICN), a unit of the giant German multinational Siemens AG, and Mike Emmons, a high-technology contract worker at the firm's Lake Mary facility, several miles north of Orlando, Florida. Siemens is a multibillion-dollar conglomerate with nearly 420,000 employees worldwide, working in businesses ranging from electrical engineering, lighting, and power to transportation, medical equipment, financing, and real estate.

In May 2000, Emmons and twenty other workers in Siemens' ICN's Lake Mary IT department were laid off. Twelve workers in the department were employed by Siemens ICN and eight, including Emmons, were working under contract. The contract workers at Siemens had worked continually for extended periods of time, and Emmons had been working at the facility for six years. Along with the others in the department, Emmons was offered severance pay in exchange for staying on for three months to train replacement workers. Because steady full-time work was hard to come by in the industry, all but one of the workers, including Emmons, accepted Siemens' offer.

Nearly all workers scheduled for replacement agree to such terms, because they need the wages, look forward to the severance pay, or are in desperate need of the health insurance. Moreover, if the U.S. worker does not accept the terms of dismissal, he or she could potentially lose eligibility for unemployment benefits, since rejecting the terms is tantamount to quitting. Nevertheless, corporations that require U.S. workers to train H-1B replacements establish a new employer-employee dynamic that is ripe for on-the-job conflict, disruption, and potential chaos.

In June, about twenty replacement workers were subcontracted to Siemens by Tata Consulting Service, an Indian-based company that recruits highly skilled workers in India to work on nonimmigrant visas in the United States. Siemens saved substantially through outsourcing the department. Emmons was told by an Indian national holding a green card that the foreign workers at the Lake Mary operation were paid the equivalent of $1,000 per month in foreign currency plus $2,000 per month in expenses, replacing an equal number of American workers who had been paid an average of $5,000 per month. Tata's replacement workers started training for programming jobs for which Emmons claims they had no preparation or qualification (interview, Mike Emmons, August 20, 2005).

In July, after giving a PowerPoint presentation showing the Tata employees how to do his work, Emmons decided to quit. Before walking out, however, Emmons and several other workers who stood to lose their jobs initiated a job action to challenge the outsourcing—through slowing down the training and work process, downloading information indicating that the Tata workers were in the United States on the wrong visas, and playing the Johnny Paycheck song "Take This Job and Shove It" (1977) on their computers, heard throughout the facility.

Investigations revealed that the replacement workers did not even hold H-1B visas, which require immigrants to have special skills that American workers do not possess—in this case, programming skills. The Tata replacement workers were in fact on L-1B visas, which require workers to have both special skills and specialized knowledge of the company. Emmons said that he and others found a management training document describing the course of study, ostensibly in order for the replacements to qualify for L-1Bs. Employees in the IT department appealed to U.S. Representative John Mica, Republican congressman representing the Lake Mary area (interview, Mike Emmons, August 20, 2005).

Before the November 2002 election, the workers received a letter from Mica's office saying that he would write a bill to protect them. By Thanksgiving, the workers were still awaiting legislative action, so Emmons and others began leafleting in Mica's neighborhood. Emmons launched what he calls an "e-mail bombing campaign" against Mica and others in Congress who paid lip service to the problem of outsourcing by introducing bills they knew would not pass (Worthen 2003).

Before leaving the company, Emmons sent workers an e-mail disparaging Siemens' labor practices that replaced skilled U.S. workers with less-skilled foreign H-1B and L-1 workers. Many workers feared losing their jobs if they complained, so the majority of them supported the e-mail campaign in unconventional ways through the computer network. Emmons recalled that most Siemens workers cheered upon receiving the e-mail and sent responses of support (interview, Mike Emmons, August 20, 2005). After reading Emmons's e-mail, one thousand workers at the Lake Mary plant shouted their approval in the facility and sent e-mails back to him approving his actions. Months after leaving the company, Emmons sent a report to Siemens ICN workers based on a news story reporting that U.S. workers who were training their replacements initiated a job action that was aired on the local CBS affiliate in Orlando, and Emmons continues to send out updates.

The controversy over Siemens' dismissal of the twenty workers continues. Emmons and other unemployed Siemens workers learned through the Federal Election Commission that Representative Mica had received campaign donations from Siemens and other high-tech companies. After Emmons complained again to his representative, Mica responded with an e-mail indicating that he would not serve as his representative on the issue any longer (interview, Mike Emmons, August 20, 2004; Worthen 2003).

In May 2003, Mica introduced legislation (HR 2154) that would block third-party contractors from issuing L-1 visas, but the bill never passed. Frustrated by the inaction, Emmons ran for Mica's House seat. Running as a Democrat, Emmons called for national health care and an end to the outsourcing of jobs to foreign contractors. Following his dismissal from Siemens, Emmons's own health care premiums rose from $804 to $1,472 per month, a serious issue because his daughter requires ongoing medical care. Emmons abandoned his bid for Congress in April 2004, unable to collect enough signatures before the deadline (interview, Mike Emmons, August 20, 2005).

The Emmons case demonstrates that the radicalization of highly skilled workers may occur when an employer informs employees that they are to be replaced by foreign nonimmigrant workers. This situation presents opportunities for micro-organizing. The standard procedure for replacing high-wage U.S. employees with IT workers with H-1B visas is to offer to retain certain employees or contractors for six to ten weeks so that they will train the replacements. Keeping workers slated for unemployment is at odds with standard human resources practices, which caution that displaced employees could become disgruntled and a source of potential conflict and dissension. Given this departure from standard practice, the informational discharge meeting is an essential part of the process of replacing U.S. workers with foreigners contracted through third-party firms. IT workers are often warned that if they do not comply with the procedure and train their replacements, they may be fired straight away and risk losing severance pay, if any is offered at all. Employers count on the fact that if they place outsourced U.S. workers in jeopardy of losing their wages and benefits, they can impose discipline that will contribute to compliance with the plan. Of course, once the workers have left the company, they are no longer under the control of the employers.

In Emmons's case, once he left Siemens he continued to fight worker displacement. He created the Web site OutsourceCongress.org, which monitored actions taken by members of Congress on issues of the outsourcing and offshoring of high-technology jobs. Before the domain was bought by another party, his Web site ran a hodgepodge of articles, congressional testimony, and angry criticism that includes commentary from the Federation for American Immigration Reform (FAIR), an antiimmigrant organization, as well as supporting testimony by the AFL-CIO's Department of Professional Employees. In the interview, Emmons stressed that he had no expertise on U.S policy toward and was not against immigrants per se but opposed the replacement of U.S. workers by foreign nonimmigrant contract workers (August 20, 2005). He is not alone in this sentiment, as the Internet allows more and more U.S.-born workers to organize protests against outsourcing and other forms of employer control (Cloward & Piven 2001).

BROKE ON THE GOLD COAST

Connecticut typically ranks first in the United States for average annual pay, a distinction the state has held into the early twenty-first century (U.S. Census Bureau 2007).[8] Apart from significant pockets of poverty in the state's major cities, such as Bridgeport, Hartford, New Britain, and New Haven, Connecticut residents have enjoyed relative stability, even during the postindustrial shift from manufacturing to services. The state is home to leading multinational corporations, including General Electric and United Technologies. The state's huge military-industrial complex has softened the blow to industrial workers. Electric Boat, a unit of General Dynamics, based in Groton, is the leading producer of submarines; Hartford-based United Technologies is parent to Pratt & Whitney and Sikorsky, two leading producers of jet engines and military helicopters. Additionally, the state economy depends on robust finance, real estate, and insurance sectors, which sustain high-wage jobs and a high standard of living. Renowned for a skilled workforce, Connecticut is one of the last states where one would expect high-technology workers to be scarce. The robust high-technology sector has given workers a confident sense of stability and constancy.

From 2000 to 2002, however, thousands of IT workers in Connecticut lost their jobs as the recession intensified and caps on foreign worker visas were raised. The majority of those losing their jobs to foreign guest workers were older workers who had been in the industry for more than ten years. Of particular concern to displaced IT workers was that large corporations in the state were using foreign contractors to find replacement workers from India and elsewhere.

John Bauman, a fifty-six-year-old high-tech worker from Meriden, Connecticut, was one of the thousands of IT workers in the state who lost their jobs. Unable to find work, Bauman called a meeting among colleagues in the industry to discuss the problem of the growing use of foreign nonimmigrant visa holders as replacements for permanent workers. To his surprise, nearly one hundred workers in the region came to the first organized meeting in November 2002. In March of the next year, the group formally established themselves as the Organization for the Rights of American Workers (TORAW), an advocacy group demanding that companies stop replacing U.S. IT workers with foreign nonimmigrant visa holders.[9]

Nativism and xenophobia against foreigners have long been deep-seated historic conventions in the United States. Virtually every new wave of immigrants has endured prejudice and victimization. TORAW claims to have steered away from the most extreme forms of U.S. chauvinism in public statements, and disassociates from nativist individuals or organizations that seek to reinstate laws that end all immigration. Still, the organization gave former CNN anchorman and syndicated national radio host Lou Dobbs its "Man of the Year" award in 2004 in recognition of his support for strict immigration controls to ostensibly protect U.S.-born workers from job loss. Dobbs—a leading neoliberal advocate—has promulgated a nativist perspective on his CNN nightly television news show and in his book *Exporting America* (2004).

Beyond ending outsourcing of good jobs, TORAW and a growing number of organizations express support for the global justice movement's opposition to the expansion of neoliberal trade policies that allow international corporations to shift production and service jobs overseas and to foreign workers at home. But this position is not shared by Indians and many others in the Global South who feel that divestment will hurt their economy. Indeed they are correct: global justice for many Indians requires advocating fair wages and decent working conditions in poor countries where abject poverty prevents human development and even a degree of respect for those who have fewer choices but to accept their fate or take up arms against the state. Increasingly, this is the case in Indian states, where the majority of the residents are living under wretched conditions without rudimentary health care and basic education, and where many live in famine. The only solution is through taking state power for the impoverished and through establishing local, regional, and global struggles that seek to provide relief and essential conditions for survival.

Signal International Workers' Direct Action

While U.S.-born workers fight their battle against guest worker programs, Indian workers face battles of their own. Even as U.S. capitalists tap into the migrant labor pool by expanding H-2B visas to exploit low-wage imported labor, Indian workers refuse to be easy prey to the U.S. corporations and the Indian contractors who defraud them through using the bait and switch technique. In the spring of 2006, after just three months on the job as welders, Indian H-2B shipyard guest workers in Pascagoula, Mississippi, began organizing and protesting low wages and their confinement to overcrowded, unhygienic conditions in barracks located on the worksite. Signal International, their employer, is an oil services and marine fabrication company with operations chiefly in the Gulf of Mexico.

In December 2003 and throughout 2004, the recruitment companies Dewan Consultants and Global International, based in India and the United States, respectively, placed advertisements in Indian and United Arab Emirates newspapers on behalf of a number of U.S. companies. Such advertisements were part of a joint effort between the two companies, which worked together to bring workers from India to the United States. The advertisements alleged that those who accepted the proffered jobs would be able to obtain permanent residence in the country. Individuals who answered these advertisements contacted the recruiters and took tests to verify their job competency. Contractor and employer inquiries on worker skills and tests were administered by the Mumbai labor recruiting companies Dewan Consultants and Global Resources, in conjunction with labor brokers J & M and Indo-Amerisoft, along with Malvern C. Burnett of the Gulf Coast Immigration Law Center LLC (*David Kurian et al. v. Signal International LLC et al.*, 2008; interview, Saket Soni, 2009). Those individuals in India and UAE who passed said tests were expressly told, both verbally and through written communication, that their green card applications would be sponsored by the labor brokers if they paid three installments totaling five to eight lakh rupees (approximately $12,000 to $20,000). The understanding between these workers and the recruiting companies was that this amount would be split between Dewan, Global, Burnett, and either J & M or Indo-Amerisoft.

In addition, the prospective workers were told that their families would also obtain future permanent residence status in the United States, at a cost of roughly $1,500 per family member. According to the terms of the workers' contracts, the recruitment and "green card fees" were to be refunded if green cards were not obtained by the signer after a processing period of eighteen to twenty-four months.

In 2004, the prospective workers paid their first installments, and in January 2006, they were informed by members of the aforementioned companies that the labor certification needed for their green card applications had been approved. Thereafter, the workers paid the remaining two installments. The financial burden the workers undertook was immense. They mortgaged and sold their homes, land, and personal belongings. They borrowed large sums of money from friends, family, financial institutions, and loan sharks, the latter charging exorbitant interest rates. In the spring of 2006, after the processing period had expired, the green cards still were not received by the prospective workers.

In May and June 2006, Signal International contacted the Mississippi Department of Employment Security, Texas Workforce Commission, and the United States Department of Labor and took the necessary steps through the H-2B guest worker program to bring 590 Indian workers to fill positions in their factory. These positions largely called for welders and fitters. During this time, the plaintiffs allege that Signal International authorized the Dewan-Global recruiting chain to claim that the company would be sponsoring the workers' green cards and would apply for two to three extensions of their H-2B visas in the interim, neither of which is legally feasible. The workers were then informed that in return for 35,000 to 45,000 rupees, or $800 to $1,100 U.S., they would each receive an H-2B visa and a green card sponsored by Signal International (Indian Workers Solidarity Congress 2008). Already substantially invested in the green card process with Dewan and Global, the prospective workers agreed to put forth the additional sums, unaware that the promises made were not legally possible. In late 2006 and early 2007, the first group of Indian guest workers Signal International hired entered the United States under the impression that they would soon be receiving green cards.

In spring, summer, and fall of 2006, Dewan and Global again placed advertisements in Indian and United Arab Emirates newspapers. This time, they sought welders and fitters to work specifically for Signal International and again promised those workers permanent residence in the United States. Again, the plaintiffs assert that Signal International approved the dissemination of these false promises on the part of the recruiting company. Once more, the prospective workers were assured that they would receive H-2B visas that would be extended at least twice, as well as green cards within two years' time, in exchange for approximately eight lakhs, the equivalent of $20,000. Another $1,500 was to be provided for each family member. Along with Dewan and Global, the labor brokers Indo-Amerisoft, J & M, and legal representative Burnett were complicit in promoting and drawing up this arrangement. A second round of Indian prospective workers signed contracts to this effect in 2006 and 2007, with the stipulation that their money was to be refunded if they had not received their green cards within a two-year period.

Throughout 2006 and early 2007, representatives from Signal International traveled to India and the United Arab Emirates and administered tests to ensure the job competence of the prospective workers as welders and fitters. Once individuals had passed the tests, and to obtain their H-2B visas, they had to be interviewed at the U.S. consulate. They were contacted by Dewan and Global employees and given instructions on what to say at these interviews. The candidates were also told they had to sign documents that redirected their passports and H-2B visas directly to Dewan and Global, preventing individual possession and control of these important documents. They were threatened that if they did not answer in the proscribed manner, they would lose their visas, green cards, and money. Travel arrangements to the United States were made by Dewan and Global. These arrangements included rushed meetings just hours before the workers' flights wherein they were not given their passports unless they paid outstanding balances and signed documents in English that many were unable to read because of both time and language constraints. They were also threatened that failure to comply would result in the destruction of their passports. Under these conditions and contracts, roughly five hundred Indian workers traveled to the United States from November 2006 to January 2007, three hundred of whom traveled to the Pascagoula, Mississippi, plant.

Many workers paid the contractors $10,000 to $20,000 in exchange for Global International's labor certification and guest worker visas for ten-month periods, renewable for up to thirty months. However, while the guest workers expected prevailing wages of $18/hour, after being reclassified as second-class welders, the company paid many workers half as much. The mandatory lodging cost for guest workers was $35 a day (approximately $1,050 a month), automatically drawn from paychecks to stay in a labor camp resembling a prison, located directly at the Signal International facility. The dormitory area consists of small and overcrowded bunkhouses. Up to twenty-four men were housed in each bunkhouse in the barracks, measuring twelve feet by eighteen feet, crowded with bunk beds and just one small bathroom.

Living conditions in Signal International's labor camp in Pascagoula, Mississippi, were substandard and their legality questionable. Originally, the workers were told that they had to live in the labor camps, and, although this position was later reversed by Signal International, the workers were told that the money would be extracted from their paychecks regardless of whether they decided to remain in the camp. This mandatory expense, coupled with the pressure they were under to repay their visa and "green card" debts, made living elsewhere an extreme financial strain, a fact that Signal International was undoubtedly counting upon in terms of continuing to exert control over their workers. Signal H-2B visa workers were told to open up accounts with M & M Bank, into which their paychecks were directly deposited. In addition, the dining hall wherein the workers took their meals was reputedly unhygienic, which led to many workers falling ill, some needing hospitalization. The labor camp took on an increasingly prisonlike aspect when one considers the behavior of the camp's security guards. The guards monitored the movements of workers in and out of the camp and conducted raids of the camp bunkhouses in which they performed invasive searches of the Indian workers' possessions. This living situation was not imposed upon their colleagues who were U.S. citizens. In addition, the guest workers allege that they were subjected to testing and retesting of skills, on-the-job discipline, layoffs, periods without work, lack of safety precautions, poor job assignments, unfair critical evaluations, and other poor employment measures that were dissimilar to those of U.S.-born workers in analogous job categories (Bauer 2008). Signal International camp workers verbally abused the guest workers by making derogatory comments on the basis of their race and alien status.

The workers were strongly discouraged from protesting these conditions by Signal International and their associated recruiting companies. As H-2B visa holders, their ability to work in the United States was completely dependent upon their continued employment with the company that registered for their visa applications. Such a reality brought a stark contrast of power between Signal International and the guest workers that the former clearly exploited. The H-2B visa program (which provides temporary visas for laborers in industries other than agriculture) suffers from an initial lack of regulatory safeguards that are afforded those with H-2A visas, such as free housing, access to legal services, a guarantee to be able to work at least three-fourths of the total promised hours, and travel reimbursement after the worker fulfills at least 50 percent of the promised working period. In addition, the Department of Labor claims that it does not have the authority to enforce the prevailing wage mandate, which holds that employers must pay the H-2B workers either minimum wage or the standard wage in that industry (this was instituted to protect jobs from wage deflation as well as to protect the workers' rights). Guest workers have virtually no protections in place and are at the mercy of their employers because being fired means automatic deportation.

But by the spring of 2007, Indian guest workers at Signal International began to complain that they would be unable to earn the money they paid to the contractors upon completion of their jobs. In March 2007, the disillusioned workers, led by Jacob Joseph Kadakkarappally—one of the contract workers—began meeting in a nearby church to discuss the poor wages and conditions. They demanded full refunds from the contractor and improved living conditions. Signal, which handpicked all the welders, fired Kadakkarappally and five other organizers, as well as cut the pay of the H-2B workers further, contending they were unqualified. The company claimed that it was dismissing and deporting Kadakkarappally and the other organizers for incompetence. While the company said officially that the six fired workers were incompetent welders, Kadakkarappally said the company vice president remarked that they were terminating them for attending the meetings. Later, they officially cancelled their licenses. In early 2008, the U.S. Department of Justice began an official investigation into Signal's practices[10] and in April 2008, a class-action lawsuit was filed against Signal that came to trial in February 2010. Signal claimed that the six workers were fired for "performance-related reasons and disruptive behavior, not for complaining to outsiders about conditions."[11]

Just after the crackdown at the Pascagoula facility, Signal International security guards locked the fired workers in the plant as they awaited deportation by the U.S. Citizenship and Immigration Services (CIS). However, after all the workers staged a protest, the Pascagoula Police Department set the guest workers free. Subsequently, the workers initiated a legal challenge to the deportation with the help of the Mississippi Immigrant Rights Alliance and the Southern Poverty Law Center. The two organizations also requested repayment of the contractor fees (Mississippi Immigrant Rights Alliance 2007; Southern Poverty Law Center 2007; Bacon 2007). The guest worker uprising at Signal International reveals the capacity and readiness of guest workers to resist oppression even if under threat of deportation and lacking the protection of U.S. labor law.

In the case of Signal International H-2B workers, their attempts to organize in an effort to change camp conditions were repressed. When Kadakkarappally and fellow worker Sabulal Vijayanbegan (Vijayan) began voicing complaints regarding their wages and the camp's housing and food, they were told by Signal International employees to desist. When these two men began organizing meetings among the workers, Signal International contacted the recruitment companies to devise a strategy to deal with the growing discontent. This resulted in Sachin Dewan of Dewan Consultants calling Vijayan's wife on March 7, 2007, and telling her that her husband must stop "making trouble. "When Vijayan was informed of this call, he in turn called Dewan, and was informed that if he continued in his efforts to organize the workers, they would all be sent back to India." On March 8, 2007, Signal International held a meeting in which management declared that the company would not extend the workers' H-2B visas if they took legal action against Signal (*David Kurian et al. v. Signal International LLC et al,* 2008; interview, Saket Soni, 2009).

At the meeting, Burnett told the workers that they were ineligible for other kinds of immigration relief and could depend only upon Signal International to maintain their H-2B immigration status and pursue their green card applications. Early in the morning of March 9, 2007, Signal International locked the gates to the camp, thus trapping the workers inside, while security guards made their way through the bunkhouses with pictures of Vijayan, Kadakkarappally, Kuldeep Singh, Krishan Kumar, and Thanasekar Chellappan, whom Signal was seeking to locate and detain as instigators of the worker action. Vijayan, dismayed by the recent calls and militant roundup, attempted suicide and was hospitalized. Kadakkarappally, who was assisting Vijayan in seeking medical attention, was forcibly brought to the "TV room," wherein Chellappan and Kumar had also been detained. Another anonymous worker, whose picture the guards had also been showing around the bunkhouses, hid and then fled from the camp. Other workers surrounded the TV room where Kadakkarappally, Chellappan, and Kumar were being held, but the guards did not allow them to communicate with the detainees.

Late in the day, Signal informed the three workers that they were fired and released them, because of growing pressure from "local media, religious advocates, and other individuals" (Indian Workers Solidarity Congress 2008) that had begun protesting the detention of the workers at the camp gates. In the hysteria and confusion, more workers deserted the labor camp. Sometime in the period between March 9 and April 10, Signal instructed M & M Banks to deny these workers access to the money in their accounts. When the remaining guest workers learned of this, it contributed to the pressure they felt to remain at their worksite, many fearing destitution or confinement if they protested against the conditions at Signal. Following this incident at the camp, Signal management, Dewan, and Burnett told the remaining Indian H-2B visa holders in a series of camp meetings throughout the spring and summer of 2007 that their visas would be extended and green cards made available if they continued to work at Signal. Nevertheless, on July 31, 2007, the H-2B visas expired. In response to their dismissal by Signal, the Indian workers began a campaign of civil disobedience and legal action, including a class-action lawsuit to restore the jobs and provide the workers with restitution.

Signal responded to the class-action lawsuit in "Signal Answer to Amended Complaint," which the guest workers filed in court on May 9, 2008. In its response, Signal claims that Michael Pol, a Mississippi deputy sheriff and president of Global Resources, contacted Signal in 2006 offering its services in obtaining foreign workers legally. Signal contends that it only authorized Global to obtain workers through the H-2B visa program. The company alleges that it did not hear about the promises made by recruiting companies on its behalf to obtain green cards until the workers themselves made inquiries about green cards after having arrived in the United States. Signal also argues that the devastation caused by Hurricane Katrina made it such that the workers could not have obtained housing independently. It says that the $35 a day covered "the cost of lodging; three meals per day of catered Indian food . . . ; laundry service . . . ; satellite television (featuring North and South Indian programming); internet access; transportation available 24 hours per day, 7 days a week to and from shopping areas, churches, medical appointments, and other local destinations of choice; free local telephone calls and access to long-distance services" (Purkayashtha 2008).

The company took a critical view of those workers who left Signal after the events of March 9, 2007, saying that though some left because of what they felt were broken green card promises, others left because they had originally "come into the country under false pretenses" (Purkayashtha 2008) to work for other companies to which Burnett redirected them and who would sponsor their green cards. Signal also maintains that some workers left Signal because they were advised by a third party to claim they were victims of illegal trafficking so that they might remain in the United States.

From May 14 to June 11, 2008, more than a year after the sit-down strike, Indian workers employed on the U.S. Gulf Coast, who migrated chiefly from Tamil Nadu and Kerala, staged a twenty-nine-day strike to protest Signal's "modern day slavery" practices (Freeman 2008), demanding a U.S. government investigation into the trafficking practices of Signal and its labor contractor. The strike was supported by the Indian Workers Solidarity Congress (IWSC), a non-governmental organization (NGO) in New Delhi, which organized hunger strikes in Tamil Nadu and Delhi (Indian Workers Solidarity

Congress White Paper 2008). In an interview, Ananya Bhattacharya, director of the IWSC, an affiliate of the workers' organization Jobs with Justice, said the Signal workers' sit-down and hunger strike gained wide support among migrant welders who had previously worked in the Arab gulf states, under better working conditions than in the United States (interview, Ananya Bhattacharya, December 14, 2008).

Since the incident on March 9, 2007, many workers remained with Signal International. Following criticism in light of the events of March 9, Signal fired Global and contracted with S. Mansur and Company to bring more workers to the United States.[12] A year later, on March 5, 2008, approximately one hundred workers quit to protest their living conditions, an effort supported by the New Orleans Workers' Center for Racial Justice, headed by Saket Soni and the Alliance for Guest Workers for Dignity.[13] When about five hundred workers protested in 2008, media attention was garnered. This spurred action on the part of the U.S. government and the government of India. On March 11, 2008, the Ministry of Overseas Indian Affairs (MOIA) suspended the licenses of Dewan consultants and S. Mansur and Co. while they investigated the trafficking allegations against the recruiting companies.[14]

Workers Organizing Workers

U.S. guest worker programs that serve as models for a new immigration policy evoke the essence of bad nonstandard jobs: low-wages, social isolation from the general workforce, indentured servitude, and, upon completion of the job, forced deportation to one's home country. While opponents of immigration do not share the same philosophy, Sona Shah and TORAW have set up models for lobbying federal officials to place restrictions on nonimmigrant visas that displace U.S. IT workers. Their campaigns have had some success. In 2004, "outsourcing" became a ubiquitous, household term, and Congress could not agree on the number of worker visas to be issued. Another sign of Shah and TORAW's campaign's effectiveness is that a bill that extended H-1B visas to 195,000 foreign workers expired in 2004. When the legislation was not renewed, the limits reverted back to the pre-2000 level of 65,000, despite enormous political pressure from high-powered industry lobbyists. This outcome reflects the work of activists such as Shah, Rob Sanchez, Mike Emmons, and John Bauman, as well as the emergence of grassroots lobbying groups ready to oppose any bill that increases caps on guest workers in a range of professions. The situation remains tense as some members of Congress insist on using the issue of outsourcing and offshoring as a way to demonize immigrants and to exploit xenophobic and nativist sentiment, though they have yet to pass any laws. The Internet has emerged as the primary means of unifying skilled electrical engineers, programmers, and new media workers to share common experiences and relay information on vital legislation and labor market trends. In addition, high-technology workers who are unaffiliated with labor unions also make use of face-to-face gatherings and meetings to avail themselves of networks to locate employers and contractors needing work. Some groups, without constituting themselves as formal organizations, meet regularly for dinner to chat with friends and get updated on the employment conditions within the industry. As steady jobs become harder to find, and IT workers are increasingly channeled into contract work with definite beginning and ending dates, this organizing is gaining momentum throughout the country.

IT workers are also engaged in autonomous organizing against their current and former employers. In early 2002, emerging high-tech organizing gathered steam, with IT workers forming organizations across the country, especially in regions with large high-technology workforces. As the labor resistance that I have discussed in this chapter reveals, to date, almost all of this organizing has occurred independent of labor unions. The portrait of micro-organizing in this chapter is that of workers organizing themselves. Still, it remains to be seen whether workers in the United States or India will be successful in preserving good jobs, as the structure of high-tech work increasingly shifts toward nonstandard arrangements like contracting. More likely, in the near future, work in the United States will reflect jobs in India, as they are converted into irregular tasks as traditional standard wage employment is replaced by contract and temporary labor.

While outsourcing is most often associated with India, especially the Indian IT sector, as we have already seen, it is a practice that is growing and spreading into lower-wage labor markets and among even more countries with declining public services for the working-class and poor. We will now turn to another case study to examine the role of Caribbean guest workers in the rapidly growing U.S. hospitality industry.

5

The Migration of Low-Wage Jamaican Guest Workers

Every March, as the winter storms turn into spring breezes on the U.S. mainland, the temperature in the Caribbean islands becomes scorching hot. Right after spring break at U.S. high schools, colleges, and universities, the Caribbean tourist season comes to a close, business slows, and resorts operated by corporate hotel chains lay off tens of thousands of housekeepers, cooks, waiters, busboys, and porters. Traditionally, most of these workers would then remain jobless for the next six months, until throngs of tourists descended once again on the islands' beaches to escape the northern winters. This changed for many, however, in the late 1990s, when an increasing number of hospitality workers in the Caribbean began making six- to nine-month sojourns to the United States and Canada to work in hotels and restaurants, performing work that North American employers say is necessary to their businesses. Those *lucky enough* to find jobs up north are highly trained in all the facets of hospitality—from cooking or waiting on customers to landscaping and cleaning guestrooms.

A number of factors in Jamaica push hospitality workers to participate in this temporary guest worker migration. Among the first of the independent countries in the area to be targeted by the IMF in its efforts to force liberalization of the economy and reduced spending on social needs, the Jamaican economy plunged in 1977 following an IMF-imposed program of structural reform and economic liberalization. This program compelled President Michael Manley to sign an austerity repayment plan of more than $4.5 billion in debt to a number of lenders, including the IMF, the World Bank, and the Inter-American Development Bank (IADB). The repayment plan called for severe monetary penalties if Jamaica failed to repay the loans for money spent on building public infrastructure during the country's first fifteen years of independence in order to support the development of the tourist industry. As a result of that program, the national government regressively discontinued providing essential public services that had been a mainstay for the working-class and rural peasant populations from independence in 1962 to 1975. In the 1980s, soaring inflation reduced the capacity of the national and county governments to provide free education, preventive health care, medicine, and affordable housing. Now, most Jamaicans rely on the private neoliberal market to provide essential services. High inflation wreaks havoc on the precarious economy and on the working class, which continues to grow ever more dependent on tourism and hospitality services, which became increasingly important after bauxite mining for aluminum declined in the 1970s.

Turning to private solutions for Jamaica's economic woes has not created prosperity in the country, but instead has exacerbated class divisions and intensified poverty in both urban and rural areas. For example, a good education in Jamaica is not free; almost all highly regarded primary and secondary schools are private institutions. Education is essential to getting a job, but many parents of working-class children cannot afford secondary schooling. The private preparatory schools that children aged four to eleven attend are considered far superior to public schools, now considered a luxury too. This kind of preparatory education is essential for getting into secondary schools and then on to postsecondary institutions, which are called *tertiary* schools for vocational training. But too many of the country's children are excluded from this system altogether. It is clear that, contrary to the prevailing wisdom of the leading multilateral agencies (World Bank, IMF, and WTO) that a market economy is the way to achieve national affluence, privatization has visibly impaired most occupational sectors. At the same time, however, the private sector has relied on government investment, and tourism and private security have flourished.

Jamaica's paradox is that this privatization has eroded even the private sector as the declining value in the country's currency has sharply reduced investment in productive activities, thereby turning Kingston—the nation's capital and population center—from a bustling commercial hub into a veritable ghost town. Even in broad daylight, few locals and tourists venture to walk through the center of the city, which under British colonial rule and the formative years of independence in the 1960s had been home to banks, hotels, commercial shipping, finance, major sporting events, tourism and entertainment, and education. A half-century later, the most-visible political-economic activity in downtown Kingston today consists of government ministry offices and a maximum-security penitentiary on Tower Street. At dusk, downtown Kingston is transformed into an actual battleground as competing gangs fight for turf and control over the drug trade. But since independence in August 1962, the commercial and government buildings built by the British in the mid-twentieth century continue to dominate the city's landscape, as construction seems to have come to an abrupt halt when the country was faced with economic crisis. Thus, the overriding change a visitor returning to Kingston after a thirty-year hiatus will find is the dearth of people. Though Jamaica does not have Cuba's reputation for vintage colonial buildings, sojourners to Kingston will get a sense that time is standing still in the 1970s without the availability of basic necessities prevalent in Havana.

The vast transnational hospitality industry in the Caribbean basin generates revenue from tourism that is essential to the private sector, and is a source of taxation for government services. Unfortunately, the dynamics of globalization have not served well the economic needs of the working class; they produce a flexible labor market but warp the traditional job and the view of "a fair day's wages for a fair day's work," a historical phrase originating in 1840s England.[1] The neoliberal paradigm produces a dual labor force in the Caribbean hospitality industry that accommodates vacationers to the region in the winter and sends experienced workers to hotels, resorts, and restaurants in the United States and Canada during the spring and summer. Furthermore, increasing numbers of Jamaican and other Caribbean laborers are working in the United States *throughout the year* to accommodate the demand for low-wage labor in ski resorts and the like.

As a result of multilateral agencies of the North withdrawing public and private investment, a vibrant economy has failed to emerge in the Caribbean, and as a result, poverty plays an important part in the need for many to migrate to the United States and Canada. The success of business lobbying efforts in the United States has increased visa caps on guest workers, helping to shape a regional temporary migration agreement. In reality, the promotion of regional migration through expanding seasonal guest worker programs creates a permanent peripatetic working class, tearing at the social fabric of Caribbean communities. As we saw in our look at India, a nation cannot build *social capital* if a considerable share of its population works in transient guest worker programs that separate families and send off youthful labor to cater to the demands of another country's corporations.

Government and industry advocates of expanding the hospitality guest worker program make two primary claims: (1) U.S. workers are uninterested in housekeeping, waiting tables, and other jobs, so the growth of the U.S. hospitality industry depends on significantly expanding H-2B guest worker visas; and (2) guest worker programs are the remedy for poverty and the means to economic prosperity for poor countries through remittances sent home by migrant laborers. Conversely, this chapter contends that (1) employers do not intend hospitality guest worker programs to fill scarce jobs but rather to reduce labor costs; and (2) remittances do not bring prosperity to countries in the South but instead line the pockets of corporate leaders in host countries of the North. That most guest workers are legally sanctioned to work in the United States does not make them better off than undocumented immigrants who frequently establish transnational communities there (Fink 2003; Smith 2006).

However, a 2006 U.S. General Accounting Office (GAO) study found that the J1 Summer Work Travel Program was not regulated suitably by the government to prevent recruiters and training programs from misleading and drawing on students for work-related tasks. The GAO reported that: "discoveries by consular officers overseas suggest that some sponsors do not consistently carry out their oversight and monitoring responsibilities." For example, one group of recruiters fraudulently misrepresented their association with a financial institution, another official found that "the company was a topless bar," and schools frequently used students in trainee programs in the United States "to work as kitchen help and wait staff." The GAO found that the U.S. State Department "does not offer any guidance on how the sponsors should carry out their monitoring and oversight responsibilities" (GAO 2005, 11).

On the whole, the principal institutional structure and operation of J1 training serve mostly the interests of employers, who generally extract money and all too often labor from unsuspecting students seeking to gain meaningful work experience in the United States. As such, the summer training program mirrors jobs training programs for U.S. citizens. In *The Job Training Charade,* Gordon Lafer concludes "the assumptions underlying job training policy are fundamentally flawed" owing to the inherent conflict of interest between employers and workers:

> On close examination, it is simply not the case that low-income Americans can rely on the profit-maximizing behavior of private firms to serve their interests. On none of the central issues of the labor market is there a simple convergence of employers,' employees,' and poor people's interests. On the contrary, in the determination of wages, the institution of job security, the threat of layoffs, and the quality of working life, the interests of management and those of workers are largely in conflict. . . . Thus the implied promise of

job training ideology—that workers can trust that when firms pursue their selfish interests they are also seeking the best interests of employees, appears unfounded (Lafer 2002, 222).

Jobs programs for foreign students are all the more exploitative and transparently reflect the interests of employers and capitalists. As such, proponents of foreign job training programs are even more apt to overstate the benefits of training in the U.S. hospitality industry. The stated objective of training programs in the United States is to develop the region's economy through educating and training a workforce for the Caribbean economy (interview, Charles Calvert, University of South Carolina, Beaufort, Department of Hospitality Management, January 20, 2006).

Through a historical, comparative inquiry, this chapter casts serious doubt on the neoliberal capitalist propaganda that expanding guest worker migration to affluent countries in the Global North will transform the Caribbean into an engine of economic growth and prosperity. This research challenges the dominant regional economic dogma by probing three salient questions. First, how are guest worker programs for hospitality laborers traveling to the United States developing the economy of Jamaica and the Caribbean basin? Is there any evidence that remittance programs formulated by the North are improving living standards in Jamaica? Finally, how is the Caribbean working class responding to U.S. and multilateral plans to expand guest worker programs touted to advance the region's economic development? This chapter examines these important questions through interviews as well as narratives of guest worker organizing to improve conditions.

New Imperialism in Jamaica: Crime and Security

Since the late 1970s Jamaica has had to come to grips not only with its transition from colonial rule to independence but also with the austerity policies imposed upon it by the IMF. Central to their efforts has been the privatization of their criminal justice system to deal with growing drug violence. At the center of Kingston is the nation's maximum security prison. Jamaica, with one of the highest crime rates in the world, has found that privatizing the police is the most efficient means of fighting crime and gang violence. The growing inequality in Jamaica and the discrimination against Afro-Jamaicans in favor of nationals of Asian descent for jobs in banking, tourism, and sales has raised unemployment in Kingston and increased the crime rate (Gray 2004). This trend is feeding into the need for Jamaican workers to find em-

ployment as guest workers in other nations. The one industry that is growing in Jamaica, however, is urban policing and security. From 1990 to 2010,
this industry has grown more rapidly than any other in the country—even
more rapidly than the hospitality industry. In Kingston and Montego Bay, an
entire cottage industry is emerging around security: from training guards to
recruiting the most skilled to safeguard private homes on the city's mountain-
ous outskirts and protecting the primary monetary installations. On almost
every thoroughfare, billboards advertise security businesses to protect the
wealthy from the growing poor. As Jamaica's impoverished population grows,
security is essential to counter the rise of gangs and to protect the wealthy,
foreign consulates, and drug kingpins.

Indeed, services are far and away the largest sector of the Jamaican economy,
and hospitality and security—among the fastest-growing labor markets—are at
least indirectly related. The growing ranks of security guards protect not only
the homes of the rich but also the island's resorts. As income inequality grows,
demand for security guards has grown so rapidly that the Jamaican government
is now seeking to regulate entry into the industry (Jamaica Information Service
2010). Thus, both industries are growing in tandem. Given that the Caribbean
is less populated than Mexico, Central America, and South America, in general, migration to the United States is not as large as that from Mexico, Central
America, and the north coast of South America. Still, a disproportionately
larger share of the Caribbean and especially Jamaican population migrates
to the United States. However, while the Jamaican Ministry of Labour has set
the minimum wage for private security guards at more than twice that of all
other workers, the hospitality industry has not fared as well. Hospitality work
remains the largest occupation in the private sector, but only one-tenth of the
80,000 workers in hospitality are members of the union (National Workers
Union 2010; interview, Vincent Morrison, president, Jamaica National Workers
Union [JNWU], February 17, 2006). The government has almost no resources
to reduce unemployment through work programs, even though joblessness is
considered the major cause of crime. Rather, Jamaica has established a private
security infrastructure that flourishes through turning security into a profitable business and a means to a job. The prison-industrial complex in Jamaica
forms a vital component of the nation's economy. In January 2004, the Private
Security Regulation Authority reported that 236 companies employed 13,615
registered security guards. However, even the security system is at risk as a
growing number of companies are replacing guards with electronic security
systems (Blair 2004). For the time being, however, the industry continues to
provide one avenue of work in which Jamaicans can find employment at home.

Even so, the slim prospects for a decent job in this one fairly stable industry force many to seek work overseas.

The Political Economy of Caribbean Labor in Historical Perspective

The idea of guest work is not new in Jamaica. Historically, those not lucky enough to find ample work there have left the country for temporary employment elsewhere. From the early nineteenth century to the present, the United States used the Caribbean labor force to work in construction, mining, agriculture, and hospitality. For example, the vast majority of workers hired to build the Panama Canal were drawn from Jamaica and Barbados. From 1905 through 1914, well more than 100,000 Caribbean workers provided the most strenuous labor in the building of the canal. Much like today, Jamaican and Barbadian laborers then were guest workers, to be sent home upon completion of the canal. According to historical accounts, the work was arduous and dangerous and many workers died from malaria and accidents on the job.[2] However, in the 1920s, shortly after the completion of the Panama Canal, the U.S., Cuban, and Brazilian governments passed restrictive laws preventing migration. In some cases, West Indians were repatriated to their home countries, further straining the economies of these regions. By the 1930s, declining prices of sugar and regional commodities further reduced the standard of living of the Caribbean working class, which led to growing tensions and regional insurrections.

It was not until the onset of World War II in the 1940s that agribusiness clamored for the lifting of barriers to regional migration. As a result of these corporate pressures, a guest worker program was instituted for Mexicans in the southwestern United States and British West Indians in the eastern part of the county. The institution of the Bracero program in the Southwest, discussed in chapter 1, prompted large eastern agribusinesses to request that the U.S. government institute a similar program that would fill a farm labor shortage on the East Coast. In response, from 1943 through 1947, the U.S. government instituted Public Law 45 as a wartime plan to import laborers from the Caribbean British West Indies (Hahamovitch 2001; Martin 2009; U.S. House of Representatives 1999, 29564).

Operated in the Caribbean by the British West Indies Central Labor Organization (BWILCO), the British West Indies Program allowed the legal importation of workers from the English-speaking Caribbean islands of Jamaica, the Bahamas, St. Lucia, St. Vincent, Dominica, and Barbados. As

Jamaica has become the major source of Caribbean workers to the United States and Canada, the name of the program has been changed to Jamaica Central Labor Organisation (JCLO).

The program was considered even more convenient because the majority of the migrant workers spoke English, whereas the Bracero program imported Spanish-speaking Mexicans. Still, by comparison, significantly fewer migrants from the Caribbean worked in the United States than did Mexicans. In total, the BWI Program permitted about 19,000 workers to migrate to the United States during the wartime era.

The largest recipient of Caribbean workers was Florida, which needed laborers for its orange industry. Ten other states on the East Coast participated in the program, hiring agricultural workers for the tobacco industry and servants in regional hotels. Almost as soon as the program was introduced, resort operators began hiring workers. Despite the fact that the BWI Program was brought to an end in 1947, businesses continued to hire workers until 1952, when the Immigration and Nationality Act (INA) was passed into law. The INA specified that West Indian migrants were to work on a seasonal basis and then return home at the end of the fruit-picking season. It was modeled after the Immigration Act of 1917 that established the Bracero program.[3]

At first, workers were employed exclusively in the agricultural sector, but some continued to work as H-2 "other temporary workers" in the seasonal hospitality sector. A clear distinction was made: those with H-1 visas were considered to be of *distinguished merit or ability* and workers on H-2 visas were regarded as second-class migrants, in the United States only to pick fruit as well as tend guesthouses and hotels. No formal distinction between agricultural and hospitality laborers had been established, but in effect two categories of Caribbean labor had been created. This distinction was in many ways reminiscent of slavery: field slaves picked fruit and tobacco, whereas house slaves cleaned and cooked for white businesses, née business owners. In the 1980s, the extensive mechanization of farm machinery diminished employment opportunities, but to this day, it has not completely eliminated agribusiness' demand for H-2A laborers.

Workers entering the H-2A guest worker program in the late 1980s were forced to pay a 5 percent fee to BWILCO and set aside 30 percent of their wages to be collected and deposited into a Jamaican savings bank accessible only upon successful completion of the job and return from the United States. From the start in 1988, guest workers were angry, because many could not afford basic living expenses. Many were also suspicious that they would not receive the 20 percent of their wages upon their return. Given that employers could at any time threaten workers with deportation and nonpayment into the fund, the deduction served to hold workers in check. Additionally, returning workers were paid interest on their deducted wages by the Jamaican bank *only when they complained about the missing interest* (Martin, Abella, & Kuptsch 2006). Typically, in the winter season, as the Caribbean's tourism industry expanded, guest workers returned home to their menial jobs at resorts as housekeepers, cooks, and low-skilled laborers.

The Modern Jamaican Foreign Hospitality Work Program

The H-2B Alien Labor Certification Program (ALCP) began in 1986. It was intended to increase the number of Caribbean nationals who worked in U.S. hotels, resorts, and restaurants on a seasonal basis. The program allows many skilled and unskilled workers to enter into the United States to work in nonagricultural occupations. It purports to be a program that is mutually beneficial to all actors involved. That is, Caribbean countries supposedly benefit from exporting hospitality workers who are unable to find stable employment at home. According to this reasoning, Jamaica and other countries benefit through remittances sent back home, which provide a source of foreign exchange revenues for the region as a whole. And U.S. hospitality companies benefit from the supply of a large pool of low-wage laborers to employers who claim they are unable to find local workers to fill jobs in the industry.

Notwithstanding the hype promoted by the World Bank and the U.S. government, both of which insist that guest worker remittances advance the economies in the Global South, the evidence shows that only a small amount of funds are transferred back to home countries. For example, the Caribbean Regional Labour Board reported that from 1996 to 2002 only $33.2 million was remitted by foreign guest workers—barely enough to build a school, and far too insufficient to expand educational opportunities in Jamaica. Though the U.S. government extols the H-2B ALCP as a temporary opportunity to work and earn significantly more than at home, workers returning from the United States complain that they barely have enough with which to support themselves. Some have even claimed that they *lost* money working in the program. Despite the very low pay, migrant workers are expected to cover all their own expenses: air transportation, bus transportation to specific locations, food, and lodging (interviews, former Jamaican guest workers, Kingston, Jamaica, March 6, 2006).

Most Jamaican guest workers maintain a yearly routine around the cyclical H-2B program. Recruitment into the program occurs from March through July, and the typical period of employment lasts from six months to one year. Most applicants are introduced to the program either by reading an advertisement about it in the local newspaper, receiving complimentary invitations to apply from area politicians, or, frequently, through referrals from family members or past participants. Veteran guest workers are permitted to recommend up to two persons each time they reregister. Processing usually takes place at the island's Kingston and Montego Bay offices, which are designated for overseas employment. Jamaica also serves as the processing center for other Caribbean islands that do not have an American embassy. Applicants from the Cayman Islands, for example, are required to complete their processing in Kingston. Processing may take from seven to ten days. Once the application is approved and the applicant is registered and screened for a police record, he or she is then sent across the island for an interview with U.S. and Canadian contractors and employers. Successful applicants must provide proof of training and experience in the hospitality industry. In Jamaica, applicants typically must also provide proof of either the completion of the nine-month Heart Foundation hospitality training program in Kingston or demonstrate a record of work in a hotel or guesthouse.

Since 1989, the number of participants in the H-2B program has increased steadily, a trend that continued until 9/11, when demand in the United States declined. The official number for Jamaica grew rapidly from a low of one hundred persons working in hotels in the United States in 1989 to a high of more than ten thousand workers today (Regional Labour Board 2004). Demand for H-2B workers grows, and the U.S. government, despite pressure from labor groups to limit entry, admitted 79,000 workers from all foreign countries in 2002. In recent years, the official annual quota of 66,000 workers has been increased by the USCIS to accommodate the summer seasonal tourist industry, but following the economic crisis, the total quota was capped again at 66,000. This cap on entry was set, in part, as a response to security concerns in the aftermath of 9/11. Recently, the demand for H-2B labor has rebounded, as more and more businesses are seeking to cut costs. One factor is that in the post-9/11 era, fewer U.S. citizens are traveling overseas, many opting instead for domestic destinations. As a result, business demand for Jamaican guest workers, who make up the majority of H2-B workers in hospitality, has remained strong—in the range of eight to ten thousand per fiscal year—with the exception of FY 2006 and FY 2008, when U.S. H2-B visa caps were strictly enforced for all countries (see tables 5.1 and 5.2). In addition,

Table 5.1. Jamaican Nonimmigrant Visas Issued by the
United States Government, Fiscal Year 2001 to Fiscal Year 2008

Fiscal Year	Temporary Guest Work Visas Issued
FY 2008	8,461
FY 2007	4,638
FY 2006	4,727
FY 2005	8,507
FY 2004	7,784
FY 2003	9,488
FY 2002	10,573
FY 2001	8,919

Source: Department of Homeland Security, 2009 (http://www.dhs.gov/files/
statistics/publications/YrBk08NI.shtm).

Table 5.2. Top Ten Sending Countries for H-2B Visas, 2008

Country	Temporary H-2B Visas 2008
Mexico	74,938
Jamaica	8,765
The Philippines	3,686
Guatemala	3,275
Romania	1,942
South Africa	1,743
Israel	1,491
United Kingdom	1,451
Australia	964
El Salvador	755

Source: Department of Homeland Security, 2009 (http://www.dhs.gov/files/
statistics/publications/YrBk08NI.shtm).

approximately six to seven thousand Jamaicans are sent to the United States
through independent contractors (Taylor & Finley 2009).

Corporate Restructuring in the Hospitality Industry

In the hospitality industry, profitability is obtained by drawing affluent customers and lowering labor costs by hiring temporary guest workers and restructuring relations of production. In the immediate aftermath of the 9/11
terrorist attacks, the hospitality industry faced significant challenges to its
efforts to regain the domestic and international business that was lost as a
result of travelers' reluctance to fly to the United States. In November 2001,
consumer confidence reached a nadir as 79 percent of travelers considered
another terrorist attack "likely," leaving hotels and resorts in a state of disar-

ray (Meetings Net, 2001). Bjorn Hanson, an expert in the global hospitality and leisure industries for Price Waterhouse Coopers Consulting, notes that although occupancy rates in the United States reached a fifty-year high (84 percent) in 2000, in 2001 occupancy rates declined by 70 percent. And while the hospitality industry lost an estimated $5.7 billion as a result of the 2001 attacks, industry observers claim that the upside to the attacks was the ability to reduce the number of employees hired compared with the preceding decade (Meetings Net 2001). The chaos produced by 9/11 surely added to growing unemployment in the industry, as jobs would be permanently lost. But industry experts predicted that cost savings would lead to increased growth as the tourist environment stabilized. However, the global economic crisis of 2007–2010 has intensified a further downturn in Caribbean tourist industry revenue. Even the 9/11 terrorist attacks overstate the influence of larger industry forces on tourism. Since 2005, the state airline, Air Jamaica, has been unable to upgrade its fleet, because it is mired in financial crisis, potential bankruptcy, and worker unrest.

Just four years after the 9/11 events, the U.S. industry did in fact revive as a growing number of tourists chose domestic destinations. In 2005, earnings in the hotel industry soared 25 percent over 2004, according to Hanson. He noted that the rise in room rates through the expanded use of five-star hotels had boosted sales (*Business Travel News* 2006). But the global economic downturn has battered the global hospitality industry, which contributes further to the drive to promote importing larger numbers of foreign guest workers who work at lower rates than U.S.-born workers.

Thus, in a relentless pursuit of profits, the future of the hospitality industry appears bright for operators; labor costs are expected to be reduced as more and more guest workers are imported from abroad, further eroding wage standards. In the last five years, hotels and resorts have consolidated into fewer companies and converted into all-purpose recreational facilities offering guests a growing number of services and amenities—from minibars to massage parlors—in order to maintain their market share. Profits are maintained by holding labor costs down and by cornering the regional and national markets.

Guest worker Recruitment:
Jamaica's Overseas Employment Center

Many young Jamaicans imagine going to the United States and elsewhere as an opportunity to travel—even if it means working in the tedious hospitality industry. Indeed, for many lifelong residents, living on an island can be isolating and boring. At the same time, economic and governmental restrictions on travel to North America from the Caribbean are disconcerting, and there are few sources of gainful employment in the Caribbean. As a result, many Jamaicans are driven by the misconception that working in the United States will improve their standard of living and allow them to earn enough money to pay for education, health care, and housing. The perception that many working-class Jamaicans have—that working abroad is the *only* means to becoming successful—fuses fact and fiction. Hope of finding a better future through guest work in the United States leads countless Jamaicans into being pushed by the government into hospitality vocational training institutes that proliferate through the island to make the most of their knowledge and experience in the industry. The Ministry of Labor and Local Security Overseas Employment Center (OEC) then helps foreign companies recruit workers from Jamaica, serving as the U.S. H-2B Labor Certification Program office to recruit qualified seasonal workers into guest worker jobs.[4]

The H-2B visa program was designed to recruit men and women with training and experience in hospitality to work overseas. Nearly everyone seeks a way out, but few get past the first interview. Vendors on the outskirts of the premises find a captive market for the food they sell through the fencing—breakfast, lunch, and dinner are all prepared and sold there, suggesting that applicants should prepare to spend the entire day at this office. Upon completion of the interview by potential employers and contractors, all applicants are fingerprinted and informed if they have been chosen. Applicants anxiously wait to hear their names called and gain acceptance into the program. Next, successful applicants must go through medical examinations in New Kingston, after which they are escorted by guards to the U.S. embassy, where they are issued an H-2B visa.

Emukile and McDermott observe that among the applicants for the H-2B program at 110-114 East Street in Kingston, many have fought dire poverty and are desperate. This program will send Jamaican hospitality workers thousands of miles from home, friends, and loved ones to work in low-wage hospitality jobs. Jeremiah, who was a temporary worker for several seasons, calls the program a "blessing" even if he must "clean their shit, wash their dirty clothing, sweep their big yard, make their unmade beds, and cook their food," as he knows it will provide some funds for his family to pay for food, health care, and other basic necessities.[5]

Of fourteen new applicants to the United States that the H-2B program interviewed, almost every one shared a desperate anxiety and aspiration to be accepted to survive and escape a plague of poverty, hunger, and joblessness (anonymous interviews, Kingston, Jamaica, February 17, 2006). Applicants ranging from recent graduates of the prestigious University of Technology to peasants who completed a hospitality course at a local school had all given up the hope of obtaining employment in Jamaica. Consequently, those selected are happy to leave their kith and kin to get even a minimum-wage job in the United States. Some Jamaicans from the countryside are so desperate that they are willing to pay more than half their wages for shelter. Most that are selected are not even provided information on their departure date. Some return every day to the OEC in Kingston to see if they have been chosen to go. They occasionally discover that they must be ready to depart for the United States with one day's notice. When sitting and observing the crowd of people at the OEC in downtown Kingston, one cannot help feeling a sense of disdain for the system that has led so many people to trade their hunger and tears for more hunger and tears. As they spend the day sitting and waiting, workers share stories about previous experiences. Some are laughed at, but they depict the seriousness of the situations that many Jamaicans face. Nadine from Ocho Rios, who has traveled to work in the United States twice, tells a group of applicants what they will face upon reaching their destination: "Trust me it is not easy you know. I don't have enough time to sleep because when my work is done I worry about not having enough money to send home to take care of my children. And I don't have any left to pay my rent here. I work so many hours that when my day is done I'm tired like a horse. I think the employer should give the workers somewhere to live or help them to pay their rent. We can't rent expensive—we don't have enough money. We even have to pay for our own transportation to work. Trust me it not easy but when I go back to stay in Jamaica there is no work" (interview, Nadine, May 19, 2006).

Nadine, who already knows the H-2B guest worker system, tells some of those accepted into the program for the first time the ominous truth that the program may do no more than just help them survive in Jamaica. Another veteran man says, "What keeps me coming back to the program is the illusion of having something. But the program really . . . makes slaves [of those] who have consented to their own bondage" (interview, anonymous, February 16, 2006). But too many feel that they must repeat this process to keep their family fed. Jeremiah Jackson knows this feeling well. For nearly a decade, from 1995 to 2005, he has gone overseas for seasonal work. Chosen once again to make the trip in 2006, looking tired but relieved for another opportunity, he states "I'm happy, but hope one day I will be able to work here in Jamaica near my family and friends" (Emukile and McDermott 2006, 23).

Wilma, who did a stint as a waitress while allegedly training on an F-1 visa, sees the hospitality and tourism industry contributing to a societal brain drain, the dissolution of families, and increased violence: "Being away from our families is contributing to crime and violence in Jamaica. You hardly find a home with a whole family of a father and mother. Even in my neighborhood you have to search long and hard to find families with both parents. Some don't have either—they stay with relatives. In safer neighborhoods where I live you are starting to see more crime and violence. I want to start my family soon, but if I work overseas, this is one of the challenges" (interview, Wilma Patterson, Kingston, Jamaica, February 15, 2006).

Leaving Jamaica for the United States in 2006, guest workers like Jeremiah and Nadine go to the compound to catch one of two big white buses—reminiscent of those used for prisoners—to take the successful candidates to the airport. Those on the buses have had to submit to a urine test and then check their luggage before leaving the OEC. Men and women ride together. Those having made the journey several times are usually somber and say little to others. Guest workers leaving for the first time wear bright colored clothing and sneakers. As the buses leave for the airport, the hustle and bustle continues at the main building of the OEC.

Why Go?

Only about 25 percent of Jamaican guest workers return for more than one stint in the United States. In the post 9/11 era, fewer jobs are to be found, but the stark reality for many old hands is that they must go back to the United States to support their families. Interviews among eighteen guest workers living in the Kingston metropolitan area revealed that many go with high hopes, but after returning, all but one expressed disappointment.

Gilbert Peterson, who just turned fifty, represents a relative success story among guest workers. He has worked as a cook in the Jamaican restaurant industry since the 1970s. When Gilbert first started working, he could make a living in Jamaica, but the deterioration of the economy has made it impossible for him to pay his bills without spending most of the year working as a cook in the United States. While Gilbert has steadily improved his skills as a cook, the declining economy has made work in Kingston inconsistent and unpredictable. In 1994, Gilbert was laid off; a year later he landed a job at the Sutton Place Hotel in Kingston, where he became a line chef, cooking lunch and dinner on both morning and evening shifts. Eventually, he lost this job because of the declining economy. Gilbert's experience is typical, for in the early to mid-1990s, business in downtown Kingston had plunged to a nadir, where no steady full-time work could be found for workers in the hospitality industry. When the overseas guest worker program for hospitality workers started to take off in the late 1990s, he said he had no choice but to split his work between Jamaica and the United States, leaving his family for most of the year just to be able to pay basic living expenses.

In 1998, Gilbert was hired as a cook at the Fairmont Dallas, a large luxury hotel in Dallas, Texas, catering to business guests. At first, he was paid $5 an hour for forty hours a week, but gradually the Fairmont raised his compensation to $10 an hour, without overtime. Guest workers from Jamaica comprise nearly half the staff of 130 at the Fairmont Dallas. Still, the hotel promotes itself as having a uniquely Texan atmosphere where bigger is better: "Combining hospitality, luxury and that special Texas flair, The Fairmont Dallas can accommodate grand events in lavish style as well as smaller, more intimate meetings. With mouthwatering dining and regal guest rooms, nothing compares to The Fairmont Dallas" (Fairmont Hotel 2007). The Fairmont has nearly six hundred guestrooms and serves as one of the leading business hotels in Dallas. In fact, the hotel is one of a chain of nearly fifty luxury hotels, catering to customers doing business or on vacation, mainly in North America.

Like other guest workers, Gilbert gets no special perks for being a veteran employee, since workers are hired on a year-to-year basis. To work at the Fairmont, all workers must pay for airfare, ground transportation, lodging, food, and other expenses. He works a ten-month schedule from February to December before returning to Jamaica. Still, because he brings home so little money, to make ends meet while at home, Gilbert has to work from December through February as a cook at a hotel in North Kingston. He earns just enough to pay for his rent and utilities, though frequently he does not have enough to pay for his daughter's elementary school education: "since I can't afford to pay for education, she had to take two years off from school." By February, Gilbert is preoccupied with preparing for his trip to Dallas and saying goodbye to his family for yet another year. Though Gilbert is resigned to his fate as a peripatetic cook, in no uncertain terms, he would prefer to remain in Jamaica: "If I have a good job here I would definitely stay with my family but I have to support my family, pay school, and rent."

As if being separated from his family were not enough, Gilbert claims that the conditions at the Fairmont Dallas are poor for most employees: low wages, abusive managers, surly customers, and even racism toward guest workers: "I always, always tell the youngsters that this is not a life for them." Initially calm and tranquil while interviewed, Gilbert suddenly became agitated and excited when speaking of his Jamaican colleagues working at the hotel. Asked if things could be changed, he says, "I would like to see a union here, but I don't think we are in a position for a union. I would support a union with my friends at work. Last June, we helped out a worker they fired and all of us made a complaint to the manager together" (interview, Gilbert Peterson, February 15, 2006, Kingston, Jamaica). The fired worker was allowed to stay on.

Gilbert is not the only worker to realize the need for collective action. Even as organized U.S. unions decline in the hotel industry, nearly half the workers at leading international hotel chains are collectively organizing informal associations. Unfortunately, organizing will come to a halt and alliances will be disbanded when the high season ends and guest workers are sent home to Jamaica for the holidays.

Guest Worker Labor Conditions

Spirit Cultural Exchange, a Chicago-based foreign seasonal worker contractor, screens and arranges transportation (and sometimes housing) for H-2B workers for a range of service employers, placing H-2B participants in a range of seasonal, manual labor positions, such as in housekeeping at a hotel or working at a factory. The company works with employers from across the United States to place seasonal workers in amusement parks, restaurants, grocery stores, hotels, and factories. They try to accommodate special placement requests, but they warn that applicants "must be open to considering a position in any industry across the United States." Positions generally last five to nine months and offer an average of thirty-five work hours per week over the course of the program (Spirit Cultural Exchange 2006).

While formulating the H-2B program as a great opportunity for traveling and earning money, Spirit—one of many such contractors—clearly states that workers should expect to come to the United States with money, sometimes more than they can expect to earn under the program.[6] With few exceptions, most guest workers have to pay all the travel, food and lodging expenses. In many instances, workers take out loans to travel to the United States, which are paid by deductions in wages. Some even wind up losing money or owing the program or lenders money.[7]

Though workers must go back home for several months every year, employers frequently speak favorably of the ties they build with *submissive* guest workers. Some employers say that lasting relationships are built between employers and workers who do not complain and provide reliable services for customers frequenting the same destination every year.[8] However, the contradiction inherent in the program is that although guest workers are viewed by employers as indispensable, they are not considered employees and therefore do not have the government protection that even undocumented laborers possess, such as the right to form unions. While U.S. free speech rights permit guest workers to form associations and unions, the seasonal nature of the work and haphazard assignments leaves little time to organize. Indeed, job placement efforts on both ends work to ensure a compliant labor force that will allow employers to avoid the specter of worker organization altogether. According to one worker interviewed in February 2006, the overseas labor processing centers in Jamaica permit U.S. employers to screen out workers who support unions and hire guest workers whom they believe will be most compliant and willing to work long hours without complaining. Consequently, on many occasions, such workers are rehired when they reapply for the program.

Because the H-2B program does not have a formal mechanism to monitor places of work and living standards, conditions for guest workers are abysmal. Without pressure to improve conditions of work and living, employers frequently force guest workers to work for twelve hours or more daily, paying them below minimum wage with no overtime compensation. Some workers secretly find other workplaces to supplement their incomes (interview, Clarence Muldrow, April 24). Thus, the caps on the program are imprecise.

Because regional Caribbean administrative bodies that run the program do not have the resources to monitor every employer, illegal practices continue at many work sites. The Regional Labour Board is vested with the authority to investigate charges of employer abuse, but with insufficient funds and no clout with which to sanction employers, it cannot enforce the law. No mechanism or organization is in place to resolve conflicts that inevitably occur between guest workers and owners. U.S. employers are aware that they can always circumvent laws stipulating that temporary workers have the right to free speech and to avail themselves of U.S. law. Failure to monitor workplaces and the lack of enforcement power combine to allow employers to take advantage of workers and to ignore rules and practices stipulated in the guest worker program by the regional Caribbean boards. The workweek for one laborer from Kingston was fifteen hours a day, four days a week. Because his employer refused to provide a fixed work schedule, this individual did not know day to day whether he would be working. He sharply criticized his treatment: "Mr. Carrington never ever gave me a schedule. All the time I end up never knowing if I was to work the next day.

I had to stay and sleep at the hotel because there was no time to go home and relax. This happened all the time. When I complained things got better but Carrington put me on the night shift. My whole day was wasted because the last bus leaves four hours before I start working again. I can't take this disrespect and I am never going back" (interview, May 18, 2006).

Jamaican Hospitality Workers:
Guest Workers and Katrina Victims

Mississippi, which has the highest poverty rate in the United States, legalized gambling in June 1990 to improve housing, education, transportation, health-care services, and increase the tax base, while also providing more jobs for local residents. Ironically, despite the Mississippi Gulf Coast's reputation of holding the highest annual state unemployment rate in the nation, H-2B hospitality workers are in high demand there. In 2008, twenty-nine commercial casinos operated in Mississippi, employing 28,740 workers, grossing $2.7 billion in revenue for the businesses, and generating nearly $327 million in taxes. Owing to the devastating effects of Hurricane Katrina on the Gulf Coast, Mississippi fell from the second largest gambling state in the United States to third largest.[9] Despite the perceived benefit of the gaming industry to reducing high rates of unemployment in Mississippi, Jamaican guest workers are a major source of the Gulf Coast labor market, above all, since they have no rights as workers. In interviews, guest workers said they were subjected to a pattern of exploitation, prejudice, and even subjected to physical danger.

In 2005, Nina Parsons—a thirty-five-year-old trained hospitality worker and single mother of two children—took on a seven-month stint working at a casino on the Mississippi Gulf Coast. Recounting her travails upon returning from the United States, she evokes a shared experience of burdensome work, low wages, isolation, and even danger that all seasonal workers are familiar with. A graduate of Kingston's B & E Catering and Training Institute, one of many vocational schools specializing in educating cooks, waiters, bartenders, and other food service workers, Ms. Parsons has a long record of food preparation job experience in Jamaica, having worked for the leading resorts and hotels in and around Kingston. Before reaching what she called the "difficult decision" to work in the United States, Nina was employed at the once bustling Jamaica Pegasus, Hilton Kingston, the former Ternover Suites Hotel, and the Crowne Plaza–Kingston, where business declined as the tourist industry moved from the capital and to other Caribbean islands. After the Chinese-owned Crowne Plaza Hotel and Resort Kingston closed in the late 1990s, the city effectively lost its economic capacity to support the threadbare working class. At just this time, overseas employment opened up as a new opportunity for Nina, who, like so many other workers in the country, is trained in all aspects of catering and hospitality.

In 2004, Nina responded to an advertisement in *The Jamaica Gleaner,* the country's leading newspaper, advertising supposedly high-wage guest worker jobs in the United States. As a highly experienced hospitality worker, Nina was hired by a labor contractor. After taking a mandatory physical exam and blood test, Nina got word in April that she had been accepted into the guest worker program and was offered a job in the United States. Full of enthusiasm, Nina expected that working at an American hotel on an H-2B visa would provide the opportunity for travel, and, more important, higher wages to support the educational and health-care needs of her children. But while Nina had many catering skills, the H-2B visa program is designated for unskilled laborers, and was limited to a term of seven months—through December 15, 2000. Nevertheless, Nina left Kingston in July and arrived in Miami, where she met the U.S. immigration and Jamaican work agents.

Recruited through her independent agent placing an ad in *The Jamaica Gleaner,* and cleared by the Jamaican Department of Labour Guest Worker Program, Nina was assigned to work at the Beau Rivage Hotel and Casino in the Gulf Coast city of Biloxi, Mississippi. Nina was put on one of two chartered Greyhound Buses for the long and arduous 725-mile, eighteen-hour trip up the Gulf Coast of Florida to Biloxi, a city whose economy is driven by the hospitality industry, augmented by gambling.[10]

Upon arrival in Biloxi, Nina was quartered in an efficiency apartment in a complex for guest workers. She was to share a three-bedroom, one-bathroom unit with five other Jamaican women, also on H-2B visas. She was disappointed and alarmed to learn that she had to pay $10 a day to share her room with a complete stranger. Because there was no supermarket nearby, she would be required to buy prepared food at fast-food outlets outside the premises. Or, she could purchase meals at the Beau Rivage's cafeteria. Before having time to get settled and unwind from the three-day trip, she was asked to join her coworkers at the sprawling hotel.

In keeping with the gambling culture, managers asked H-2B workers to hold a drawing to determine where in the hotel complex they would work. Nina drew a job as a waitress during the graveyard shift from 12 A.M. to 8 A.M., where she would work at $7 an hour—starting immediately. During her six-month stay, Nina was frequently required to work overtime without pay. She was told by U.S. workers that guest workers could not keep tips, which were pocketed by coworkers and managers. After paying $300 a month for rent, less than $100 was left for food, travel, sundries, and any entertainment; little money was left to send home to her family. Travel to and from work was also difficult because buses did not run late at night. Frequently, Nina ended up walking the three miles from the apartment to the hotel. Or, to avoid the long walk, Nina would leave two hours early for the twenty-minute ride to work.

Nina did not expect such low wages and poor conditions. She had entered the H-2B program to pay for her eleven-year-old daughter Samantha's secondary education. Samantha had been left with the child's paternal aunt in Spanish Town—a suburb fifteen miles northwest of Kingston. Nina related: "When I spoke on the phone Samantha wanted me to come back right away. You know, her aunt was a little rough with her and wouldn't let her go out. Her father was working in Florida near Orlando. When I called Samantha she said she wasn't happy at all. I wanted to come back early but they forced us to stay until the end of the year" (interview, February 17, 2006, Kingston, Jamaica). In addition to the disparity in pay between H-2B workers and others, Jamaicans were asked to work longer in the more grueling jobs than were U.S. citizens. Again, Nina describes this inequality: "In every occupation Jamaicans were doing harder work—much harder. Let me tell you. I remember I had to work in the laundry or as a dishwasher whenever they needed me. When Americans were there, you would have two or three workers on the dishwashing machine. When we came, only one Jamaican was assigned. They did this all the time, all the time. We always did more" (interview, February 17, 2006, Kingston, Jamaica).

At the Beau Rivage, management dealt differently with H-2B laborers than they did American and other foreign workers.[11] Nina noted that, "[Workers from] other countries don't have it as hard as us. Sometimes the owner makes us responsible for things that happen—if a customer sees us touching a spoon or a table not set right." Even undocumented laborers from Mexico and Central America were paid higher wages and had more flexibility in their work schedules: "Our average work week is six days. If you work three or four days the bosses don't like it and they threaten to call the authorities." Nina recalled one incident where a group of undocumented Latino workers demanded that the hotel increase wages from $7 to $9 an hour: "When their wages increased, we also asked for a pay raise, but they didn't give us any more. They were doing the same work and paid better. It wasn't fair to us. My life was work all day long. I got up in the afternoon and work until I have to go home and sleep again, all for very little money. But other workers got more when they complained. We could not pay them any mind because they would send you back by Greyhound Bus and we would not be paid anything."

Nina also said that many customers were rude and sometimes hostile:

"Most Mississippi people were not so friendly. Racism was very, very, very strong. Once a white guy would get into it with me and use words that were unfriendly—mainly racial remarks. They used to say: 'You know—you are taking away our jobs.' Whenever I listened to customers talking with other black waitresses and waiters, they would pass strong remarks." Meanwhile, African Americans treated her with respect and some even took groups of Jamaicans on entertainment and shopping trips to New Orleans, Mobile, and Jacksonville. Despite the harsh conditions and resentment, Nina does not regret working in the United States, because she was able to put $2,000 (U.S.) in the bank each year for educating her two children.

Even so, in 2001, Nina decided not to reapply for an H-2B visa in the United States, opting instead to work in the Bahamas, where, she said, conditions were considerably better. Still, if economic conditions continue to deteriorate in Jamaica, Nina said she will be forced to return to the United States to earn money for her children's education. Later, sitting under a tree in St. Andrews, due north of Kingston, Nina mused: "Our country is so beautiful. We have nature that does a lot to our country. We are educating the young in a lot of different areas—to work in local and international fields. People can work here but most of the time people have to leave because you can't get jobs" (interview, February 17, 2006).

Pay to Work: Hospitality Education

Workers hired through agencies are not the only Jamaicans exploited by the U.S. hospitality industry. Perhaps even more shocking, many firms in the industry employ vocational hospitality students on F-1 visas who remain at U.S. resorts for a semester or two, and some employ college graduates from Jamaica under the false belief that they will gain management training in the United States. Jamaica has an expansive private education system in hospitality and tourism, training everyone from cooks and housekeepers to accountants and managers. The leading postsecondary schools provide vocational training in hospitality to students as a passageway into the domestic and international occupations that will provide remuneration through foreign spending at home and remittances from abroad. At the University of Technology of Jamaica (UTech) and the University of the West Indies, Mona (UWI Mona)—the largest postsecondary schools in the country—hospitality and tourism are primary majors (Middlehurst & Woodfield 2004).[12] To qualify for a degree in tourism and hospitality management studies, students must travel to and study in the United States through an educational and internship program. This program supposedly provides extensive instruction, but in reality, it amounts to a new form of exploitation whereby students may attend one class a week and spend the rest of their time doing menial work in the hotels and restaurants of South Carolina, New England, and Michigan resorts. In Kingston, Jamaica, and in Brooklyn, New York, many students have complained that they only have one or two hours of contact in class per week. Their remaining time is spent working as waiters and housekeepers or organizing activities for hotel and resort guests. Student workers are unpaid by hotel employers and many are required to pay for this so-called education.

In the fall of every year Jamaican students on F-1 visas return to Kingston with complaints of extreme exploitation. Students go to the region with the expectation that they will learn front-office management but instead spend almost all their time housekeeping, waiting tables, and dishwashing. Marcia traveled to Myrtle Beach, South Carolina, in 2002 through an Internet advertisement offering degrees in hospitality. But she complains that she had to pay for the course, and she exhausted so much of her traveling and living expenses that she had to return after three months: "you pay for everything before you start training: airline transportation, accommodation, insurance, even the shuttle bus." She was assigned to the Embassy Suites, a three-star hotel that is part of the Hilton chain, and adds: "I never spent any time in the classroom, but became a part of the waitress team working full time five days a week."

Embassy Suites claims to run an equal-opportunity college—enrolling eight student workers from Jamaica, Ireland, Poland, and Morocco. According to Marcia, all the students came with high expectations, only to be deflated by the fact that they were working full time rather than learning. Also, she adds, "we had to pay insurance through AIG if we were injured on the job." Still, those who have spent time overseas are considered to be more marketable upon their return to Jamaica: "Now maybe I can work at Couples in Ocho Rios. I'm interested in human resources but I will be exposed to all the departments—housekeeping, kitchen, accounting, waitressing." Finally, Marcia reached the conclusion that though she gained no experience through her work in Myrtle Beach, upon completing the course, she was fortunate to find a decent job as a supervisor at a mid-range hotel in Jamaica. For Marcia this guest worker program is a mixed bag (interview, Marcia, February 15, 2006).

Elizabeth Gibson, a twenty-eight-year-old from North Kingston, was a college graduate specializing in hospitality from the Mona Campus of the University of the West Indies and, like Marcia, she expected to gain practical experience in the front office of a hotel. However, Elizabeth's expectation was not met, and she claims to have endured exceptionally harsh conditions at her job. Unlike most H-2B guest workers, Elizabeth had traveled to the United States in 2001 on an F-1 student visa, where she was assigned to the guest activities division at a resort near Orlando, Florida. Two years later, with a college degree and a year of practical experience in the industry, Elizabeth was happy that she would not have to pay for her trip, and she believed that her background in hospitality services would translate into a higher-level position paying at least four times as much as she could have earned back home. But contrary to her expectations, Elizabeth was in for an onerous job that paid so little that she could not even afford to pay her travel and living expenses.

Elizabeth, assigned to work at Myrtle Beach's Quail Marsh for nine months, said in no uncertain terms, "I hated the job and I regret going. It cost me money and dignity." From March to November, Elizabeth complained of "harsh and grueling" conditions and a work schedule that was "haphazard." Given one week's notice that she was assigned to the job in Myrtle Beach, Elizabeth had to pack her bags without advance notice to prepare for the long assignment in the United States. If she declined the job, she would be disqualified from the program. Upon arrival in Miami from Kingston, Elizabeth was "processed by the Jamaican government" and dispatched on a chartered Greyhound bus for a two-and-one-half-day journey up the east coast of Florida to Myrtle Beach. Elizabeth anticipated that with her college degree, she would work the front office as an assistant reservation clerk. However, she was assigned only house-keeping and dishwashing.

Told in Kingston she would work thirty-five hours a week, Elizabeth protested that most of the time, "I was required to work six days a week without getting overtime pay to mop floors and clean toilets." Elizabeth knew that if she worked a second job that she would have to pay the money she earned back to the government, but she felt that she had no other choice but to work elsewhere to supplement her income at the Quail Marsh. Because she had to pay $140 a week to share a room with three others, "I had so little money that I had to work" at a nearby fast-food restaurant. Although Elizabeth remained for the entire period, she "had to borrow money to get to the U.S. At the end of the program, I ended up owing money to lenders" (interview, Elizabeth, March 12, 2006, Brooklyn, New York).

Employer Abuse of Temporary Workers and Labor Resistance

New guest workers are aware that labor contractors and resort owners seek out two qualities in applicants for the guest worker program: (1) submissive and docile men and women who they believe will be too afraid to complain, and (2) those with requisite skills in housekeeping, cooking, and other kitchen work. So many Jamaicans have skills in the hospitality industry that recruiters go to Jamaica to seek them out (interview, labor contractor, February 16, 2006). Prospective Jamaican workers are evaluated on the basis of skill and temperament by contractors and human resource professionals looking for those workers who will do all they are asked without complaining. Even so, some Jamaican guest workers, toiling under the most repressive conditions, sometimes defy the rules and regulations of the hotels and resorts that hire them.

In 1999, a contractor from Long Island selected Abigail Steadman, a twenty-seven-year-old single woman from St. Andrew, a suburb just north of Kingston, for a job at Gurney's Inn, a resort on the vast sandy beaches just outside Montauk Point, New York. To be cleared for the trip, Abigail was required through the Jamaican Ministry of Labour to take obligatory prescreening exams for pregnancy and communicable diseases.

Upon Abigail's arrival at Kennedy Airport on the outskirts of New York City, she paid for transportation on a minibus for the four-hour, 110-mile trip to Montauk Point, on the eastern end of Long Island. Abigail was placed at Gurney's Inn, Resort, Spa & Conference Center, which represents itself as among the premier year-round resorts in the world: "Stressed" upper-class New Yorkers travel to Gurney's Inn to "escape the pressures of the city."[13] Despite the fact that all ocean beaches in the United States are ostensibly available to the general public, Gurney's portrays itself as "On the Brink of One of the World's Finest, Private, Wide, White, Sandy, Ocean Beaches" (Gurney's Inn 2010).

Gurney's Inn is remote and accessible only by Old Montauk Highway, an isolated road on the oceanfront. The resort is five miles east of Amagansett and three miles southwest of Montauk Point, Long Island. On the pristine beaches of the Hamptons, on the South Shore of Long Island's East End, Gurney's charges customers $1,655 a night during peak season in the summer for oceanfront cottages. From October through April, when temperatures typically drop below freezing, the guest room rate is reduced to $1,385 a night. Lower rates are charged for those farther from the beach.[14]

Since the late 1990s, Gurney's has contracted low-wage H-2B and J1 student workers through an immigration lawyer. The lawyer travels to Jamaica in search of workers, many of them duped into paying for the "opportunity" to work in low-wage jobs. Like most resorts, Gurney's stopped offering employment to local residents and began aggressively contracting Jamaicans to fill jobs. All housekeepers, cooks, dishwashers, laundry workers, and landscape workers at Gurney's are foreign laborers. The inn has a system that divides workers according to the basis of national origin, ethnicity, and migration status. Irish students work at Gurney's on J1 visas for management training while Mexicans and others from Latin America work the kitchen and as landscapers.

Abigail was one of these workers. She said that management's conduct was sickening, and that she would "never do it again," and let everyone know that the resort unabashedly subjects many of its workers to wretched conditions. Abigail is incensed that she was charged $1,200 by a private agency to find the placement and was required to pay government visas and a one-way plane fare. The fee was paid through deductions from her hourly wage. Her housekeeping job paid $6.50 an hour without overtime. Dishwashers were paid $4.80 an hour, below the state and federal minimum wage. Abigail never expected to be placed in a job with repressive work rules and very little freedom of movement: "Daily living conditions for the twenty guest workers was intolerable. The most terrible part of the work was the housing. At Gurney's Inn, we all had to pay $65 each a week for housing but had no privacy at all. I tell you that we were given six rooms and one bathroom for more than twenty guest workers. We had four or five people in every room and the bathroom was almost always occupied. We weren't allowed to use the public bathrooms!" (interview, Abigail, March 12, 2006).

Under the H-2B program, employers are not required to provide workers with food. Because the nearest store was a forty-five-minute walk, guest workers had to call George's Yellow Cab in Montauk. But workers rarely went to Montauk during winter months, because most of the city was shuttered and only one or two groceries were open. Given that guest workers were restricted from using any of the facilities, they were encouraged to eat leftovers and scraps that would otherwise go to waste: "During my three-month stay, I went to town to pick up groceries maybe five times" (interview, Abigail, March 12, 2006). Because Abigail arrived after the close of the tourist season, most of the grocery stores and restaurants in the city were closed. Abigail said that she made friends with a Colombian chef who made sure that she had enough to eat and sometimes cooked meals for the staff.

After staying for nine months in 1999, the next year, Abigail surprisingly went back to Gurney's. She offered few explanations other than that the contract and transit fees were reduced and that customers usually tipped hospitality staff fairly well. But she maintains that working conditions at Gurney's deteriorated significantly in 2000 to the point that many workers started to complain among themselves. After working for two months into the spring 2000 season, about half of the Jamaican housekeepers began what amounted to a job action, frequently skipping out on work through calling in sick.

In 2000, Abigail said that she frequently worked two or three shifts a week rather than the standard five. "They were mad at us but there was nothing they could do but send us home." Indeed, when workers at Gurney's and other resorts *are* sent back to Jamaica, they are never allowed to return again as H-2B guest workers. "When one man got fired, they didn't even take him to the airport. He just had to find his own way. That scared us all, so we returned to our five day a week work schedule." But four months into the job in 2000, Abigail quit and went back to Jamaica: "I couldn't take it anymore. They sent me directly to Kennedy Airport for a return flight to Jamaica and deducted the trip from the 40 percent of the wages that they set aside for me. My sister said that she was so surprised that I took the job. I thought that I was going to get a lot of money but all I got was misery."

Unremitting complaints are ignored or disregarded by U.S. and Jamaican authorities, including objection to wages paid below the local industry norm and, in some instances, under minimum wage. On the whole, like U.S. workers, guest workers complain that low wages do not allow them to save for educating their children or buying a house, but they do not even provide sufficient funds to pay basic expenses for their families or living costs. Even if employers pay minimum or more, the local cost of living is significantly higher than back in their home countries. For many, the lure of $5 to $8 an hour coaxes them to join the program without realizing they will incur high local living costs in the United States.

Those Jamaicans earning as much as $10 an hour typically work overtime (anonymous interview, February 14, 2006). Others say that they *lost* money working in the program because some pay recruiters' fees on top of transportation, temporary lodging, and food. Workers are not permitted to supplement their income by taking on other jobs while working in a hotel or resort they have been assigned by the H2-B system. However, several workers interviewed said that insufficient income for personal expenses such as lodging fees, transportation fees, and food force them to take on additional work. Male workers have a greater propensity to breach their contracts and suffer the consequences of being deported and banned from the program, but since many women joining the program are single mothers, they are more reluctant to abandon their work, even under unbearable conditions (Thomas 2005; anonymous interviews, February 14–16, 2006). Several returning guest workers interviewed in February 2006 say they remain in the program just to pay for daily living costs, elementary school education for their children, and health care for their families (anonymous interviews, six returning workers, Kingston, Jamaica, February 14–15, 2006).

Under the guest worker program, employers are required to deduct 23 percent of guest worker wages, to be paid upon their return to Jamaica. This compulsory savings program is intended to provide savings to returning workers, but the money is also withheld if the workers are discharged from the program.[15] In interviews, some workers said that they did not believe they received the full 23 percent (Benjamin McGuiness, interview, February 14, 2006). Surely the decline in the Jamaican dollar reduces the funds workers eventually receive. In every one of twenty-two interviews conducted in Jamaica and the United States in February 2008, guest workers objected to the deduction. Some even claimed to have never received the money. Still, eager to expand the H-2B program, the Jamaican government rarely takes into consideration worker complaints. In lockstep with the World Bank notion that foreign remittances sent home by contract workers are a viable source of economic growth, officials hope the program will generate revenue to develop the country.

The Social Cost of Jamaican Low-Wage Migration

In the last decade, independent employment contractors have avoided the formal H-2B system in some cases through illegally recruiting guest workers to bypass the annual cap, adding a new dimension to the hospitality industry, and increasing the number of foreign workers vulnerable to exploitation. Many contractors simply ignore the stipulations limiting the number of guest workers of the H2-B program, threatening to undermine conditions even further. U.S. employers prefer to pay foreign workers off the books and the agencies and their corresponding practices make it difficult for the Jamaica Central Labor Organization and the Regional Labour Board to negotiate for more acceptable conditions of work for these employees.[16]

Because the H-2B visa fails to protect the rights of guest workers, thereby threatening the legitimacy of the program, some see the Regional Labour Board as a shield for the labor abuse and malpractices of corporations in the United States. The Jamaican authorities believe the system could be improved through the creation of employment cooperatives in the United States that would process workers efficiently and serve as clearinghouses for the hospitality industry employers. A plan would be established that would provide a way for workers to transfer to new businesses if they are dissatisfied or when their work assignments come to an end. Following the dictates of the World Bank and other multilateral agencies, the Regional Labour Board proposes creating alliances within the U.S. government to market the H-2B program as a reliable and viable tool for contribution to the northern economy.

The Labour Board, which represents workers in the Global South, seems intent on sending its workers to the North as a means of generating jobs overseas, reducing unemployment, and increasing foreign remittances. It has put forward a plan to "exhaust at its highest level, its diplomatic and political capabilities and lobby to have the H-2B visa 'cap' expanded each year by an agreed percentage to reflect the growth of the program and its usefulness to the U.S. economy" (Regional Labour Board 2004, 9). The plan would also ensure that a portion of the temporary worker's earnings be deducted and placed in interest-bearing escrow accounts in the participant's country. Upon the successful completion of the program and return to the homeland, the funds—plus interest—would be returned to the individual guest worker. The plan seeks to place all potential guest workers on an Internet database, providing U.S. employers the opportunity to start selecting workers long before designated deadlines. This database would both ease the process for employers and provide guest workers with ample advance notice of assign-ments. The Labour Board contends that the new process will greatly reduce the time now spent in the recruitment process. However, owing to the fear that the United States may seek guest workers from lower-cost countries, the deliberations by the Jamaican Labour Board has not permitted the inclusion of workers who would benefit from a multilateral plan that would provide guest workers equivalent wages and rights as unionized workers in the U.S. hospitality industry. If a guest work program is necessary, the only means to alleviate their draconian treatment and poor conditions is through rank-and-file participation in transnational unions.

The Regional Labour Board is seeking an expansion of the program through inducing employers to hire employees through contractors. The Jamaican government is training workers in housekeeping, waiting tables, staff build-ing, and hospital maintenance—jobs that it considers in high demand in the United States. Jamaica seeks to encourage the Heart Trust and other training institutions to expand curriculums covering new areas beyond hospitality, including computer skills, health-care training, and even golf caddying. All of these proposals, spurred by the IMF and World Bank, are seen as means of expanding the H-2B program and using guest worker remittances as the new development model.

The evidence collected from interviews in 2005 and 2006 with guest work-ers demonstrates that the U.S. H-2B migrant labor plan, and the J1 hospitality training program, does not appreciably benefit the Jamaican economy, peasants, or working class. The programs provide marginal pay, and few workers or students earn enough to improve their living standards, let alone start a business of their own. However, most workers are driven to the United States by necessity of providing for basic needs. Those younger guest workers are drawn by the misleading allure of making it rich in the United States. In most cases, Jamaican guest workers earn just enough to pay for their expenses while in the United States—a paltry sum of money. However, because employers must deduct 30 percent of worker wages for deposit into Jamaican bank accounts, workers seem to come back to Jamaica with a lot of money. Interviews with veteran workers who have traveled back and forth reveal a sense of resignation that housekeeping, landscaping, cooking, waiting on tables, and dishwashing is as far as they will go up the corporate ladder. In return, they may earn a small nest egg that is enough to pay for their child's education for one year; but while recent research by Gonzalez and Smith on Mexico shows that remittances have a perverted effect on the economies of workers' hometowns, Jamaican workers do not even earn enough to provide the basis for community development (Gonzalez 2006; Smith 2006, 18–52).[17] The tourist industry and hospitality guest worker programs redound to benefit corporations in the United States and western Europe.

Caribbean Hospitality Workers in the H-2B Guest Worker Program

The U.S. H-2B guest worker program is perhaps the most comprehensive example of how foreign labor is abused to benefit the U.S. hospitality industry. Directly operating under the Department of Homeland Security, United States Citizenship and Immigration Service (USCIS), the H-2B program supposedly certifies that employers have made significant efforts to find local workers, but without success.[18] In most cases, employers are not scrutinized at all by the USCIS or the Department of Labor. The H-2B nonimmigrant working visa allows foreign nationals from the West Indies and Mexico to enter the United States temporarily to work in nonagricultural employment. In recent years, foreign contractors have independently recruited guest workers from Jamaica and the Caribbean outside the official U.S. government H-2B program, or by falsely filing tourist and student visas on behalf of workers. Those employed in hospitality outside the official H-2B program are under even greater danger of employer abuse and come to bear a resemblance to indentured servants. Like IT guest workers from India, guest workers from

Jamaica reported that resort employers promised sponsorship for green cards and legal status in the United States in exchange for as much as $5,000, working without pay, or long-term commitments to their businesses (anonymous interviews, Myrtle Beach, South Carolina, September 10, 2006).

According to economic geographer Anna Lee Saxenian, demand for guest worker services of all skills is growing because global corporations are drawing more extensively on technological innovation (Saxenian 2006). However, though Saxenian reveals the ways in which technological changes create new labor requirements, she fails to explain a key dimension: that the motivation is not improving services to the public, but rather forcing down labor costs in all occupational sectors. Additionally, in the low-wage sector of the economy, entrepreneurs do not transform the world just through skill and technology, resourcefulness, intelligence, and access to capital, but through undermining labor markets and lowering wages to expand corporate profitability (Isard 2005). In this case, technology is not used at all—and individual skills do not produce advantages, but profit is created through crafting new policies that exploit desperately poor workers around the globe who are seeking to survive. In this context, those bearing the cost and risk are both U.S. workers *and* global migrants.

The restructuring of hospitality services on a global and national scale is being enacted by corporations seeking increased profitability in what has become the world's largest industry, where wages represent a considerable share of total costs. However, occupational wage scales and work conditions suffer erosion when new labor-saving strategies aimed at reducing these labor costs are used. In the United States, the hospitality industry has drawn on the large pool of workers predominantly from the south. Most Jamaican H-2B guest workers would prefer to stay home rather than leave their families every year for six to nine months, but are compelled to leave because of their economy's deterioration and the availability of work at any wage in the United States.

Many guest workers are recruited by U.S. business to enter the country through other channels than the H-2B guest worker program. Continuously searching for profits, a growing number of hotels and resorts in the United States recruit students on F-1 visas. As written earlier, most students are initially enthusiastic about learning and gaining experience in the U.S. hospitality industry, and some entertain high hopes of landing a job. In other cases some businesses go so far as to recruit undocumented migrants independently or use contractors to transport workers to their facilities.

In sharp contrast to undocumented workers in manufacturing and service industries, H-2B guest workers do not have the opportunity to develop roots and establish transnational foundational communities. Therefore, as previous migrant labor programs show, even if the United States enacts a new immigration law permitting most *undocumented* migrants to stay, a new draconian *guest worker* law supported by Republicans and Democrats will allow entry only for a defined period of time. Because guest workers must return home upon completion of their "tour of duty," they leave scant evidence that they had ever lived and labored in resorts, hotels, and restaurant chains, as numerous accounts of today's authorized and undocumented immigrant workers in cities throughout the United States demonstrate (Cordero-Guzmán et al.; Fink 2003; Foner 2000, 2005; Kasinitz 1992; Mink 1986; Ngai 2004; Smith 2000; Smith 2006; Waldinger 1999; Zolberg 2006).

To be sure, enacting an expansive H-2B guest worker labor program will add a new dimension to the vast literature that depicts transnational migration as a factor in forging bonds between disparate communities around the globe. However, the only memories of guest workers and their countries of destination is the human indignity they endure. Only some desperate laborers return for another season if they are obedient and work extraordinarily hard without complaining. Nonetheless, unlike undocumented immigrants, temporary workers are never permitted to permanently settle in the United States.

Who benefits from the guest worker scheme? The key institutions and organizations supporting guest worker programs are the finance and banking industries, large hotel chains and resort owners, contractors, and government officials in Jamaica who profit financially from the program (Jamaica Information Service 2007; Taylor & Finley 2009). Even some opponents of unregulated migration oppose H-2B guest work as exploitative, deceptive, and often fraudulent toward temporary workers (Seminara 2010). Almost all Jamaican guest workers interviewed for this project from 2004 through 2010 regret that they must participate in the program, but reason that they have few other choices for alternative employment at home. Jamaicans on F-1 student visas have greater aspirations than guest workers. They aspire to someday operate or even own a hotel in Jamaica, but upon pondering the shortage of finances, the majority of the ten students interviewed are skeptical that they will eventually own property. Instead, they foresee working for a multinational firm—if they get a job at all. Furthermore, most students returning from the United States do not even believe they will rise to manage a hotel (interviews, Jamaican students in Kingston, Jamaica, February 14–17, 2006; interview, anonymous, Brooklyn, New York, March 8, 2006).

Plainly, as shown in the introduction, the U.S. government is indifferent to the treatment of guest workers; what is more surprising, however, is that the Jamaican government itself has not taken any action to protect the rights of its own citizens who are involved in guest worker programs. Jamaican officials in the Department of Labour and Social Security conform to the dictates of the U.S. guest worker program and consider its growth vital to raising foreign exchange. Even union leaders buy into the system of guest work as Jamaican development policy. For example, Vincent Morrison of the JNWU actively sits on the Regional Labour Board that supports expansion of the H-2B program.

Essentially, once the workers arrive in the United States, they are on their own. The Jamaican government only recently expanded its Miami consulate to operate the guest worker program: most of its work involves ensuring that migrant workers reach their destinations in the United States and contracting with Greyhound Bus Company to transport workers to worksites within a 1,500-mile radius of Miami. To date, the Jamaican National Workers' Union has no presence in Miami, nor does it monitor guest workers' fortunes. Utter neglect by the union toward guest workers' issues raises serious questions about representation and human rights monitoring in the United States itself. Absent any protection, it is argued here, Jamaican workers are subject to abuse and neglect by unscrupulous employers. As this chapter illustrates, despite abysmal and often dangerous conditions, migrant workers from Jamaica and the Caribbean basin have no recourse but to quit and return home at their own expense.

To be sure, the U.S. hospitality industry embraces a broad new guest worker program as a substitute for the vast numbers of undocumented laborers, who may, under traditional immigrant programs, be forced to return to their home country. The guest worker program provides a legal basis for exploiting workers and curbing unionization. And though undocumented workers are ubiquitous in the United States, business prefers an official guest worker migration program in order to remain insulated from government scrutiny. Guest workers would be approved by the USCIS, work from three to ten months, and then be forced to go home.

A key inquiry in this chapter regards the inability of guest workers to resist intense state controls and employer surveillance and scrutiny, and therefore the absence of resources to resist. In chapter 6 we will discuss the use of transnational labor representation as a vital means in advancing the rights of migrant agricultural workers. The precedent-setting organizing victory of migrant farm workers in Mexico and the United States, with the vital support of the Farm Laborers' Organizing Committee (FLOC) in

2003, challenged North Carolina's powerful growers' association to agree to standards covering thousands of H-2A agricultural workers (Smith-Nonini, 2009). What leverage do H-2B guest workers have against the immense hospitality industry that ineluctably seeks to cut labor costs? Is U.S. labor capable of intervening to build worker power through providing guest workers resources and power to organize unions of their own? The growing low-wage hotel, laundry, and restaurant unions have much to lose through an expansive guest worker program. Absent a resolute labor movement, U.S. and foreign-born worker rights will continue to disappear in the United States and around the world.

Corporate Domination and Economic Disparity in the Hospitality Industry

The fundamental quandary that besets the Global South is the fact that capital and ownership of the leading industries are controlled by multinational corporations that dictate employment policies—backed with the threat of relocation or withdrawal of vital economic resources. The absence of capital and economic resources diminishes the capacity of states in the Global South to alter the policies of the Washington Consensus—the IMF, WTO, World Bank, and multinational corporations—which demands structural adjustment policies that lead to open markets, privatization of all industries, and reduction of public benefits for the poor and working classes. For the weak economies of the Caribbean Basin, tourism is the major source of jobs and revenue. Those countries with economies dependent on tourism are unable to initiate developmental policies and generate promising new industries. Almost totally dependent on tourism, any island that does not go along with the directives of the multilateral agencies is in danger of losing market share and revenue, crucial for many workers. The state developmental model of the Pacific Rim—in which government leaders direct economic growth—is not an option for Caribbean Basin island nations.

Remittances to Jamaica and the entire Caribbean Basin region are not re-invested at home for infrastructure, education, and social programs, but used to pay for education, health care, and other essential needs. As a whole, independent researchers demonstrate that remittances "do not include notable degrees of investment in productive projects or community-based development such as infrastructural works" (Phillips 2009). While the World Bank estimates that remittances to Jamaica accounts for an average of $700 for every resident annually, the funds do not finance development projects that may develop the country (Fajnzylber & López 2008). In addition, Jamaica is a prime example of a country of 'leakage' as temporary workers who return often spend their earnings in United States commercial establishments and airports to pay for consumer goods brought as gifts to their families. As such, the remittances fail as a development strategy for small states of the Caribbean that desperately require rebuilding of their infrastructure (Puri & Ritzema 1999).

Some of the same U.S. companies that employ guest workers in the United States own or have interests in the resorts of the Caribbean. Anthropologist George Gmelch, a leading authority on the Caribbean, argues that foreign corporate control in the Caribbean is systemic:

> Unfortunately, the advocates of tourism did not realize, or did not care to admit, that much of the profit from tourism leaves the region. This "repatriation of profits," or "leakage," as it is referred to in the tourism literature, means that there is a large discrepancy between gross and net tourism receipts. Hence, the real economic benefits of tourism to a country are not revealed by gross foreign-exchange earnings but what is left over after deducting the amount which stays or returns overseas. Most of the leakage is due to foreign investment and foreign control of the Caribbean's tourism industry. Two-thirds of the hotel rooms in the region are foreign owned, and the tour companies who arrange the visitor's activities are often foreign owned (Gmelch 2003).

Nearly all the major airlines that transport vacationers are U.S. and western European carriers, and the leading hotels, resort chains, and prime beachfront real estate are concomitantly owned by corresponding interests in the Global North. Although several regional carriers provide service between the Caribbean and the United States and Europe, the majority are used for island hopping and do not generate significant revenue (Pattullo 2005). Foreign multinational hospitality firms are omnipresent in the resorts, accounting for about two-thirds of all hotel rooms in the region, and have even a greater share in the established tourist islands of Barbados, Jamaica, and the Bahamas. Today, foreign ownership over prime resort property in Barbados hovers at 90 percent (interview, Trevor Rowe, March 1, 2006).

The U.S. Hospitality Guest Worker Jobs Scam

In South Carolina, regional colleges that are supposedly training students for careers in the hospitality industry maintain a close connection with the hotels and resorts that line the state's coast. One case in point is the University of South Carolina at Beaufort, which offers bachelor of science degrees in hospitality management. Located 2.3 miles from exclusive Hilton Head, South Carolina, USC–Beaufort educates a large and growing number of foreign students on eighteen-month J1 training visas. In the 1960s, Hilton Head Island had a sizable African American population, living in segregated communities and planting on their own small plots or working for large tobacco plantations. Well before the island was developed exclusively for tourism, plantation owners paid African Americans bused in from Savannah, Georgia, $7.00 to work nine-hour days. One worker recalls: "Even then the money was no good, but we had no choice, man. For many of us, we either worked or starved" (interview, Steven—anonymous worker, June 18, 2006). By the 1980s, the majority of African Americans living on the island were bought out by land speculators, leaving the island primarily an enclave of upper-class white tourists. By the 1990s, with few exceptions, the only black population remaining on the island was comprised of Caribbean guest workers.

Tourists of all socioeconomic classes go to South Carolina to relax on the state's eastern beaches, known as the Strand. Lodging costs in South Carolina's Grand Strand vary widely—from roadside motels in Myrtle Beach on the northeast coast of South Carolina to exclusive resorts of the southeast region of the state, dominated by Hilton Head Island. The tourism industry is concentrated on Hilton Head, a seventy-two-square-mile island that benefits from guest workers, foreign students, and workers who are brought in by outside contractors. Charles Calvert, associate professor of hospitality management at USC–Beaufort, maintains that using the H-2B program offers a competitive advantage to resorts (telephone interview, Charles Calvert, Beaufort, South Carolina, February 2006). He argues that U.S. workers do not want to work in the industry. With the school so close, the resorts on Hilton Head and on the South Carolina coast benefit greatly. All the leading hotels—the Hilton, Westin, and Marriott—use the H-2B program and the J1 student visas from around the world. While Calvert maintains that the various visa programs drive wages up and keep better jobs for locals who do not have to do manual labor, Will Moredock, a journalist and historian of the Strand, the coastal resort region nearby Myrtle Beach, said that the programs are designed to keep local wages down (interview, Myrtle Beach, South Carolina, February March 2006).

Moredock contends that tourism in South Carolina (a state claiming one of the highest poverty rates and the lowest levels of education in the United States) would be enhanced if wages were raised for every employee in this industry that overshadows all others, especially with the outsourcing of textile manufacturing overseas in the 1990s. From 2001 to 2003, South Carolina's three-year average poverty rate (14.0 percent) was one of the highest in the United States and remains perennially among the highest in the nation. In the early 2000s, many underground agencies have emerged that hire workers outside the formal guest worker program and transport them to the United States without proper documentation. Thus, the caps on the program are wildly inaccurate. Moreover, many workers in the industry employ students on F-1 visas who remain at U.S. resorts for a semester or two. As discussed above, students on F-1 visas working at U.S. resorts are sorely disappointed that most of their training is spent cleaning or cooking rather than in the classroom. The remaining time is spent working as waiters, dishwashers, or housekeepers, or organizing activities for guests of hotels and resorts.

Regarding the guest worker program component of students in the United States on J1 visas, Calvert noted how pleased the hospitality industry is as a J1 sponsor to help staff resorts and hotels in the U.S. Southeast. He claims that South Carolinians do not want the jobs in the industry and Jamaican H-2B workers and students are enthusiastic to work in the state's tourist economy. Oblivious to the adversity and suffering of migrant laborers who must leave their families for most of the year, he praises the H-2B visa as a means to support guest workers back home. Because local labor is not required to work in menial tasks, Calvert maintains that U.S. workers pursue higher-wage jobs and prefer not to clean and cook at hotels and resorts, positions that temporary Jamaican guest workers are capable of performing.

Conclusion: The Hospitality Industry and Guest Workers

Since the H-2B program was established in 1987, workers from the Caribbean have represented the second-largest cohort of guest workers. Jamaicans comprise almost all of the Caribbean's guest workers, according to the Regional Labour Board, which found that in 2002, 11,700 Jamaicans participated in the U.S. H-2B program. As the farm sector has mechanized, more workers are entering the U.S. hospitality industry. The Jamaican government projects that the continued expansion of the guest worker programs to the United States and Canada will reduce unemployment in Kingston and other major cities.

Jamaicans can enter the U.S. guest worker industry through three primary streams. The usual means of entry is through the Jamaican Ministry of Labour U.S. Hotel Workers Programme. All Jamaicans are routed through the Ministry of Labour, but a growing number of labor contractors are directly recruiting and screening Jamaicans for work in the United States. Subsequently, guest workers are required to go through the Ministry of Labour for approval.[19] Jamaican guest workers are recruited directly by agents that screen applicants to the program for possible work in resorts and hotels that require low-wage workers or by the hotel managers themselves.

In reality, the agents are contractors who charge hospitality companies for establishing programs in Jamaica and elsewhere and selecting workers for their programs. The company screens out applicants who are untrained and others that may be more militant. Then the workers are subjected to general health examinations. Still, most contractors portray the program as an international cultural exchange program where Jamaicans are afforded the opportunity to travel abroad (Taylor & Finley 2008). Other employers go to Montego Bay—a city on the north coast of Jamaica—to select housekeepers, cooks, landscapers, and others without the assistance of outside contractors.

As the hospitality industry's attempts to reduce labor costs continue to demand low-wage workers, the U.S. government accommodates the industry by advancing a comprehensive guest worker program for low-wage labor. Many consider this neoliberal labor program essential to expanding profitability in the hospitality industry, which by and large is unable to lower capital costs by imposing new technology on its workers. For example, while *speedup* is always a means of improving worker productivity in any industry, most of the labor in the hospitality industry is essential to its operation. Only modest technical gains may be derived from new technology in housekeeping, for example, which requires workers to change linens and towels, make up beds, empty trash, vacuum, and clean bathrooms. No new technology has emerged to change the nature of the work. Therefore, because profits cannot be obtained from technological change, the industry seeks to redefine the conventional postwar job as a "non-job" by restructuring worker relationships with their employers from employees to contract laborers. That is, instead of directly hiring hotel staff, they use contract and student labor to sharply reduce wages and increase profitability. As a former U.S. worker at a major luxury hotel chain states: "As sous-chef I enjoyed my job, and was paid well by industry standards, but when they hired contract labor from Jamaica, I was a mere step above my counterparts who are great cooks. Still, while my take-home earnings declined, my replacements from Jamaica are paid very little for very long hours even by their standards" (anonymous interview, H-2B worker, July 17, 2006).

The labor thus no longer represents conventional employment, but work for which the employer has absolute control over the workplace and may dismiss the employee as soon as the worker is no longer needed—without any penalty to the employer. Employers benefit by reducing downtime, eliminating unemployment compensation, and shifting the overall burden of reproduction—paying the bills and staying alive—to the worker. Unlike conventional employment, in which *employers* assume responsibility for benefits, unemployment insurance, health care, disability, and other social costs, guest worker programs place full responsibility onto the *employee* for such social expenses.

So, to put this new regime into place, the hospitality industry actively recruits guest workers to staff a growing number of seasonal positions. In effect, the guest worker is *leased* for a defined period of time and then sent back home when they are no longer needed. Typically, in the hospitality and resort industry, guest workers serve between six and nine months in positions formerly held by full-time workers—or U.S. workers who would have to be paid social benefits during the off-season. Guest workers from the Caribbean with experience in housekeeping, preparing food, and waiting on guests comprise an ideal group for satisfying the industry's appetite for low-wage labor. Further, this new labor regime in the United States is consistent with multinational efforts to restructure the global economy for the purpose of reducing the cost of labor. So, what can be done to help the workers?

In chapter 6, we explore the importance of advancing new forms of transnational labor solidarity within extant trade union organizations and the even more urgent significance of new modes of labor organization that emerge out of U.S.- and foreign-born worker struggles and are founded on principles of solidarity and uncompromising resistance to neoliberal capitalist dominance. Guest worker programs only repress rank-and-file organizations, paving the way to degenerate and immoral employer despotism over both U.S.- and foreign-born workers. Through recognizing the crucial importance of solidarity and rank-and-file control, workers can develop experience in successful resistance to employers and expansion of their collective power.

6

Who Can Organize? Trade Unions, Worker Insurgency, Labor Power

The appearance of the modern guest work program in the United States is in many ways an extension of the long-standing labor migration policies of the early twentieth century. But it is also a crucial aspect of the neoliberal globalization policies that have unfolded since the 1990s. In both senses it is an example of the state bowing to the demands of capital, which regards labor as a tradable human commodity. While government officials and immigrant rights advocates wrestle with framing a new migration policy that would permit many of the undocumented entry into the United States, if a new law effectively ends all immigration, business leaders and their sponsors in both the Republican and Democratic Parties consider the creation of a vast guest worker program essential to expand the pool of low-wage labor in the United States. The principal purpose of guest work is to restructure wages and working conditions in the United States and other labor markets of the advanced capitalist Global North. Even if workers were allowed to organize into labor unions, guest work programs are inherently a form of transitory labor migration that will permanently undermine forms of solidarity that profoundly endure in migrant societies and allow for worker organization.

To make the system more palatable, according to Stephen Castles and Raúl Delgado Wise (2008), proponents of greatly expanded guest work programs are now using the euphemism "circular migration" to remove any harmful undertone to such policies that are intrinsically deleterious to workers in sending and receiving countries. However, establishing a new semantic of guest work as a positive type of "circular migration" establishes an affirmative imprint on policies that only intensify the social and economic marginalization of workers in both the developed and the developing worlds. Guest worker status translates into subordination of the worker as a human commodity, and irrespective of the etymology of the term—as demonstrated in the case studies of Indian and Jamaican migrants—the system sharply erodes living standards in both the sending and the receiving countries. A more accurate and truthful depiction of the most significant consequence of guest work must encompass neoliberalism's ineluctable demolition of stable lives and labor markets that subordinate both migrant and native-born workers. Though some labor unions—such as those for teachers and nurses—ensure that all workers (even guest workers) are represented, the overall effect is the relegation of guest workers to a marginal and inferior status. While in rare instances labor union representation is compulsory—especially in the case of skilled workers—most employers will prohibit guest worker union membership and resist their unionization.

This book contends that formerly established labor markets that were built upon class struggle, conferring to workers a modicum of power in developed countries, have been targeted by capital for slow destruction through the onslaught of documented and undocumented labor migration. As Karl Marx argued, the advances of the working class produce the conditions for further marginalization through capital's outlay of surplus value into new forms of less-expensive production. In this case, guest workers are an integral means to reduce the standards in a wide range of skilled and unskilled labor markets just as new machinery replaced workers in the late nineteenth century (Marx 1915).[1]

Labor market shortages are fashioned both by capital and the state. Withdrawal of the state from financing education and labor training allows global capital to seek out ever lower-cost labor outside regional and national labor markets in the United States and the Global North. A prime example is the steep reduction of state-administered technical training institutes for postsecondary students, which was once viewed as a means of advancing to higher wage working-class positions in construction, nursing, plumbing, electricity, welding, maintenance, and beyond.

Dramatic confirmation of the shift from productive manufacturing, health care, and service functions to financial education in high school and postsecondary schools is found in U.S. government statistics from 1982 to 1994, when the number of high school students in curriculums with vocational concentrations declined 25 percent. Over the same period, high school graduates specializing in vocational curriculums declined from 13 percent to 7 percent of all students, according to the U.S. Department of Education. As a result, vocational training shifted from concentrations in manufacturing, construction, technology, and communications toward business and trade, which together had the most graduates. Even as educational programs have dwindled dramatically in the 1970s to 1990s, the number of students graduating in the health care industry increased from 0.6 to just 1 percent in the period 1982 to 1994, a marginal expansion even during a period of dramatic growth in medical demands (Levesque et al. 2000).

I argue further that even under draconian conditions, most workers—both nationals and immigrants—will not accept their diminished earnings and conditions without resistance and direct action, typically occurring at the point of production. Because of concessions to management and a focus on full-time members, contemporary trade unions that had been founded upon worker militancy and direct action in the early to mid–twentieth century and consolidated as the primary source of labor protection in the United States and Europe from the 1930s to the 1980s are now in shambles. In the neoliberal era (mid-1970s to present), more often than not, organized labor has failed to defend labor market standards for the working class. Unions have voluntarily engaged in concessionary bargaining to curry favor with management, who incessantly threaten to move enterprises to lower-cost production facilities or through incapacity to oppose capitalist restructuring of labor markets through offshoring and guest worker programs.

Even if their leaders are at the forefront of strategic organizing campaigns in new unorganized industries, the decline of traditional trade unions has permitted the destruction of established organized labor markets, through willful disregard or lack of power vis-à-vis capital to defend their own members. But this book has also demonstrated that in the absence of trade unions, new forms of resistance have emerged to confront capitalist enterprises, some effectively, but frequently temporarily, similar to the IWW (Industrial Workers of the World) model of organizing that was at the forefront of rank-and-file labor activism in the United States, Canada, central Europe, and Australia from about 1905 to 1920. While the IWW is disparaged by some historians for its idealism and limited membership, the unions comprising the federation refused to negotiate contracts with capitalists and challenged dominant labor federations through the rejection of hierarchies—whether based on skill level, race, nationality, and/or gender—in the workplace.

The IWW's brand of labor organizing increased momentum among low-wage industrial and service workers who were excluded by the American Federation of Labor (AFL) and other traditional unions. But as businesses reinvested surplus value into mass production industries, traditional trade unions recognized that they too had to organize a mass base—as at its peak in 1917, the IWW expanded to 100,000 dues-paying members (Dubofsky 1969). While traditional trade unions disparaged the IWW's inclusive, syndicalism, and anticapitalist rank-and-file democratic unionism, most unions finally accepted organizing on the basis of factory type rather than skill level, and ultimately embraced immigrants, who formed the basis for the vast expansion of organized labor in the 1930s and 1940s.

Labor Organization: Strategy over Form

Traditional labor organizing models based on collective bargaining have failed to defend and advance worker rights and power in the contemporary neoliberal era. Since the mid-1990s, labor strategists have recognized the breakdown of traditional organizing and collective bargaining. In response to the assault on wages and labor rights, strategists have advanced an array of proposals that have been largely futile.

In 2004, the AFL-CIO began a major national legislative campaign to pass the Employee Free Choice Act (EFCA) as a means of easing unionization through amending the National Labor Relations Act. The legislation would bypass the most demanding requirements of labor law that included elections, where employers have typically intimidated workers from joining through firing worker organizers and threatening closure of plants and facilities. Democrats in the U.S. Congress, under pressure from nonunion employers, reneged on promises of support once the legislation seemed a possibility following the Obama election. While EFCA would have expanded labor union worker recruitment efforts, the legislation did not include provisions for expanding rank-and-file power to determine the union of their choice (Lynd 2008). By the spring of 2010, the most substantial elements of the legislation—which would waive the requirement for an election—was off the table, and EFCA seemed on the brink of collapse. Correspondingly, in 2010, amid the longest economic downturn since the Great Depression, even plans to reform immigration law, through creating a large guest worker component, seemed off the table, because of high unemployment and growing xenophobia.

The second significant form of increasing worker power has been through labor union expansion and reorganizing labor markets. The rapidly growing SEIU (Service Employees International Union) and its labor union acolytes had proposed streamlining the unwieldy unions that represented workers across labor markets into ten to twelve unions in discrete occupational categories: health care, hospitality, food production and services, heavy manufacturing, construction, trucking, and so on. Representing health care workers, the fastest-growing major segment of the national labor market, SEIU stood most to gain by recruiting new members with such a strategy of labor market consolidation. But even labor market consolidation initiatives have proven largely illusory, owing to rank-and-file opposition to deals with corporate managers that for the most part exclude workers, and have led to greater internal divisiveness among unions who see the SEIU effort as a form of poaching members.

What is lost in most top-down labor union organizational efforts are union leaders' grasp of the absolute necessity to include workers in organizing struggles. If labor unions are to gain genuine power, they must have a strong rank-and-file that has emerged out of struggle and is prepared for future clashes with management, when necessary. It is impossible to organize workers in the absence of the rank-and-file; yet building organizations is seen as developing a stronger bureaucracy of political operatives inside the union who are loyal to leadership but care less for members and workers.

Yet, why is the bureaucratic form of labor unionization relevant to understanding migrant worker labor organizing campaigns? Migrant workers have a propensity to engage in labor organizing, more so than native-born workers, who do not have the equivalent bonds of solidarity deriving from their communities and labor-market niches. Both documented and undocumented migrant workers are likely to spend time at the same job for a longer period of time than native-born workers, who are not bound to jobs and subaltern communities.

As such, because of the deregulation of labor markets, low-wage, native-born workers ironically experience more precarious work and living arrangements than most migrant laborers, who frequently risk arrest and expulsion by state immigration authorities if they seek employment outside their assigned jobs or community. Thus, as precarious labor (referred to in Europe as "precarity") is institutionalized by the neoliberal deregulated state, migrant workers have gained new ways to defend their subjectivities. Papadopoulos, Stephenson, and Tsianos assert that "precarious subjectivities are being contested from two conflicting sides: the regime of precarious life and labour aggressively tries to systematize the insecurity of precarious subjectivities; at the same time the embodied experience of precarity constitutes a drift leading away from these subjectivities" (236). Clearly, the native-born working classes of the Global North who are under assault from neoliberalism can learn a great deal from the mobilization of migrant workers who are asserting new forms of freedom and resistance outside the formal regulation of traditional labor markets and the state.

Organized labor's failure to provide a convincing counterforce to corporate exploitation of the labor shortage debate and its initiatives to extensively expand a temporary migrant labor program is placing workers in the United States and on a global basis at an unprecedented risk to further erosion of wages, disruption of labor markets, and loss of work. Furthermore, the inability to develop a coherent strategic position on migration is leading to labor's irrelevance as a credible advocate for the U.S. working classes. Three crucial factors account for this inertia among labor unions:

1. Cautiousness and fear that challenging capital through mobilizing workers in the United States and abroad will be countered by new corporate action against unions. Furthermore, union leaders are conformists and anxious that migrant workers' active participation may pose a threat to their positions of power and jeopardize typically harmonious relations with management.

2. Latent divisions within organized labor on the migration question muted in 2000 when the AFL-CIO shifted its historical antiimmigrant position to welcome foreign-born workers as potential new members. Though not all unions approved of this shift, labor supporters of immigrant rights pushed for the elimination of employer sanctions, amnesty, and other efforts to promote foreign-born labor rights, and in particular, their unionization. A faction of craft and professional unions remained opponents of immigrant incorporation, even as more unions have increasingly diverse members.

3. Only a segment of unions in narrowly restricted occupational labor markets stood to gain through lifting the restrictions on undocumented workers. Leaders of national unions promoting amnesty from 1986 to 2010 were motivated not only by altruism but also by the potential of increasing union density in low-wage health care, building services, hospitality, and other labor markets where immigrants work in large numbers. The new policy of the major leaders in organized labor was forged by activists or unions seeking to advance their organizing opportunities among labor markets that had become dominated by immigrants. While in the short term, service unions stood to gain by immigration reform, most manufacturing unions hemorrhaging members to offshoring heavy industry are in most cases not in a position to increase membership through recruit-

ing immigrant workers, and have not represented migrant workers in the United States on visas.

Capital and Immigration Reform

In the United States, organized labor's divisions and disunity that erupted in 2005 contributed to corporations maintaining absolute control over migration policy initiatives. Led by SEIU, the departure of eight unions to the Change to Win (CTW) labor federation, comprising some eight million members from the AFL-CIO, which initially created a schism among organized labor, has largely unraveled. Divisions on policy remain as the private sector has declined to its lowest point since 1900, according to the U.S. Bureau of Labor Statistics. In 2009, owing to a steep decline in manufacturing, union membership declined by 771,000 to 15.3 million, and for the first time public sector labor union membership outpaced private sector employment.[2]

Divisions on the migration question reappeared again from 2005 to 2009, when the SEIU and seven other national unions left to form CTW. The SEIU and subsequently UNITE-HERE testified to the U.S. Congress in favor of a new immigration law that included expanded guest workers, while the AFL-CIO (and even most CTW unions) opposed the program. But in 2009–2010, a fraying CTW and weakened AFL-CIO both agreed to oppose expanded guest work programs proposed by the McCain-Kennedy immigration reform bill.[3]

Still, it is not improbable that comprehensive immigration reform will enlarge a guest work system tantamount to contract labor for foreigners entering the United States. Correspondingly, the challenge to U.S.-born workers will be intensified by competition from guest workers who may have no legal or labor rights under the majority of proposals proffered in Congress that are crafted by corporate business interests—from Microsoft to Hilton Hotels.

The labor legislation created through the National Labor Relations Act of 1934 in response to the expression of solidarity and militancy of workers fighting to protect their rights on the job is now barely relevant to the U.S. working class. New proposals for amending immigration law call for restricting foreign-born workers from engaging in self-activity and work stoppages. As such, national labor law that is already in shambles will be even less effective as foreign-born workers seeking to engage in freedom of association and unionization—as is the case today—will likely be sent back to their home countries.

Unless further restrictions are placed on the First Amendment, guest workers—like all U.S. workers—are not prohibited from associating and forming organizational bonds grounded on the First Amendment protection of freedom of speech and assembly. However, if nothing prevents employers from firing U.S.-born workers organizing unions, why would an immigration reform bill include legislation to protect the rights of foreign-born workers to organize?

For the first time since the National Labor Relations Act (NLRA) was enacted in 1935, employers will unequivocally revoke from a segment of the labor force the rights to organize into unions, restrict collective bargaining, and withhold labor through striking. State labor law will replace federal courts if guest workers file complaints of almost any kind (Compa 2004, 38–39). While guest workers will have the legal right to form associations, any employer will have the right to fire any worker without cause, and workers will have no institutional system to file grievances against unfair labor practices. Guest workers will not be subject to the National Labor Relations Board (NLRB) and will have no legal mechanism for protesting poor conditions, human rights violations, and discrimination.

LABOR UNIONS AND FOREIGN-BORN WORKERS

From the founding of the American Federation of Labor (AFL) in 1886 until 2000, peak labor organization in the United States and national affiliates consistently opposed policies and initiatives that would increase the number of migrant workers from other countries. The federation and its members took a restrictive stance toward the foreign-born, ostensibly to protect the U.S.-born from labor market competition from migrant workers, who typically earn less.

In February 2000, then-president John Sweeney announced a far-reaching change in the AFL-CIO's policy to support the elimination of the major provisions preventing undocumented immigrants from working in the United States. Sweeney and national union leaders primarily representing service-sector workers recognized the fact that newcomers to the country were already working in a range of manufacturing and service jobs ripe for union organization. Still, this position of inclusion was not wholly embraced by unions representing manufacturing workers.

The AFL-CIO's expectation was that the policy reversal would help facilitate efforts by service-sector unions to organize documented and undocumented migrants who, overall, have enthusiastically supported joining unions as a means of improving their wages and working conditions as well as gaining greater advantage and respect from their employers (Bacon 2000; Bacon 2008; Haus 2002). This policy change, eliminating the "employer sanctions" provisions of the 1986 Immigration Reform and Control Act, and supporting amnesty for undocumented workers, the federation thought, would considerably improve the labor movement's reputation among immigrants, and thereby increase support for union organizing. This new policy has improved labor's standing, facilitated goodwill, and assisted organizing drives targeting immigrant workers.

A year earlier, in March 1999, the INS (Immigration and Naturalization Service) announced that it would reduce enforcement of the employer sanctions program by diminishing the number of raids and focus agency resources on I-9 enforcement to appeal to employers to refrain from hiring undocumented immigrants. Instead of raiding workplaces where suspected undocumented migrants were employed, the INS said it would shift resources to policing the border and the prevention of immigrant smuggling. According to *Migration News,* the new directive resulted in a sharp decline in INS workplace raids during the 1990s to a low of 14,000 in 1998 (*Migration News* 1999; Bacon 2000).[4] The new policy reflected the AFL-CIO's influence over the Clinton administration to prevent businesses from using employer sanctions as a means of firing undocumented workers when they were seeking to organize into unions. Unions hoped that the federal government's new policy would prevent employers from calling in the INS during the heat of organizing campaigns to prevent the drives from succeeding.

While President George W. Bush supported amnesty and a new immigration bill in 2006, the inclusion of a vast guest worker program was opposed by many populists, and nativist political leaders sought to mobilize the electorate to support a more draconian policy toward undocumented workers. Even union leaders saw the proposed McCain-Kennedy bill as the basis for further eroding wages and working conditions. Following the 2006 mass immigrant protests for amnesty, support dwindled among Republicans worried that they would lose much of their socially conservative base and supporters of the "war on terrorism" who considered foreigners residing in the United States a threat to national security (Cutler 2006; Edwards 2005).

Despite the supposed tilt of government policy toward immigrant workers, employers facing union organizing have invoked the "employer sanctions" provision of the 1986 Immigration Reform and Control Act (IRCA) to combat unionization. The government invokes the employer sanctions provision mostly to stymie worker organizing rather than to penalize employers violating the act. Typically, employers have called in the U.S Department of Citizenship and Immigration Services (USCIS)—formerly the INS—to raid their shops and arrest and deport undocumented workers. The so-called employer sanctions penalties are rarely enforced, and if enforced they amount to a fine of up to $3000 for each undocumented immigrant and a prison sentence of up to six months on the employer. Employer sanctions were rarely implemented, even in cases where employers provided undocumented immigrants counterfeit green cards and Social Security cards (Calavita 1990).

In 2007, as Congress was negotiating a Comprehensive Immigration Reform, the USCIS began raiding a larger number of establishments hiring undocumented migrants to provide cover for Republicans who might support the passage of a new law. Notably on March 6, 2007, the USCIS raided a factory in New Bedford, Massachusetts, arresting some 361 workers, primarily Latinos from Guatemala, and began deportation procedures. Ironically, the factory was manufacturing backpacks for the U.S. military (Abraham 2007a; Abraham 2007b; Shulman 2007).

By 2008, with Bush's immigrant reform legislative initiative all but dead, the administration began demonstrating toughness toward undocumented immigrants through dramatically expanding the number of ICE (Immigration and Customs Enforcement) raids and arrests of workers at enterprises employing undocumented immigrants. As the debate shifted from immigrant rights to enforcement, the number of workplace arrests soared. From fiscal year 2002 to fiscal year 2008, the number of U.S. ICE arrests increased nearly twentyfold from 485 to 5,184. The growth in workforce enforcement raids came as the Bush administration was under greater pressure by Republicans and social conservatives waging single-issue campaigns to enforce border security by detaining and expelling immigrants.

While national unions are more welcoming of foreign-born workers, they maintain divergent policies toward legislative efforts to create comprehensive immigration reform. When guest worker programs ended following the two world wars, typically foreign migrant labor has been recurrently absorbed into the United States. While foreign labor undercut union wage rates, organized labor has always come to terms with the fact that many migrants in the working class have been at the vanguard of the union movement. In the first two decades of the twentieth century, nativist sentiment against foreign labor commonly provided the basis for the conservative unions in the AFL to break organizing drives sustained by foreigners from Europe as well as African Americans. In the 1930s, foreign-born workers in manufacturing were a major force in the establishment of the National Labor Relations Act sanctioning union membership.

Consequently, national unions in U.S. labor must catch up with ever-changing government law to improve the odds of recruiting new workers. Both the AFL-CIO and CTW eagerly seek to recruit new members, including foreign-born workers both within the National Labor Relations Board mechanisms and informally through pressuring employers to agree to union recognition. But they generally consider foreign guest workers a threat to organizing drives and their members' jobs. This contradiction reflects the different statuses maintained by undocumented workers and workers in the United States on temporary visas. In view of the fact that undocumented workers are not under constant scrutiny by the government, contractors, and employers, unions can legally organize them. Unlike undocumented workers, the U.S. government assigns most guest workers on visas to specific employers before their arrival to the United States. Because guest workers on H-2B visas can only work in the United States for a specific time and employer, it is exceedingly difficult to organize into traditional unions, adding to the importance of new forms of cross-border solidarity to advance the rights of workers.

ORGANIZED LABOR IN DISARRAY

Organized labor has been unable to frame a migration policy, despite the substantial influence immigrants have had on worker and union political-economic power. The fundamental claim of the chapter is that since the 1950s, national labor unions have formulated policy positions in response to their relation to salient interests of their members' occupational labor markets. This practice mirrors organized labor's structural differentiation on the basis of industry, labor market, and occupation rather than considerations of workers themselves, and ideological and political positions. This book argues that since their inception in the United States, labor unions have organized on craft, and then industrial and occupational grounds—and that this history prevents building broader regional and community-based worker coalitions that could sustain direct challenges by businesses used to undermine wages and working conditions.

Labor unions' failure to mobilize both internal and foreign migrant laborers has diminished the capacity of workers to maintain and advance their interests in the workplace. Thus, just as the migration of U.S.-born workers to the country's South has eroded wage standards, foreign-born migrants to the United States erode labor standards for both organized and unorganized workers. The peripatetic nature of the U.S. labor force from job to job makes it all the more compelling for unions to organize internal as well as foreign workers. Thus, distinguishing foreign-born workers from the U.S.-born fails to take into account the expanding itinerant employment life of most workers, as fewer workers can expect to have one or even two careers during their lifetimes. While mobilizing and organizing foreign migrant workers is crucial to rebuilding labor's political and economic power, in recent years, the capacity for unions to organize the working class across racial and gender categories has declined. Most U.S. workers are told they must work and subsist nomadically through moving to new jobs to and from cities, and across state borders (Block, Danziger, & Schoeni 2006; Burtless, 1990; Kalleberg, 2003; Neumark 2000). Significantly, in most developing nations, internal migration to urban areas is understood by political economists as the most significant factor in comprehending the living standards of workers. In some cases, displaced rural migrants are forced into urban zones without authorization, intensifying social instability and poverty. In other contexts, urbanization is viewed as a vital source of income for impoverished rural migrants. However, as urban areas fail to provide employment and services, a growing number of migrants are returning to rural areas (Jha 2008; Massey et al. 1993; Munck 2005).

In the neoliberal environment of accelerated capital transfer and industrial relocation, workers are forced to migrate to new locations and form new bonds of solidarity as they enter new workplaces and communities. Labor is fragmented, and as it is organized on an industrial/labor market basis, it is incapable of responding to capital movement, which in turn contains the capacity of workers to mobilize into unions. Thus, the growth of guest worker programs based on circular return migration will further erode worker power through reducing the institutional capacity of labor unions to organize workers. Yet, guest worker programs are especially unfavorable to organizing migrant laborers, who are unlikely to form sustainable communities based on permanence and constant representation. As workers gain power vis-à-vis capital, Ernest Mandel argues that the capitalist class *can and must* challenge "the partial conquests of workers in the sphere of distribution and the sphere of production" (Mandel 1995, 74).

Thus, within the sphere of distribution, capital seeks to contest wages and benefits, trade union representation, and the right to strike. In the sphere of production, capital seeks to increase the workday and the intensity of the labor process. From 1990 to 2010, capital has strengthened its efforts to divide workers through expanding labor mobility, while seeking to reclaim control over the workplace through doing away with labor unions—often without significant institutional opposition. Worker power in the workplace is conditioned by capital, which, Mandel asserts, relentlessly seeks to impose wage competition from "the outside" to erode labor "cooperation and solidarity" (Mandel 1995, 79). Migration, rather than freeing labor, confines and restricts its capacity to engage in its struggle to achieve class solidarity (Ness 2005).[5]

If Marx sees ideas and culture as the barrier to social transformation, can we envision organizing on the basis of concrete human economic interests expressing contrasting forms of class struggles on a regional basis? Even if it is possible for organized labor to move from "trade unionism" to "community unionism," is it possible to replace "class appeasement" with "class struggle unionism," or even on an interim basis genuine "class compromise unionism," now a legacy of the 1930s New Deal concessions that is all but wiped out? If trade unions are incapable of resuscitating themselves, how can we expect a coherent policy on labor migration?

PLAYING HIGH STAKES WITH WORKERS

Historically, organized labor has been unwavering in its opposition to foreign guest workers, who may compete for jobs with U.S. workers and drive down wages for union and nonunion workers that are potential union members. Since 2000, just as national unions have directed attention to immigrant workers, business has successfully lobbied Congress and the president to raise the cap on skilled and unskilled guest worker visas. The guest worker program allows business to maintain a reserve army of workers abroad in a range of service professions. Upon arrival, the U.S. government and contractors closely monitor guest workers, who have few legal rights. With or without cause, employers can fire H2-B guest workers, and contractors must send them home at their own expense. Some workers are sent home if they are no longer needed by their employers. Because documented and undocumented immigrants frequently settle in ethnic communities, they are not under the government's radar screen. The USCIS has few resources to monitor and deport undocumented workers. Some national unions in labor markets where the undocumented work in large numbers support immigration reform to promote their organization.

Unions that have grown rapidly through organizing the low-wage undocumented workers in the building service, home care, cleaning, and hospitality industries face serious obstacles to organizing new workers following passage of a broad guest worker law. As a result, even if some national unions may gain members over the short term, union density may decline even further as employers opt for guest workers whom unions cannot easily organize. To increase profits, employers will favor guest workers who may work during busy seasons. In a tight labor market, the redundancy of foreign labor in the service sector may create high unemployment among naturalized foreign workers as employers begin to hire seasonal H2-B workers in greater numbers. Unless the hotels are organized and have agreements covering all workers, including guest workers, it is doubtful that they will grow.

In view of the high stakes posed to workers by an enlarged guest worker program, it is astonishing that the U.S. labor movement is deafeningly silent in the electoral and legislative arena, aside from presenting policy positions on a basis equivalent to the hotel industry. National labor unions are incapable of consistently pushing unified policy positions—reflecting the narrower interests of occupational labor markets of their respective organizations. Consequently, the debate on migration policy takes on a scattershot appearance. At best, the AFL-CIO is reacting to ad hoc national union objections to the present program and plans for expanding legal migration through contracting guest workers from abroad. In 2007, the CTW federation coalition was unable to reach consensus as the SEIU and former UNITE-HERE union supported a law that provided amnesty for some undocumented workers, who were potential members, and a vast expansion of a guest worker program, while the other major unions viewed neoliberal globalization as altogether a dangerous threat to the job security of their members.

Authentic strategic differences among service and manufacturing unions over U.S. immigration policy revealed crucial fissures that drove a wedge between the two factions. Not all AFL-CIO national unions supported organizing undocumented workers, especially in the aftermath of 9/11, when conservative union leaders drew parallels between undocumented workers and terrorists. The Teamsters (nominal members of the CTW) and other conservative national unions displayed apathy or sometimes open opposition over new immigrant organizing. While the AFL-CIO and organizing unions were enthusiastic, a rising number of rank-and-file members vociferously opposed undocumented immigrants, including professional workers and African Americans, who had in some cases legitimate reason to oppose the AFL-CIO's new policy. In the 1990s and 2000s, labor markets once dominated by U.S.-born workers were converted into jobs to be filled by undocumented, contract, and present and future guest workers.

Thus while the incorporation of all immigrants is widely viewed as essential to union growth, and a human rights issue, resentment among U.S.-born labor, especially those employed in bad jobs that do not provide wages that can support basic living standards, and where workplace conditions are onerous, has been escalating. Ever since the formation of the Knights of Labor union movement in 1869, trade unions and their members recognized the moderating force of immigrants on wages. The new argument posited by unions, parroting the line of corporations, was that U.S.-born workers did not want low-wage jobs. But concurrently, because of federal government cutbacks and corporate restructuring of labor markets, the traditional job had become ever more casual and unsteady. Labor and its superficially leftist advocates had adopted the position of capital that undocumented immigrants become regularized and absorbed into the labor force. Labor unions saw the new immigrants employed in low-wage jobs as organizing targets requiring less financial commitment and organizational challenge.

Advocacy for immigrant labor union organizing as the antidote to declining union density proliferated, especially among academics, where such organization is significantly less challenging than in New York, Chicago, and other large cities, because of large ethnically homogeneous communities and low union density (Delgado 1993; Fine 2006; Gordon 2007; Milkman 2006). For example, Roger Waldinger claimed that immigrants were not taking jobs from African Americans, but rather, filling essential low-wage jobs that African Americans eschewed because of poor wages and lack of prestige. In the process, he argued that the newcomers reinvigorated New York City, which since the 1970s was in economic decline, with new vibrancy and energy (Waldinger 1999). Perhaps. However, the stunting of job opportunities among African Americans and Afro-Caribbean New Yorkers who would enthusiastically take these new jobs at even minimum wage was lost upon Waldinger. When white ethnic New Yorkers moved away, they left a range of essential private-sector jobs that could have been filled by U.S.-born blacks, but they were never given the opportunity. The newly restructured service sector was ready-made for foreign-born workers living in dire poverty. New York's capitalist class seized on the chance to employ migrants below minimum wage in labor markets essential to the city's economy (Sassen 1991).

Deterioration of Organized Labor

A summary of the positions of national unions clarifies the internal division over policy, discord, and contradictory responses rooted in bald-face opportunism even as organized labor is declining to a historic nadir in membership among workers and national political influence. More important seems to be internecine conflict among organizing unions and relative indifference, ossification, and bureaucratization among exclusionary professional, craft, and building trades unions.

The historic decision by the AFL-CIO in its February 2000 convention in Chicago to embrace undocumented immigrants signaled the growing power of the SEIU in the AFL-CIO and organized labor and the unambiguous need for unions to expand organizing into new communities. From 1989 to 2000, the SEIU along with UNITE proposed resolutions at national AFL-CIO conventions to eliminate the exclusionist policy of the federation toward immigrants. The policy shift reflected the reality that SEIU and a growing number of unions were already representing migrant workers. If successful, the AFL-CIO's policy shift to remove the "employer sanctions" provision of the 1986 immigration law would regularize a large and growing segment of workers and potential union members in low-wage service industries. The change in policy may have been more rhetoric than reality from the AFL-CIO, as lifting even mild penalties on employers hiring undocumented migrants without addressing the decline in decent jobs for the entire working class was not politically feasible. The policy shift was intended to support union efforts to organize undocumented workers.

Most AFL-CIO national unions were indifferent to the policy shift, indicative of the exaggeration that "organized labor" had genuinely turned from supporting restrictions to opening its arms to all immigrants. But organized labor's new shift to a policy favoring amnesty for undocumented immigrants must also consider the fact that as a peak organization, the AFL-CIO has little influence over national unions and tepid support from professional and construction unions (Bacon 2008; Guskin & Wilson 2007; Haus 2002). No less, the policy shift recognized the efforts by SEIU and UNITE to organize labor markets with large percentages of migrant workers. In the absence of a unified position among unions on migration and a comprehensive analysis of the complexities, the issue of eliminating employer sanctions and then support for amnesty remained nothing more than slogans. In spring 2000 and 2001, the AFL-CIO held celebratory meetings of "successful" organizing among immigrants in Washington, New York City, Chicago, Houston, and Los Angeles. In some cases the events displayed neglect and disregard that many immigrants suffered, even as union members. With the exception of several notable campaigns—such as SEIU's Justice for Janitors—organizing the events revealed that migrant workers largely organized their own networks to counter abject exploitation.

Underlying a failure to formulate a vigorous policy on migration is the inherent contradiction in the system that exploits both U.S.- and foreign-born workers. Both a "legal" system permitting naturalization of unauthorized immigrants and the erstwhile failure to enforce the 1986 immigration law with harsh penalties for the wreckage of entire labor markets by employers would devastate the U.S. and foreign migrant workers.

The weakness of the AFL-CIO to influence national policy is evident even before the breakaway of CTW unions. Because unions in the United States are mostly organized on an industrial and regional basis, the federation is politically fragmented. Further, even if the AFL-CIO had clear ideological positions, the craft nature of industrial unionism in the United States weakens the capacity to influence the actions of autonomous national unions, and it is impossible to convey unified unambiguous principles to the U.S.-born and migrant working class. In April 2009, the AFL-CIO and CTW joined together in support of an overhaul of the immigration system that limits guest workers (AFL-CIO 2009). The AFL-CIO accurately cast blame on the government for failing to enforce labor law in the United States and charged NAFTA with undermining economies in the hemisphere, forcing millions to migrate north searching for work.

The AFL-CIO impugns the government for failing to enforce laws, legal decisions denying worker rights, and emasculation of labor law. Because the government does not enforce, but rather undermines, labor law, "corporations have been able to create a secondary class of workers numbering in the millions—whose inability to meaningfully exercise their labor rights has allowed employers to lower working standards for all workers" (AFL-CIO 2006). The AFL-CIO opposes proposed guest worker programs that "essentially create a second class of citizens who remain marginalized with no voice in our democracy" (AFL-CIO 2006).

Curiously, this position mirrors that of most critics of migration. The government is at fault for the declining conditions for workers in the United States and abroad, but missing is a systematic explanation of the neoliberal capitalist forces that set in motion government policies that the AFL-CIO criticizes disjointedly. The government does not even appear as a mediator between capital and labor, and it does nothing to prevent "law-breakers that are employers and contractors who have been employing undocumented workers to maximize their profits at the expense of established workplace standards" (AFL-CIO 2006).

Essentially, the AFL-CIO is living in a prehistoric age desperately chasing the good old days when unions had a scrap of power to influence government labor policy. The AFL-CIO could never influence the federal government with testimony or position papers decrying the erosion of labor rights. By pushing for evenhandedness, the federation will get law that is inimical to the interests of the working class. The growing exploitation of migrant workers that AFL-CIO officials and lawyers correctly disparage is a symptom of neoliberal capitalism that the U.S. government has been instrumental in devising and applying on a global scale. Failing to articulate multinational capital's colossal influence over government's neoliberal policy, the AFL-CIO is complicit or at best naïve in believing that federal legislation to increase the ability to organize unions will appreciably expand rank-and-file membership and power.

It is likely that the AFL-CIO and its affiliate unions are too weak to influence government policy against corporate interests, but it is discreditable to posture that such speeches, despite good intentions, will make much difference when most workers do not even know where the federation stands on migration and neoliberal capitalism. Indeed, the AFL-CIO spends more time disparaging the CTW coalition than devising an approach to migration that will engender greater U.S. and foreign-born worker participation. Characteristically, the federation does not direct indignation toward rapacious capitalists and multilateral organizations that have greatest influence over government. Rather than specifically denouncing corporations for their antiworker policies, the federation appeals to the government to stop them from undermining worn-over labor codes.

Conducting activities as an interest group, the AFL-CIO avoids condemning national unions for undermining erstwhile and present labor markets through failure to enforce collective bargaining agreements. So many union leaders, particularly in the private sector, fear criticizing employers more than alienating their own members. The low-intensity debate on migration policy by the AFL-CIO and the CTW in 2007 was an indication of this fear of defending members of all backgrounds at the expense of upsetting companies where they retained bargaining relationships. Better to lose a bargaining unit than alienate the entire company that is slowly but surely in the process of replacing union workers through closing firms and establishing new low-wage labor markets. If organized labor is to regain its lost credibility that has, in part, been a cause of its catastrophic loss in membership over the past fifty years, national unions must honestly recognize that top-down bureaucratic leaders engaged in concessionary bargaining leads in many cases to two-tier agreements that have further stratified workers inside plants, positioning older, higher-paid workers with pensions and health care against younger workers, who have lower wages and few benefits. These changes, pushed by business without much opposition from unions, has alienated and disaffected major segments of the working class who are prospective union members but have lost confidence that unions could, in fact, protect them from neoliberal capitalism. By the 1980s, the rise of permanent replacement workers for strikers demonstrated that unions had lost the institutional and moral capacity to defend their members. Ironically, many workers in meatpacking lost their jobs to undocumented workers.

While unions now commendably seek to defend and organize new immigrants, this policy shift has intensified nativism among U.S.-born workers against foreign-born undocumented workers. The disaffection has obscured the reality that all those who work are members of the U.S. working class, irrespective of their nationality or immigration status. As the older workers have aged out of the labor market, and younger workers lost their connection to labor unions, moving to and fro from one job to another, labor shortages of skilled workers have emerged in nursing, construction, and professional jobs. Business has sought to undermine pay rates for low-skilled workers and has restructured labor markets through promoting expanding migration to gap a void left by American workers who do not wish to toil in factories, drive vehicles, wait on tables, clean and maintain buildings, and care for children (Waldinger 1999). Though labor market shortages have emerged, they are products of businesses seeking to undermine wages and benefits or suppress new labor organizing that would increase the wages and status of arduous jobs that do not require extensive training.

On the Issue of Comprehensive Immigration Reform

When evaluating specific policy differences on immigration, it is crucial to abstain from analysis rooted in conflicts in organized labor, ideological differences, or appraisals of personal integrity of union leaders. Rather, this book asserts that material and class-based interests of unions and their members provide the best means of assessing action. As the immigration debate gained steam in 2006 and 2007, individual union expressions offer hollow explanations of union policy.

Notwithstanding the purported differences between the CTW and AFL-CIO, this book argues that migration policy exposes a useful lens from which to view the political-economic basis for union action. Owing to the intense differences among competing national unions on reforming immigration and migration legislation, significant fractures appear in both the AFL-CIO and the CTW coalition. The divergent positions make a strong case for understanding migration through the lens of unambiguous occupational and class difference filtered through the interests of labor union leaders. Still, virtually all the guest labor programs proposed by Congress will compromise the rights of U.S.- and foreign-born workers in the United States.

In country after country, labor unions are in a defensive posture against capital relocation to new low-cost producers, subcontracting of work, and the replacement of union members with guest workers. The prevailing wisdom is that the distinctive histories of labor movements inform the history and culture of national institutions. While historical institutions are crucial to understanding political and economic traditions, even in the conservative culture of the United States, few could have envisioned the far-reaching market reforms that have eroded the power of organized labor through transcending national boundaries. If the past twenty years are a prelude to the future, proposals for a guest worker program that deports laborers upon completion of their specific job is likely to grow while migration with a path to citizenship will dramatically decline.

Workers on nonimmigrant visas labor under more oppressive conditions than undocumented laborers. The guest worker program allows foreign contractors to exercise near-total control over their hiring, work, and leisure time. This system is equivalent to indentured servitude, outlawed in the late nineteenth century as the "free labor" movement helped abolish contract labor (Orren 1991).

The second Bush administration and neoliberal politicians promulgated plans to convert almost all new migrant workers, regardless of skill level, into guest workers as a means to further bend to corporate demands for low-cost labor. Such a policy would weaken the power of all foreign workers and their unions by limiting the time guest workers could stay in the United States. The program would transform steady jobs into guest work programs that hire workers on a seasonal basis. In 2004, President Bush introduced legislation for a program that would designate all migrants as temporary workers:

> I propose a new temporary worker program to match willing foreign workers with willing employers when no Americans can be found to fill the job. This reform will be good for our economy because employers will find needed workers in an honest and orderly system. A temporary worker program will help protect our homeland, allowing Border Patrol and law enforcement to focus on true threats to our national security. I oppose amnesty, because it would encourage further illegal immigration, and unfairly reward those who break our laws. My temporary worker program will preserve the citizenship path for those who respect the law, while bringing millions of hardworking men and women out from the shadows of American life.[6]

This scheme would favor corporate interests by undermining the capacity of unions to organize workers. Despite this clear threat to workers, divisions remain among unions supporting and opposing such immigration reform.

Before the bill failed in the Senate, the creation of a new program that included guest workers was President Bush's last major legislative initiative before leaving office. Passing the legislation was also crucial to SEIU and its president Andy Stern, who joined business, religious, and government leaders at a press conference in Washington on January 19, 2006, to denounce a Republican bill that would have criminalized undocumented immigrants.

Supporting the McCain-Kennedy bill, Stern said that "[B]y establishing a legal, orderly process, we can bring immigrant workers in this country out of the shadows and under our laws, connect those workers with willing employers (EWIC 2006)." In May 2007, the SEIU position was echoed by business organizations, including the American Restaurant Association, which supported comprehensive immigration reform under debate in the Senate that included a guest work program that would provide low-wage labor (Gay 2007). However, it should be noted that while SEIU supported the McCain-Kennedy immigration reform in its Senate testimony, in a letter sent to Senator Ted Kennedy, disseminated to the immigrant rights community in January 2007, SEIU leaders Stern, Anna Burger, and Eliseo Medina opposed enlarging a guest worker program, favoring instead a pathway to citizenship to all foreign workers (SEIU 2007).[7]

In the spring of 2007, UFCW, the Teamsters, and the Carpenters indicated resolute opposition to efforts at immigration reform. UFCW adamantly opposed guest workers that "only turn permanent jobs into temporary ones, create an underclass of exploited workers, and lower workplace standards for all workers" (Wilson 2007). This position was echoed by the Teamsters' general president James P. Hoffa in 2006, who was pleased that the legislation stalled in the Senate. In an official statement, Hoffa asserted that the legislation would create "a modern day 'Bracero' program" (Hoffa 2006). Though the Teamsters are focusing on government efforts to oppose easing of the Mexican truck flow into the United States, the union demonstrated concern for all workers, including migrants. "Time and again, it has been proven that guest worker programs lead to the exploitation of workers. These workers are captive to their employer and often exploited . . . which brings wages down for everyone" (Hoffa 2006).

The primary cause of the rift within the CTW is each national union's effort to safeguard the jobs and material interests of its members. Pondering the possible immediate membership gains that could result from amnesty, UNITE/HERE, which split with CTW and joined the AFL-CIO in October 2009, did not consider the long-term economic adversity workers employed in the hospitality and restaurant industries would confront by the corporate-dominated immigration reform (Feinstein 2007). By contrast, the SEIU has little to lose through expanding the program to unionized health-care workers, as the program already mandates that guest workers join their union facilities.

PROFESSIONAL LABOR UNIONS

The guest worker program (like the Bracero program before it) is a form of virtual indentured servitude, for workers across skill levels. Under the

H1-B program, skilled foreign guest workers may stay in the United States to work for at least six years (two successive three-year renewable terms). The ultimate reward for guest workers who do not complain and who obediently accept indentured servitude for six years is the remote possibility that their employers will sponsor them for green card status. Unions prefer undocumented immigrants to migrant workers holding green cards because they stand a better chance at recruiting them into their organizations, since guest workers must return home through the process of circular migration. In the high-technology sector where labor unions have few members, organizing guest workers is nearly impossible. Employers and contractors prefer to keep guest workers—no matter the skill level—in subordinate, temporary positions so they can continue to lower wage costs (interview, Gregory J. Junemann, September 17, 2005).

Thus, employer attestations regarding their so-called "good faith" efforts to recruit U.S. workers are laughable. Employers establish qualifications and skill sets that are most often tailored to a specific guest worker. Attestations regarding the payment of the prevailing wage are equally insufficient. The law has the effect of greatly aiding corporate efforts to lower wage rates for IT and professional workers.

The labor movement seeks to end the guest worker program, which it sees as a contract labor system. To facilitate unionization, organized labor demands a reduction of the number of high-technology guest workers, or else a change in the status of guest workers to permanent employees who can be organized into unions. Currently, foreign guest workers hired for a temporary period by third-party labor contractors are often dismissed and forced to return to their home countries if they seek improved wages and conditions.

Having failed to improve immigrant status legislatively, organized labor has called for federal enforcement of the law to verify that employers need to hire foreign guest workers and penalizing employers who fraudulently hire nonimmigrant workers. Organized labor argues that to stem the tide of worker displacement, the government needs to improve oversight of the labor certification application (LCA) program. If oversight is not implemented, working conditions and job security will deteriorate for both guest workers and native IT workers. According to former WashTech president Mike Blain, conditions have already declined. He asserted that in many cases, years of sixty-hour weeks and taking classes on your own dime to keep up with technology leaves you in the unemployment line, after being laid off with no notice (interview, Mike Blain, July 6, 2004). Gregory Junemann, president of the International Federation of Professional and Technical Engineers (IFPTE), points out that his members are directly affected by H1-B workers:

Junemann said that IFPTE had members whose jobs were lost when General Electric, Boeing, and Lockheed brought in foreign workers willing to accept low wages and were fearful of complaining for fear of deportation (interview, Junemann, September 17, 2005).

By definition, the program that SEIU proffers would extend migration rights to citizenship to a growing sector of foreign workers. While the union opposes permanent guest workers, it supports legislation that would expand these programs. The union never mentioned time constraints that are clearly defined as "seasonal" in the H-2A and H-2B programs. The H-2A guest worker program in agriculture and beyond has been in place since World War I in the southwestern United States and since World War II in the eastern part of the country. In each case, workers are forced to return to their countries of origin upon completion of their job stint, or when they are no longer needed by their employer. If enforced according to plan, the program would operate on the basis of forced contract labor—a departure from the "immigrant freedom rides" of 2003, which were organized with extensive support of HERE.

FARM LABORERS ORGANIZING COMMITTEE

The Farm Laborers Organizing Committee (FLOC), a farm workers union founded in 1967 by Baldemar Velasquez, who remains its president, is an affiliate of the AFL-CIO and has put forward a program that would provide for the most far-reaching and encompassing protection for migrant labor. By virtue of protecting the rights of foreign labor, the employer incentive to replace U.S.-born labor with foreign-born labor would be minimized. FLOC is an ardent opponent of efforts to hastily pass flawed "comprehensive immigration reform" through just eliminating the employer sanction provisions of the 1986 immigration legislation and providing amnesty for those who entered the country without authorization during the past two decades.

In June 2007, FLOC represented twelve thousand workers in North America, of which more than six thousand were in the H-2A guest worker program. Over the past twenty years, FLOC has been more successful than any other union in reaching agreements protecting farm workers. In 1986, FLOC successfully waged a campaign at Campbell's Soup that provides greater power to farm workers in Ohio and now extends to farm workers employed for subsidiaries of the Heinz Corporation in Michigan.

The most notable victory is FLOC's effort to organize farm workers employed for the North Carolina Growers Association (NCGA). FLOC's Mount Olive campaign in the state succeeded in achieving labor agreements for foreign guest workers in the H-2A program who migrate from Latin America to pick vegetables in North Carolina. In 1998, FLOC initiated a five-year organizing campaign for farm workers hired to work in the pickle, sweet potato, tobacco, and Christmas tree industries. In 2004, after a five-year boycott, FLOC won an agreement that covered eight thousand workers in North Carolina, now represented by the union in the United States and Mexico.

FLOC's agreement with the NCGA is the most far reaching of any union to date, as it covers all workers, without discrimination on the basis of nationality. The seriousness of the Mount Olive campaign is the initiative to create what it calls an "active voice" for workers in determining their own conditions. FLOC asserts that the contracts "set labor history, not only by changing the agricultural system but also in bringing in H-2A 'guest workers' under union contracts. Formerly, these workers had little say in who employed them or in the conditions of their work." The program allows workers to engage in negotiations, grievances, health care, and transportation from Mexico to the United States and back (interview, Ken Barger, September 18, 2005; Greenhouse 2004; Smith-Nonini 2009; Velazquez 2007.)

To win significantly higher wages, health and safety guarantees, and improved working conditions, FLOC sees education as integral to its mission. While many unions use the nomenclature of cross-border organizing, FLOC organizes workers in the U.S. agricultural workplaces and in Mexico, where workers are recruited by contractors. The union has an office in Monterrey, Mexico, where contractors seek low-wage laborers. The presence in both countries has assisted workers with a range of obstacles—including help with obtaining a visa and educating them on the contract that is in place in North Carolina. The organizing presence in Mexico and in the United States has increased the power of workers and the growers, who may now negotiate directly with the union and its members on wages, conditions, and productivity. Concomitantly, the power of contractors that regularly exploit unsuspecting workers is reduced, because they do not have the capacity to serve as brokers between workers and corporations. The fact that contractors do not have the power to charge workers for jobs and sell laborers to employers has significantly reduced exploitative relations. Now that FLOC has a direct relationship with employers and workers before they arrive in the United States, as noted, they are able to ensure higher wages and safety while expanding productivity for farm growers.

The FLOC victory in North Carolina translated into immediate gains for Mexican workers, but not without the harassment of contractors. Some of the advantages were that workers did not have to pay for applying to the program and were not responsible for transportation expenses to the United States.

Also, the companies paid for visas, rather than the workers themselves. The transportation costs, which averaged about $350, were paid by the growers. Without strict oversight, contractors may continue to be able to exploit workers to ship them across the border and pay wages significantly below the standard collective bargaining agreements signed between FLOC and farm growers. Nevertheless, even Velazquez recognizes the path-breaking work of FLOC in negotiating a genuine cross-border program: "The unusual feature of the NCGA workforce was that they were almost entirely H-2A workers. Eight-thousand workers employed on some one-thousand farms after year-end transfers. The agreement compelled FLOC to open up an office in Monterrey, to oversee the seniority clauses in the agreement and serve as an education center for workers about the rules, obligations, and rights before coming to the U.S. With the exception of NCGA, we soon discovered the corruption endemic to the recruitment of workers in their villages and towns" (Velazquez 2007).

Nonetheless, farm growers still prefer the guest worker model where regulations are not enforced and workers can be fired without cause. Through transnational organizing, FLOC serves as a guardian of immigrant workers, which reduces the capacity of growers to divide workers. Those recruited in Mexico can rely on the union that they know to monitor wages and working conditions that were historically flouted and ignored by the growers association.

At its September 2006 convention, FLOC passed a resolution that would create a "Freedom Visa." The visa severely undercuts employer incentives to replace U.S. and foreign-born workers with new guest workers through three provisions:

1. The Freedom Visa grants the right for citizens of countries bound by trade agreements to cross borders for jobs with full working rights, just as corporations and capital can move across borders.
2. Workers would also have the right to change employers and seek improved jobs at new locations.
3. Workers would have the right to organize and join unions and be covered by civil and labor right protections.

Velazquez asserts that regularizing and legalizing the H-2A worker is a simple task that must be instituted and enforced immediately: "If Congress can suggest the likes of a Z visa," Says Velazquez, "why not a visa to travel and work with . . . labor rights." While specifically envisioned to cover farm workers, FLOC seeks similar guarantees for "guest workers" in other occupations.

According to Velazquez, the pressure of FLOC has led both to success and continuous harassment from farm businesses and contractors. On April 9, 2007, organizer Santiago Rafael Cruz was bound and beaten to death at the organization's office in Monterrey (Velazquez 2007).

TEMPORARY AND PERMANENT US WORKERS

How can organized labor in the United States resist the corporate onslaught on U.S. workers initiated since the early 1970s that has dramatically reduced union density in the labor market and curbed union political influence? Labor union density continues to decline despite the fact that John Sweeney and his successor, Richard Trumka, and the other new leaders of the AFL-CIO are more enthusiastic about organizing new workers. Only a minority of national unions dedicate greater resources to organizing, led by SEIU, which recruits rather than organizes workers. As a consequence, most unions are still losing members. From 1995 to 2002, union density has declined in eight out of ten leading occupational classifications. The only industry groups where unions have increased density are hospitals and public administration (Hirsch and Macpherson 2010).[8] The rapid decline in union membership as a share of the labor force has generated a calamitous debate among national labor leaders over the future direction of organized labor. Some unions are calling for the AFL-CIO to restructure through devoting resources to organizing on an industry basis.

Union decline reflects capital mobility to move production and services to lower-cost regions, weakening the power of unions that do not have local or regional control over industries that cannot move. Hence, unions representing health-care and public service workers are somewhat more insulated from capital flight. But while these industries are expected to grow dramatically over the next decade, unionization in the last seven years has remained relatively stagnant. From 1995 to 2002, union density has increased by 1.4 percent in hospitals and declined 1.4 percent in education (Hirsch and Macpherson 2010). The Bureau of Labor Statistics (BLS) projects that between 2002 and 2012, education and health services will grow by 31.8 percent. BLS predicts that "[a]bout 1 out of every 4 new jobs created in the U.S. economy will be in either the healthcare and social assistance or private educational service sectors" (U.S. Bureau of Labor Statistics 2004–2005).

Now that corporations have placed high-technology workers under increased domestic and foreign competition, unions are finding professional workers more amenable to organization. Still, even if professional workers express interest in forming unions, fear of employer resistance and intimidation impedes organizing efforts in a slack and highly competitive labor market. The corporate restructuring of work through nonstandard work arrangements (casual labor, outsourcing, part-time, and temporary work) further complicates workers' ability to unionize. Indeed, this is reflected in the rhetoric of human resource professionals arguing that workers will take on multiple careers throughout their lifetimes, requiring retraining and adjusting to a myriad of employer needs.

Even human resource professionals are girding for change. According to Steve Bates of *HR Magazine*, "[h]uman resource management is undergoing a massive transformation that will change career paths in as yet uncertain ways" that may include the outsourcing of HR departments. The journal notes that corporations "are placing greater emphasis on business acumen and are automating and outsourcing many administrative functions" (Bates 2002). If professional workers must again and again retrain for new occupations, their prospects for organizing into unions are greatly diminished. Because guest worker programs are expanding from skilled to unskilled workers, the stability of labor markets are constantly under assault, and gone are the days when workers could spend their entire lives in one industry, let alone company.

Migrant Workers and Organized Labor in the United States

While some unions are correctly expending resources and energy on advancing the rights of foreign-born workers—demonstrated by the Immigrant Workers Freedom Ride of September and October 2003—the government is directing energies toward ameliorating their plight by sending them home and establishing a guest worker program that in many ways is akin to indentured servitude. On the one hand, in 2000, the AFL-CIO—pressured by the Union of Needletrades, Textiles and Industrial Workers (UNITE),[9] the Service Employees International Union (SEIU), and other service unions organizing low-wage workers—declared support for undocumented workers in the United States. On the other hand, the AFL-CIO Department for Professional Employees (DPE) categorically opposes legal migration through the nonimmigrant visa program under current conditions. If nonimmigrant visa holders, or guest workers, could stay in the United States permanently, union leaders say, they would be welcomed. Because foreign visa holders are here for a defined time, however, the national unions have opposed skilled and unskilled guest workers that undermine wage standards in a range of labor markets.

Today, organized labor unions in the United States are in danger of losing members to both high- and low-wage foreign guest workers. It will be difficult for unions to argue that undocumented workers be provided greater legitimacy than guest workers, even if they have been working in the United States for many years. Politically, unions will be unable to defend the undocumented—even if they are in unions—against guest workers who enter the United States legally but are not subject to labor law and wage and hour regulations.

In the short run, organized labor may have to demonstrate that foreign labor is expendable and that employers should focus on hiring U.S. citizens and authorized immigrants. Therefore, the two federations could successfully argue that that both foreign workers on nonimmigrant visas and the undocumented are competing for jobs with U.S. workers, undermining wage rates, and increasing unemployment in the industry. Until the present, unions have focused on legislation opposing guest work programs for high-skilled workers, but as the number of H2-B workers grows, more and more unions will oppose guest work programs aimed at low-wage workers, especially in health care, hospitality, and other services.

In regard to professional H1-B workers, the Department of Professional Employees of the AFL-CIO claim that rather than filling spot shortages, nonimmigrant visa programs flood the labor market with more than 200,000 guest workers each year. Despite restrictions on working in the United States, many foreign laborers on nonimmigrant visas, like their undocumented counterparts, seek green cards and permanent employment. Unions opposing the guest worker programs argue that, unlike undocumented workers laboring in low-wage jobs, nonimmigrant visa holders are in fact competing against U.S. workers. However, it is increasingly apparent that undocumented workers have also displaced formerly unionized workers over the past two decades in the service sector because of government antiunion policies and a feeble response from organized labor.

GUEST WORKERS, LABOR LAW, AND CLASS SOLIDARITY

The sweeping restructuring of the U.S. labor market illustrates the obsolescence of the NLRA and the failure of unions to defend worker interests. Nevertheless, the NLRA that supposedly defends all workers regardless of their status in no way prevents employers from abusing guest workers. No provisions of the labor law require employers to abide by U.S. labor laws that provide for payment of minimum wages, a standard work day, child labor, and payment of overtime when workers exceed the eight-hour workday. No

section of the law grants migrant workers the unconditional right to organize unions of their own. Even undocumented workers are protected under
labor law, and under the NLRB, have the right to form unions of their own.

The term "guest worker" is a misnomer. Migrant laborers do not have
rights equivalent to U.S.-born workers and the majority are not covered
by contractors and associations representing employers. If workers seek
safeguard from predatory employers, the only option is to turn to civil law
that is supposed to permit guest workers or any individual to file civil and
criminal claims. However, in all practical fact, the H2-B guest worker program requires foreign laborers to leave the United States as soon as they
are no longer working for the original contractor. Given that prosecuting
civil or criminal cases takes a long time and requires legal representation,
lawsuits and criminal charges are filed infrequently.

Nonetheless, transnational guest workers will retain a subaltern status,
because they will not have the capacity to retain their rights, and in the current context of unionization, which is on a local and national basis, in most
instances, guest workers will not stay long enough to form bonds of solidarity with others. Thus, while Jennifer Gordon and others have proposed
cross-border unionization, especially among low-wage workers, as a means
of transnational political citizenship and social rights for documented and
undocumented migrants, most workers who can even achieve unionization
will not have the opportunity to exercise the power found in labor representation (Gordon 2007). Furthermore, the desolation of labor unions in
U.S. civil society has left a large organizational chasm built on solidarity.
While undocumented immigrants may benefit from a new transnational
labor regime, it is implausible for guest workers to build bonds that would
lead to enduring solidarity. Until the U.S. native- and foreign-born working
class can reestablish its own institutions of solidarity that would expand its
bargaining leverage under capitalism, it is difficult to envision a program of
transnational labor citizenship, constructed on the foundation of new, highly
developed forms of neoliberal exploitation, which would benefit migrant
laborers.

Notes

Introduction: Guest Workers of the World

1. Boswell argues that employers have held down labor costs through segregating workers into discrete labor markets on the basis of race and ethnicity. This development of job segregation for Chinese workers in the late nineteenth century is comparable to the rapid growth of divided labor markets for immigrants in the early twenty-first century and transparent in guest worker programs that will reserve specific labor markets for temporary workers. In the late nineteenth century, labor market segregation was accompanied by anti-Chinese stereotypes and violence. In the California mining industry, Chinese workers toiling as contract laborers were considered "coolies," a derogatory term that was synonymous to slaves, despite the fact that Asian immigrants were employed as indentured servants. White anti-Asian racial hostility contributed to the dispersion of Chinese mine workers and other laborers from California to other western states and led to violent resistance, especially when used by capitalists as strikebreakers. Following the 1876 recession, Chinese workers were subject to violent repression.

2. Passage of a comprehensive guest worker program in the United States seems inevitable. Once business gains a massive supply of migrant workers, politicians are likely to whip up sentiment to round up undocumented migrants and send them home as pariahs and criminals, just as in the aftermath of 9/11. Though the government does not provide data on deportations, tens of thousands of South Asian, Arab, and Middle Eastern immigrants faced discrimination and left on their own accord or were indiscriminately deported.

3. See, for example, Thomas Friedman's *The World is Flat* and *The New Argonauts* by Anna Lee Saxenian, dean of the School of Information at the University of California at Berkeley, and Bill Gates's *Business @ the Speed of Thought*. All these best-

selling books pay almost no attention to the social consequences of the new migrant workforce and outsourcing of services.

4. What are needed are strong labor institutions capable of challenging the growing inequities of the neoliberal market economy. To strengthen workers in the United States, it is necessary to do away with much of the worker restrictions to engage in concerted activity established following passage of the National Labor Relations Act of 1935 and undermined through the Supreme Court and antilabor legislation. The Taft-Hartley Act of 1947 that hinders worker collective action has so undercut the rights of workers that labor law is irrelevant to most U.S. workers today.

Chapter 1. Migration and Class Struggle

1. See Gérard Duménil and Dominique Lévy, *Capital Resurgent: Roots of the Neoliberal Revolution* (Cambridge, Mass.: Harvard University Press), 2004.

2. Gereffi, Gary and Miguel Korzeniewicz, eds., 1993. *Commodity Chains and Global Capitalism*. Westport, CT: Greenwood Publishing Company. Chapter 6 (pp. 123–42) examines the emergence and growth of the service sector commodity chain in the international economy and its effect on national economies.

3. Under President George W. Bush, the INS was renamed the U.S. Citizen and Immigrant Services under the umbrella of the Department of Homeland Security.

4. AFL-CIO. 2009. Resolution 11: The Labor Movement's Principles for Comprehensive Immigration Reform. Accessed December 3, 2009: http://www.aflcio.org/aboutus/thisistheaflcio/convention/2009/upload/res_11.pdf.

Chapter 2. Political Economy of Migrant Labor in U.S. History

1. In two new books published in 2006, J. D. Hayworth (R-Arizona) and Tom Tancredo (R-Colorado), two conservatives in the House of Representatives, go so far as to assert that undocumented immigrants are sources of terrorism, compete with U.S.-citizens for jobs, and are barbarians harboring ideology counter to the American Judeo-Christian ethic.

2. The Immigration Act of 1875, also known as the Page Act, prohibited the entry or "importation" of immigrants deemed immoral—such as women who were prostitutes—but was viewed as an initial measure to bar foreigners, particularly Chinese and other Asians. See Ming M. Zhu, The Page Act of 1875: In the Name of Morality (March 23, 2010). Available at SSRN: http://ssrn.com/abstract=1577213.

3. Glenn Firebaugh's *The New Geography of Global Income Inequality* contends that in the 1970s, a historic transformation occurred: the income gap between the Global North and Global South reached a climax and has continued a steady process of decline. Subsequently, the differentiation in income between the North and South has narrowed. From 1970 to 2005 relocation of manufacturing and services from the Global North to the low-wage Global South has increased corporate profitability. Nevertheless, a large share of profits are repatriated to finance capitalists in the North,

and not used to increase the standard of living in the South. Concurrently, inequality began to expand within countries as the disparity of income between the rich and the poor began to grow. In both the Global South and North, income has been redistributed from the working class and poor to corporations and the upper class. In the Global South, inequality has widened further as new nonunionized industry displaces older firms that had unions that facilitated greater labor protection.

4. In 2006, the UNPD reported that almost half of all international migrants are female, and that they "outnumber male migrants in developed countries." See United Nations Commission on Population and Development, *United Nations Economic and Social Council POP/943,* April 3, 2006, 39th session, 2nd Meeting, and *United Nations Press Release POP/844,* New York, October 28, 2002.

5. Gilbert Gonzalez views U.S. guest worker programs as an imperialist strategy equivalent to historic British and French colonial policies in India and Algeria. His study of Mexicans in the U.S. Bracero guest worker program supports the position that corporate and business monoliths drive labor migration. In government-sanctioned programs, workers are employed as contract labor, and when no longer needed, they are sent back to their home countries. In effect, since 1917 the United States functioned as the labor contractor through establishing the Bracero agreements, bringing low-wage labor from Mexico to ostensibly fill jobs in agriculture and transportation industries in periods of labor shortage during World War I and World War II. In turn, Mexico performed the duties of labor recruiter for large-scale agricultural interests in the Southwest and in the East. Braceros were readily available and disposable, effortlessly controlled and efficient, and, best of all, cheap (Gonzalez 2006, 7).

6. The WTO, comprising 146 member states, was founded upon completion of the GATT negotiations seeking to lower tariffs and other obstacles to free trade. WTO adjudicates conflict over free-trade barriers. It is a forum for negotiations that seek the expansion of free trade in diverse sectors of the global economy. In the General Agreement on Trade in Services (GATS), the United States is at the forefront pushing for passage of a broad agreement covering an array of financial services and technology. While the United States operates a huge deficit in trade in manufacturing, there is a modest surplus in trade in services.

7. As deputy secretary of defense from 2001 to 2005, Paul Wolfowitz formed part of a small inner circle of strategic advisers to the president on the U.S. invasion of Iraq. Wolfowitz became chief propagandist of President George W. Bush to rally public support for the invasion of Iraq in 2003, taking the nation on a unilateral path in world affairs. He was the architect and proponent of the Bush Doctrine, which calls for *preemption*—the notion that the United States may use military force against a regime it deems dangerous to its interests. Following Wolfowitz's appointment to lead the World Bank, global remittances have become the most salient feature of development in the Global South, more revealing of the vital importance of low-wage migration to the North than a development plan for the South.

8. Duménil and Lévy see finance as the major beneficiary of the transfer of wealth. Indeed, financial companies stand to benefit from the major industry crises, for example, as declarations of bankruptcy provide the opportunity to restructure companies. During the course of corporate restructuring, a bankrupt corporation may lay off workers en masse, sharply reduce wage rates, and cut benefits to lay the groundwork for restoring financial profitability. David Harvey brilliantly makes use of Duménil and Lévy's work to demonstrate concretely the reassertion of capital—through a historical examination of privatization, market reform, and the growth of financial institutions in Chile, China, the U.K., and the United States.

9. Barbara Shailor (2007), director of the AFL-CIO International Department, notes that in the Dominican Republic, women losing jobs working in sweatshops in export processing zones frequently migrate or are trafficked into forced prostitution.

10. This growing opposition is becoming increasingly evident. IT and engineering workers and unions threatened by low-wage guest workers who may undermine established terms of trade or wages claim that opening a guest worker migration program undermines social and economic standards by driving down wages. National, state, and local organizations continue to appeal to Congress to eliminate guest worker programs and enforce the 1986 Immigration Reform and Control Act banning unauthorized immigrants from working in the United States. The intensity of the debate extends to immigrants—both documented and undocumented—who dramatically oppose a guest worker program. Immigrants see guest worker programs as a threat to their livelihood; as contract workers, they would not be protected by federal wage and hour legislation and the National Labor Relations Act that permits them to form unions. As guest workers, they are subject to employer tyranny and threats of deportation rather than simply dismissal. Though U.S. courts are diminishing the rights of undocumented immigrants to organize, most still have the ability to find a new employer. If governed by a guest worker program, migrant workers would be subject to immediate deportation.

11. Papademetriou and Yale-Loehr (1996) contend that the United States must shift its focus to stress an *economic stream* of migration to provide the labor force needed to promote industrial development. They argue that the *social stream* of migration that focuses on family reunification and the *compassionate stream* that provides asylum to refugees—historically the center of U.S. immigration policy—do not offer benefits to the economy.

Chapter 3. India's Global and Internal Labor Migration and Resistance

1. The Washington Consensus directed by the International Monetary Fund (IMF), World Bank (WB), and World Trade Organization (WTO) was formed in 1989 to implement neoliberal reforms advocated by leading global corporations.

2. U.S. Department of Labor, Bureau of Labor Statistics. Available online at http://

data.bls.gov/servlet/SurveyOutputServlet?&series_id=LNU04032237. Accessed February 26, 2006.

3. Information technology-producing industries: Extended mass layoff events, private nonfarm sector, 1996–2009. Available online at Bureau of Labor Statistics at //ftp.bls.gov/pub/special.requests/mls/mlitprod.txt. Accessed January 28, 2010.

4. A growing number of foreign labor contractors in the United States are becoming known as "body shops," given that they trade in people and control the work lives of foreign workers in the nation. See Xiang Biao, Global "Body Shopping": An Indian Labor System in the Information Technology Industry (Princeton, N.J.: Princeton University Press, 2006). Moreover, foreign contractors are crucial in securing the housing and health-care needs of foreign nonimmigrant workers. Three Indian contractors provide a large segment of the U.S. IT and business services market: Tata Consultancy Services, Infosys Technologies Ltd., and Wipro Technologies. These are Indian companies that provide IT, business consulting, and accounting services on an international basis. The companies primarily employ Indian programmers. An ongoing complaint by opponents is that U.S. government authorities do not enforce the law and permit contractors to replace American workers and fraudulently file labor applications at lower rates than U.S. workers.

TCS's client list reads like a who's who of the leading manufacturing, energy, telecommunications, financial services, and software multinationals in the world: AT&T, AXA Insurance, British Telecom, Canadian Mutual Life, ChevronTexaco, Citicorp, Deutsche Bank, General Motors, Ford, General Electric, IBM, Lucent Technologies, Nike, Nortel Networks, P&O Nedlloyd, Qwest Communications, UBS, and Verizon Communications. The firm has formed strong relationships with educational institutions in India and throughout the world, including the Indian Institute of Technology, the University of California, the University of Wisconsin, Carnegie Mellon University, the University of Humberside, the University of Waterloo, and the Rotterdam School of Management.

Infosys Technologies Ltd., founded in 1981, is now one of the world's leading IT software contractors, with 28,000 international employees and annual revenue exceeding $1 billion. Based in Bangalore—considered India's Silicon Valley—Infosys expanded rapidly only under the neoliberal reforms. In 1987, the company entered the U.S. market, opening offices in Fremont, California. By 1999 Infosys became the first Indian company to be listed on the NASDAQ stock exchange. Infosys has rapidly increased its U.S. presence, opening five development centers in 1999 and 2000 as the H-1B guest worker program expanded dramatically. The company serves clients in North America, western Europe, and East Asia—including Oracle, Intel, Siebel, Interwoven, Informatica, BEA, Star Partner, MatrixOne, Mantas, and SAP Partner Services.

5. On average, programmers in India and China earn a fraction of the average U.S. wage of $60,000 per year. As H1-B authorizations declined in 2006 and 2007, ITAA (Internet Technology Association of America) is successfully lobbying Congress on

behalf of the IT industry to provide exemptions to allow more than 85,000 workers to enter the United States. Concomitantly, IT contractors elude the cap of 85,000 by sending workers to the United States through a consortium of third countries (Matloff 2002; ITAA 2004, 2006, 2007).

6. OBC includes not only a number of castes, but also other groupings. Check out on OBCs. See A. Ramaiah, "Identifying Other Backward Classes," *Economic and Political Weekly* (June 1992): 1203–7.

7. In 2006, Gagan Global, a U.S.-based contractor, sought to import workers trained by the Overseas Manpower Consultancy, a training school in the Hyderabad region of Andhra Pradesh. Owing to Teamster union opposition, the plan to send for Indian temporary truck drivers to the United States was foiled. See Jerome R. Corsi, "Truck Drivers from India to Take U.S. Jobs? Union Protests Plan as Attempt to Undercut 'Hard-Working Americans.'" *WorldNetDaily.com,* http://www.wnd.com ?pageId=37119, accessed August 6, 2010.

8. The largest trade unions in Hyderabad represent public sector workers who are under assault by efforts to reduce wages. In addition, older garment, steel, and industrial and service sectors—such as banking workers and transport drivers—are also typically unionized (Sen 1997).

9. Because Yagar and his wife are members of a low caste, employers may not remunerate them directly, but pay contractors and subcontractors who take large cuts out of the salary.

10. Dalit is not a single caste. The lowest castes, those who used to be treated socially, if not legally, as untouchables, are even now treated as outcasts; they call themselves Dalits, meaning the oppressed.

11. A study by Uni, a transnational labor organization based in Geneva, has found that security workers in major cities are paid minimum wages by G4S, a British-based multinational security firm. The study also found that G4S workers are typically employed six to seven days a week, twelve hours a day. Without union representation, the workers are employed as contractors without job security, and are typically fired for complaining about their conditions. See G4Solidarity 2010.

Chapter 4. Temporary Labor Migration and U.S. and Foreign-born Worker Resistance

1. Established in Delhi in 1961, the Indian Institute of Technology maintains regional campuses in Kanpur, Kharagpur, Madras, Mumbai, Guwahati, and Roorkee.

2. For a petitioner list opposing the U.S. guest work programs, see http://www .zazona.com/H1BPetition/p/signatories.html. The list also includes corporate executives, unemployed technology workers, manual, and unskilled workers.

3. Available online at http://www.adpwilco.com/outsourcing/out-over.htm. Accessed February 13, 2006.

4. Shah said in an interview that H-1B workers typically worked seventy hours a

week, significantly more hours than full-time Goldman Sachs employees, where she witnessed huge differentials in health benefits and pensions. She argued that some Wilco guest workers in the United States could barely earn enough to make ends meet and certainly not enough to save significant funds. Even some normally complacent H-1B workers began to complain about their working and living conditions, as the majority of the H-1B holders lived with coworkers across the Hudson River in New Jersey in ramshackle housing obtained through ADP Wilco (interview, Sona Shah, March 18, 2005, New York City).

5. L-1 visas are intended for employees transferred from a foreign company or branch to a U.S. affiliate of the same company. L-1A visas are for executives and managers, while L-1B visas are for employees with specialized knowledge. L-1 visa holders may extend their stay for up to seven years and may apply for permanent residency in the United States.

6. In recent years, the number of L-1 visas issued per year has risen 40 percent, from 41,739 in 1999 to 57,700 in 2002. See Katie Hafner and Daniel Preysman, "Special Visa's Use for Tech Workers Is Challenged," *New York Times,* June 1, 2003.

7. Paul Brubaker. "Pascrell to Support Work Visa Reform: Resident Urged Congressman to Act," *Montclair (N.J.)Times,* January 2, 2004. Available online at http://www.montclairtimes.com/page.php?page=6757. Accessed February 13, 2006.

8. In 2007, the per capita income in Connecticut was $54,117, far higher than the US national average of $38,611 and almost twice that of Mississippi's personal income per capita of $28,845. U.S. Department of Census, 2007.

9. For more than five years TORAW called on the government to take steps to deter both outsourcing and offshoring of jobs. John Bauman, president of TORAW, said that the organization had two hundred members across the country by 2004. TORAW worked with the AFL-CIO's Department of Professional Employees to support limitations on nonimmigrant visas and advance legislation to curb and monitor outsourcing and the importation of foreign workers. TORAW worked with Democratic Representative Rosa DeLauro on legislation that she introduced to address these issues. In 2003 TORAW pushed Connecticut Democratic Senator Christopher Dodd and the state's Republican Representative Nancy Johnson to introduce the USA Jobs Protection Act, companion bills in the Senate (S 1452) and House (HR 2849) that would place tighter restrictions on H-1B and L-1 visas.

10. Debapratim Purkayashtha. "Labor Unrest at Signal International," ICFAI Center for Management Research, 2008, 2.

11. Lindsay Beyerstein and Larisa Alexandrovna, "Human trafficking of Indian guest workers alleged in Mississippi shipyard; Contractor defends 290-man camp," *The Raw Story* 3, April 2007. http://rawstory.com/news/2007/Human_trafficking_of_Indian_guest_workers_0412.html.

12. "US job racket agents' licenses suspended," 11, March 2008. 13, August 13, 2009. http://www.thaindian.com/newsportal/uncategorized/us-job-racket-agents-licences-suspended_10026348.html.

13. "MOIA probes recruitment of Indian workers for US shipyard," 10, March 2008. 13, August 2009. http://www.thaindian.com/newsportal/uncategorized/moia-probes -recruitment-of-indian-workers-for-us-shipyard_10025942.html.

14. Debapratim Purkayashtha, "Labor Unrest at Signal International," ICFAI Center for Management Research, 2008, 1; see *Thaindian News*, "US job racket agents' licenses suspended," 11, March 2008. http://www.thaindian.com/newsportal/uncategorized/ us-job-racket-agents-licences-suspended_10026348.html.

Chapter 5. The Migration of Low-Wage Jamaican Guest Workers

1. The phrase "a fair day's wages for a fair day's pay" was coined by the Victorian writer and critic Thomas Carlyle in *Past and Present*, 1843. Later, the expression was derided by Friedrich Engels as a fabrication to speed up the capitalist production process.

2. Large numbers of workers from Jamaica and Barbados contracted serious diseases and died during the building of the Panama Canal. Remittances from workers, commonly known as "Panama Money" in Barbados, did improve conditions of the black working class through improving health care, education, and conditions on both islands. See Bonham C. Richardson, *Panama Money in Barbados, 1900–1920* (Knoxville: University of Tennessee Press, 1986).

3. The INA required employers to provide temporary laborers to pay for travel expenses from the Caribbean to the United States.

4. The Overseas Employment Center is sponsored and operated by the Jamaica Central Labor Organization, a division of the Ministry of Labor and Social Security.

5. According to Jeremiah, "me rada clean mi rada clean du du and av food fi yam, dan fi clean it and don't av any food or (I prefer to clean human waste have food to eat rather than not to clean and not have food).

6. Spirit Cultural Exchange shifts all costs to the H-2B workers, who ostensibly serve as contractors. Spirit informs potential workers that "participants should expect some additional expenses before and upon arrival in the USA." The Spirit Cultural Exchange program does not include a housing deposit and rental fees, meals, international airfare, domestic transportation in the states, and airport transfers: "Generally, we recommend that participants have at least $500 available upon arrival in the USA in traveler's checks or other means to cover initial 'settling in' costs until the first paycheck. Participants should budget for an additional $500-$800 per month to cover housing, meals, and personal expenses. These amounts may vary depending on spending habits and work location."

7. According to Deborah Thomas (2004), U.S. H-2B employers are dispersed geographically throughout twenty-two states, from New England to the Deep South, from the Carolinas to California. The most popular destinations are popular U.S. tourist destinations, the Massachusetts shoreline, the Upper Peninsula in Michigan, the Mississippi Gulf Coast, the ski resorts in Colorado's Rocky Mountains, and coastal

resorts in the Carolinas and Florida. The scale of operations ranges from small New England bed and breakfasts to luxury resorts in the Rocky Mountains.

8. U.S. employers seek to recruit guest workers with skills in cosmetology, massage therapy, and other spa services. However, for the most part, very few guest workers provide these services due to lack of supply.

9. The Gulf Coast region of Mississippi, especially Biloxi and Gulfport, is a leading destination for gambling. However, the state also permits gambling in the river towns of Greenville, Natchez, Tunica, and Vicksburg. Source: Mississippi Casino Operators Association, Mississippi Gaming Commission. See http://www.americangaming.org/Industry/state/statistics.cfm. Web site accessed December 28, 2009.

10. Situated sixty-five miles northeast of New Orleans, Biloxi was severely damaged by Hurricane Katrina in September 2005. At the height of the summer tourist season, Katrina forced many hotels and casinos to close. The Beau Rivage was severely damaged by water, but survived the storm. Many other casinos, hotels, and resorts along the shore region were completely destroyed.

11. To authenticate her employment at the Beau Rivage Hotel and Casino, Nina showed me her Beau Rivage ID card, which read: "This card identifies you as a Beau Rivage employee. Use it to record hours worked. Misuse may result in disciplinary action." The card had a bar code and the name Beau Rivage: Biloxi, Mississippi.

12. The programs include degrees in food service, hotel management, hospitality, and tourism. Montego Bay Community College offers similar education in food and beverage management, hospitality and tourism, and entry-level technical skills. In addition to UWI and UTech, Northern Caribbean University–Mandeville offers advanced degrees that require students to go overseas to the United States, Canada, the U.K., and elsewhere for internships. For more information, see Robin Middlehurst and Steve Woodfield (2004), *Summary Report: The Role of Transnational, Private, and For-Profit Provision in Meeting Global Demand for Tertiary Education: Mapping, Regulation and Impact—Case Study Jamaica* (Vancouver: Commonwealth of Learning/UNESCO).

13. See www.gurneys-inn.com for detailed information.

14. In 2007, the cheapest rate for the small "Oceanview Studio," far from the cottages on the beach, is $395 a night during peak season.

15. In the 1980s, some Jamaican guest workers lost all their savings to a government labor minister who absconded with the funds.

16. At the 80th Meeting of the Regional Labour Board Conference (2004), the member ministries emphasized the importance of adhering to the dictates of the *official* program, especially where the protection of guest workers is concerned. Only by enforcing the law will unauthorized agencies be eliminated and acceptable standards of living and treatment of workers be ensured (Regional Labour Board 2004, 9).

17. In *Mexican New York,* Robert Courtney Smith provides a vivid portrait of the consequences of Mexican transnational migration from Mixteca, Mexico, to New York City over less than a decade, a pattern that "exacerbates inequalities, and creates

new possibilities, including transnational ones, for political and social action" (Smith 2006, 39). Conversely, in Jamaica, migrants' status as guest workers tends to have no effect on economic and political life. The transnational linkage between Kingston (or other cities) and the resort to which migrants are assigned does not permit settlement, whereas Mexican undocumented workers have forged ties between their local economies and emerging communities in U.S. cities.

18. Hospitality employers are required to demonstrate that workers are only needed temporarily, despite the fact that every year workers are rehired on a seasonal basis and return home, only to return the following year.

19. Concern regarding the expansion of the H-2B program is prevalent among Jamaican government and labor union leaders. The board members include: Barrington Bailey, senior director for Manpower Services at the Jamaican Ministry of Labour, and Vincent Morrison, the board chair, who is the vice president and island supervisor of the Jamaican National Workers Union. Cecil Weir, deputy liaison for the U.S. government, attended the 80th meeting of the board, in Kingston, on April 28 and 29, 2004. The board resolved that an extension of the guest worker program was essential to the Caribbean region. See Regional Labour Board, *Exporting Labour in the 21st Century—Strategic Outreach Plan for the Expansion of the H-2B Programme* (Kingston: Ministry of Labour and Social Security, September 2004).

Chapter 6. Who Can Organize? Trade Unions, Worker Insurgency, Labor Power

1. In *Capital, Volume I,* Marx contends (443–44), "Machinery possesses relative surplus-value; not only by depreciating the value and indirectly cheapening the same labour power through cheapening the commodities that enter into its reproduction, but also when it is first introduced sporadically into an industry, by converting the labor employed by the owner of that machinery, into labour of a higher degree and greater efficiency by raising the social value of the article produced above its industrial value, and thus enabling the capitalist to replace the value of the day's labour-power by a smaller portion of the value of the day's product."

2. "Union Members, 2009." Bureau of Labor Statistics News Release, January 22, 2010. Accessed February 7, 2010: See http://www.bls.gov/news.release/union2.nro.htm. As manufacturing employment plummeted, and for the first time ever, unionized workers in the public sector (7.9 million) outpaced that in the private sector (7.4 million).

3. On May 23, 2007, SEIU and UNITE-HERE provided its official position on immigration reform in testimony by Fred Feinstein to the U.S. House of Representatives immigration committee. While the United Farm Workers support the bill, the Teamsters, UFCW, and Carpenters, representing more than half the CTW, staunchly opposed the McCain-Kennedy bill. See Testimony Presented by Fred Feinstein, University of Maryland School of Public Policy on Behalf of Service Employees International Union and UNITE-HERE before the Subcommittee on Immigration,

Citizenship, Refugees, Border Security and International Law, U.S. House of Representatives, Washington, D.C., May 23, 2007. http://judiciary.house.gov/hearings/pdf/Feinstein070524.pdf.

4. The new INS directive also protected employers hiring undocumented workers from workplace raids during critical times. Particularly, the new policy allowed farming companies to employ undocumented immigrants to harvest time-sensitive crops (apples, asparagus, and so forth). Not surprisingly, employers opposed INS workplace raids during acute labor shortages. Still, employers such as Stemilt Growers Inc., a produce company in Washington state, defeated an organizing drive waged by the Teamsters. See INS: "Fewer Workplace Raids," *Migration News,* April 1999, vol. 6, no. 4. At its October 2000 convention, the AFL-CIO passed a resolution repealing its support for the 1986 employer sanction provisions of the Immigration Control and Reform Act (IRCA) that allowed employers to fire undocumented workers during organizing drives. See David Bacon, "Immigration Law Keeps Workers in Chains," in the americas.org, January 2000, http://www.americas.org/item_131.

5. For a discussion of labor unions and immigrant labor solidarity, see Immanuel Ness, *Immigrants, Unions and the New U.S. Labor Market,* 40–57.

6. President George W. Bush, State of the Union Address, Washington, D.C., January 20, 2004.

7. SEIU 2007. "Letter to Senator Kennedy from SEIU Leaders Andrew Stern, Anna Burger, and Eliseo Medina. January" 16. See http://www.workingimmigrants.com/2007/01/sieu_on_immigration_reform.html. Accessed February 24, 2010.

8. From 1995 to 2002, union density has declined dramatically in retail trade, communication, nondurable goods manufacturing, durable goods manufacturing, transportation, utilities, education, and construction.

9. On July 8, 2004, UNITE merged with the Hotel Employees and Restaurant Employees International Union (HERE) to form UNITE-HERE, a larger union of 440,000 members and more than 400,000 retirees. In 2009, even before the election of John Wilhelm as president in June, Bruce Raynor (the union's previous president) and most former UNITE leaders split to form Workers United, which subsequently became a membership division of SEIU.

Bibliography

Abraham, Yvonne. 2007a. "Up to 350 in Custody after New Bedford Immigration Raid." *Boston Globe,* March 6. Available online at http://www.boston.com/news/globe/city_region/breaking_news/2007/03/up_to_350_in_cu.html.

———. 2007b. "As Immigration Raids Rise, Human Toll Decried," *Boston Globe,* March 20. Available online at http://www.boston.com/news/nation/articles/2007/03/20/as_immigration_raids_rise_human_toll_decried/. Accessed February 16, 2010.

AFL-CIO. 2006a. "Q&As on AFL-CIO's Immigration Policy." Available online at www.longislandfed.org/IssuesPDF/Immigration_QA_October%202006.pdf. Accessed February 24, 2010.

AFL-CIO. 2006b. "Responsible Reform of Immigration Laws Must Protect Working Conditions for all Workers in the U.S." San Diego: AFL-CIO Executive Council, March 1.

———. 2009a. "AFL-CIO, Change to Win Agree on Joint Immigration Framework, April 14. Available online at http://blog.aflcio.org/2009/04/14/afl-cio-change-to-win-agree-on-joint-immigration-framework/. Accessed December 7, 2009. "Change to Win And AFL-CIO Unveil Unified Immigration Reform Framework," http://www.changetowin.org/for-the-media/press-releases-and-statements/change-to-win-and-afl-cio-unveil-unified-immigration-reform-framework.html. Accessed December 7, 2009.

———. 2009b. "The Labor Movement's Framework for Comprehensive Immigration Reform: AFL-CIO and Change to Win, April." Available online at http://www.aflcio.org/issues/civilrights/immigration/upload/immigrationreform041409.pdf. Accessed February 2, 2010.

Alkirei, Sabina and Maria Emma Santos. 2010. *Acute Multidimensional Poverty: A New Index for Developing Countries. OPHI Working Paper No. 38.* July. Oxford: Oxford Poverty and Human Development Initiative.

American Hospitality, Travel, Tourism and Franchise Industries. 2006. "Letter to U.S. Senate." February 10.Available online at http://www.aila.org/content/default .aspx?bc=6755|25669|19898|18690|21557|18692.

Amman, John, Tris Carpenter, and Gina Neff. 2006. *Surviving the New Economy.* Boulder, Colo.: Paradigm.

Amnesty International. 2000. "Jamaica: Deaths in Prison." *Amnesty International.* Available online at http://web.amnesty.org/library/Index/ENGAMR380032000 ?open&of=ENG-380.

Andrews, Gregg. 2002. *City of Dust: A Cement Company Town in the Land of Tom Sawyer.* Columbia: University of Missouri Press.

Aneesh, A. 2006. *Virtual Migration: The Programming of Globalization.* Durham, N.C.: Duke University Press.

Ansley, Frances. 2008. "Doing Policy from Below: Worker Solidarity and the Prospects for Immigration Reform." *Cornell International Law Journal* 41: 102–14.

Archibold, Randal C. 2006. "Strategy Sessions Fueled Immigration Marches." *New York Times,* April 12, section A, column 3, p. 16.

Arora, Ashish and Suma Athreye. 2002. *The Software Industry and India's Economic Development, Information Economics and Policy* 14, no. 2 (June): 253–73.

Bacon, David. 2000. "Immigration Law Keeps Workers in Chains." In the americas .org, January. Available online at http://www.americas.org/item_131.

———. 2001. "Labor Fights for Immigrants." *The Nation,* March 21. Available online at http://www.thenation.com/doc/20010521/bacon. Accessed July 1, 2006.

———. 2005. *The Children of NAFTA: Labor Wars on the U.S./Mexico Border.* Berkeley: University of California Press.

———. 2007. "Guest Workers Fired After Protesting Slavelike Conditions." *New America Media.* Available online at http://news.newamericamedia.org/news/view_ article.html?article_id=4be58daa34f9551a19abcd88608fa0c0. Accessed April 11, 2008.

———. 2008. *Illegal People: How Globalization Creates Migration and Criminalizes Immigrants.* Boston: Beacon Press.

Bagchi, Amiya Kumar. 2002. *Capital and Labour Redefined: India and the Third World.* London: Anthem Press.

———. 2005. *Perilous Passage: Mankind and the Global Ascendancy of Capital.* Lanham, Md.: Rowman & Littlefield.

Baldauf, Scott. 2005. "Power Shortages Threaten India's Boom." *Christian Science Monitor,* June 1.

Banerjee, Debdas. 2005. *Globalisation, Industrial Restructuring and Labour Standards: Where India Meets the Global.* New Delhi: Sage Publications.

Banerjee, Payal. 2006. "Indian Information Technology Workers in the United States: The H-1B Visa, Flexible Production, and the Racializaiton of Labor." *Critical Sociology* no. 2 (March): 425–45.

Bates, Steve. 2002. "Facing the Future: Human Resource Management is Changing." *HR Magazine,* July.

Bauer, Mary. 2008. "Testimony of Mary Bauer, Director Immigrant Justice Project, Southern Poverty Law Center before the U.S. House of Representatives Subcommittee on Immigration, Citizenship, Refugees, Border Security, and International Law." U.S. House of Representatives, April 16.

Beik, Mildred Allen. 2006 [1996]. *The Miners of Windber: The Struggles of New Immigrants for Unionization, 1890s-1930s.* University Park: Pennsylvania State University Press.

Benner, Chris. 2002. *Work in the New Economy: Flexible Labor Markets in Silicon Valley.* Malden, Mass.: Blackwell.

Bhagwati, Jagdish, Arvind Panagariya, and T. N. Srinivasan. 2004. "The Muddles Over Outsourcing." *Journal of Economic Perspectives* 18, no. 4 (Fall): 93–114.

Bhagwati, Jagdish N. 2005. *In Defense of Globalization.* New York: Oxford University Press.

Bhatt, Ela Ramesh. 2005. *We Are Poor But So Many: The Story of Self-Employed Women in India.* New York: Oxford University Press.

Blair, Leonardo. 2004. "Cut in Security Contracts." *Jamaica Gleaner.* Available online at http://www.jamaica-gleaner.com/gleaner/20040208/lead/lead3.html.

Block, Rebecca M., Sheldon H. Danziger, and Robert Schoeni. 2006. *Working and Poor: How Economic and Policy Changes are Affecting Low-Wage Workers.* New York: Russell Sage Foundation.

Boltanski, Luc, and Eve Chiapello. 2007. *The New Spirit of Capitalism.* London: Verso.

Boswell, Terry E. 1986. "A Split Labor Market Analysis of Discrimination Against Chinese Immigrants, 1850–1882." *American Sociological Review* 51, no. 3 (June): 352–71.

Breman, Jan. 1985. *Of Peasants Paupers and Migrants.* New Delhi: Oxford University Press.

Briggs, Vernon M., Jr. 2004. Testimony to United States Senate Committee on the Judiciary: Evaluating a Temporary Guest Worker Proposal—Guestworker Programs for Low-Skilled Workers: Lessons from the Past and Warnings for the Future. Washington, D.C.: U.S. Senate. February 5.

Brody, David. 2005. *Embattled Labor: History, Power, Rights.* Urbana: University of Illinois Press.

Brubaker, Paul. 2004. "Pascrell to Support Work Visa Reform: Resident Urged Congressman to Act." *Montclair Times,* January 2. Available online at http://www.montclairtimes.com/page.php?page=6757. Accessed: February 13, 2006.

Burtless, Gary, ed. 1990. *A Future of Lousy Jobs.* Washington, D.C.: The Brookings Foundation.

Bush, George W. 2004a. Speech. The White House, Washington, D.C., January 4.

———. 2004b. "President Bush Proposes New Temporary Worker Program: Remarks by the President on Immigration Policy." The White House, Washington, D.C., January 7.

———. 2004c. "Fact Sheet: Fair and Secure Immigration Reform." The White House, Washington, D.C. Available online at www.whitehouse.gov/news/releases/2004/01/20040107-1.html. Accessed January 7, 2004.

———. 2004d. State of the Union Address, Washington, D.C., January 20.

Business Travel News. 2006. "Hoteliers in Driver's Seat," June, pp. 1–10.

Calavita, Kitty. 1990. "Employer Sanctions Violations: Toward a Dialectical Model of White-Collar Crime." *Law & Society Review* 20, no. 4, 1041–69.

———. 1992. *Inside the State: The Bracero Program, Immigration, and the I.N.S.* New York: Routledge.

Caribbean Net News. 2003. "British companies seeking to build prison in Jamaica." October 2, available online at http://www.caribbeannetnews.com/2003/10/02/prisons.htm.

Carlyle, Thomas. 1977. *Past and Present* [originally published in 1843]. New York: New York University Press.

Castells, Manuel. 2000. *The Rise of the Network Society.* Oxford: Blackwell.

Castles, Stephen, and Mark J. Miller. 2003. *The Age of Migration: International Population Movements in the Modern World.* New York: Guilford Press.

Castles, Stephen, and Raúl Delgado Wise. 2008. *Migration and Development: Perspectives from the South.* Geneva: International Organization for Migration.

"Center before the House Subcommittee on Immigration, Citizenship, Refugees, Border Security, and International Law, U.S. House of Representatives: The H-2B Program in the United States." Washington, D.C., April 16.

Chase, Katie Johnston. 2009. "Hundreds attend rally for fired Hyatt housekeepers: Politicians urge boycott of the hotel." *Boston Globe.* September 18.

Chibber, Vivek. 2004. *Locked in Place: State Building and Late Industrialization in India.* Princeton, N.J.: Princeton University Press.

Cloward, R. A., and F. F. Piven. 2001. "Disrupting Cyberspace." *New Labor Forum* 11, 91–94.

Collinder, Avia. 2009. "Guard Services in Decline—Electronics Saving Security Sector." *Jamaica Gleaner.* May 15.

Compa, Lance. 2004. *Unfair Advantage: Workers' Freedom of Association in the United States Under International Human Rights Standards.* Ithaca, N.Y.: Cornell University Press/Human Rights Watch.

Cordero-Guzmán, Héctor R., Robert C. Smith, and Ramón Grosfoguel, eds. 2001. *Migration, Transnationalization & Race in a Changing New York.* Philadelphia: Temple University Press.

Cornelius, Wayne A., and Jessa M. Lewis, eds. 2006. *Impacts of Border Enforcement on Mexican Migration: A View from Sending Countries.* Boulder, Colo.: Lynne Rienner.

Corsi, Jerome R, 2006. "Truck Drivers from India to Take U.S. Jobs? Union Protests Plan as Attempt to Undercut 'Hard-Working Americans.'" WorldNetDaily.com. Available online at http://www.wnd.com?pageId=37119. Accessed August 6, 2010.

Cutler, Michael W. 2006. "DHS Intelligence and Border Security: Delivering Operational Intelligence," Statement of Michael W. Cutler before the U.S. House of Representatives, Committee on Homeland Security, Subcommittee on Intelligence, Information Sharing, and Terrorism Risk Assessment, June 28.

Daniels, Roger. 2005. *Guarding the Golden Door: American Immigration Policy and Immigrants since 1882.* New York: Farrar, Straus and Giroux.

Das, Gurcharan. 2002. *India Unbound: The Social and Economic Revolution from Independence to the Global Information Age.* New York: Anchor Books.

De Sarkar, Dipankar. 2008. "900 million Indians live on less than $2 a day." *Indo-Asian News Service,* June 12.

Delgado, Héctor L. 1993. *New Immigrants, Old Unions: Organizing Undocumented Workers in Los Angeles.* Philadelphia: Temple University Press.

Deshpande, L. K., N. Sharma, Sandip Sarkar, and Anup K. Karan. 2006. *Liberalisation and Labour: Labour Flexibility in Indian Manufacturing.* New Delhi: Institute for Human Development.

Dobbs, Lou. 2004. *Exporting America: Why Corporate Greed is Shipping American Jobs Overseas.* New York: Warner Books.

Dubofsky, Melvyn. 1969. *We Shall be All: A History of the Industrial Workers of the World.* Chicago: Quadrangle Books.

Duménil, Gérard, and Dominique Lévy. 2004. *Capital Resurgent: Roots of the Neoliberal Revolution* (translated by Derek Jeffers). Cambridge, Mass.: Harvard University Press. Originally published in 2000 as *Crise et Sortie de Crise: Ordre et Désordres Néolibéraux.* Paris: Presses Universitaires de France.

Dychtwald, Ken, Tamara J. Erickson, and Robert Morrison. 2006. *Workforce Crisis: How to Beat the Coming of Skills and Talent.* Cambridge, Mass.: Harvard Business School Press.

Edwards, James R., Jr. 2005. "Keeping Extremists Out: the History of Ideological Exclusion and the Need for its Revival." Center for Immigration Studies. September.

Elliott, Kimberly Ann, and Richard B. Freeman. 2003. *Can Labor Standards Improve Under Globalization?* Washington, D.C.: Institute for International Economics.

Emukile, Wynsome, and Olivia McDermott. 2006. "The Guest worker Program in the West Indies." Unpublished manuscript.

Emmanuel, Arghiri. 1972. *Unequal Exchange: A Study of the Imperialism of Trade.* New York: Monthly Review Press.

Essential Worker Immigration Coalition. 2006. "Businesses Urge Review and Consideration of Compromise Offered by Senators Mel Martinez (Rep-Florida) and Chuck Hagel (Rep-Nebraska)." Press release, April 5.

EWIC. 2006. "Coalition Vows to Defeat Harsh Immigration Bill." *Reuters,* January 19. Available online at http://www.ewic.org/index2.php?option=com_content&do_pdf=1&id=96. Accessed February 24, 2010.

Fairmont Hotel. 2007. Website. http://www.fairmont.com/dallas/. Accessed April 18, 2007.

Fajnzylber, Pablo, and Humberto López. 2008. *The Development Impact of Remittances in Latin America.* Washington, D.C.: The World Bank.

Faux, Jeff. 2006. *The Global Class War: How America's Bipartisan Elite Lost our Future—and What it Will Take to Win it Back.* Hoboken, N.J.: Wiley.

Fears, Darryl. 2005. "Immigration Measure Introduced." *Washington Post,* May 13, A08.

Featherstone, Liza. 2002. *Students Against Sweatshops.* London and New York: Verso.

Feinstein, Fred. 2007. Testimony Presented by Fred Feinstein, University of Maryland School of Public Policy on Behalf of Service Employees International Union and UNITE-HERE before the Subcommittee on Immigration, Citizenship, Refugees, Border Security and International Law, U.S. House of Representatives, Washington, D.C., May 23, 2007.

Fine, Janice. 2006. *Workers Centers: Organizing Communities at the Edge of the Dream.* Ithaca, N.Y.: Cornell University Press.

Fink, Leon. 2003. *Maya of Morganton: Work and Community in the Nuevo New South.* Chapel Hill: University of North Carolina Press.

Firebaugh, Glenn 2003. *The New Geography of Global Income Inequality.* Cambridge, Mass.: Harvard University Press.

Foner, Nancy. 2002. *From Ellis Island to JFK: New York's Two Great Waves of Immigration.* New Haven, Conn.: Yale University Press.

———. 2005. *In a New Land: A Comparative View of Immigration.* New York: New York University Press.

Frank, Thomas. 2004. *What's the Matter with Kansas? How Conservatives Won the Heart of America.* New York: Henry Holt.

Freeman, Richard B. 2007. *America Works: The Exceptional U.S. Labor Market.* New York: Russell Sage Foundation.

Freeman, Sunil. 2008. "Indian Workers' Struggle Shines Light on Human Trafficking, Slave Labor." *PSLWeb.org,* July 4. Available online at http://www.pslweb.org/site/ News2?JServSessionIdr009=v29yt8h827.app5b&page=NewsArticle&id=9509&n ews_iv_ctrl=1261. Accessed March 7, 2010.

Friedman, Milton. 2002. *Capitalism and Freedom.* Chicago: University of Chicago Press.

Friedman, Thomas. 2005. *The World is Flat: A Brief History of the Twenty-first Century.* New York: Farrar, Straus and Giroux.

G4Solidarity. 2010. *The Inequality Beneath India's Economic Boom: G4S Security Workers Fight for their Rightful Place in a Growing Economy.* Geneva: Uni Property Services G4S Alliance. Available online at www.uniglobalunion.org/ . . . /UNINews . . . /UNIPS%20Global%20Mtg%20April.2010%20mins.pdf.

Gagan Global LLC. 2006. "Indian Truck Drivers Recruited for U.S." Available online at http://webcache.googleusercontent.com/search?q=cache:gQMQRZRyljAJ :omcap.ap.nic.in/USAreq.doc+gagan+global+ltd+u.s.&cd=1&hl=en&ct=clnk&gl =us. Accessed August 6, 2010.

GAO. 2005. *State Department: Stronger Action Needed to Improve Oversight and Assess Risks of the Summer Work Travel and Trainee Categories of the Exchange Visitor Program.* Washington, D.C.: GAO. October, GAO-06-106.

Garnaut, Ross, and Ligang Song. 2005. *China Boom and its Discontents.* Canberra: Asia Pacific Press.

Gartner Incorporated. 2005. "Gartner Says Skills Shortage in India's Call Centers Has Negative Impact on Service Delivery." Egham, U.K., September 12.

Gates, Bill, with Collins Hemingway. 2000. *Business @ the Speed of Thought: Succeeding in the Digital Economy.* New York: Warner Books.

Gay, John F. 2007. Testimony of John F. Gay, Senior Vice President, Government Affairs & Public Policy, National Restaurant Association, before the Subcommittee on Immigration, Citizenship, Refugees, Border Security and International Law, Judiciary Committee, U.S. House of Representatives, Washington, D.C., June 6.

Gereffi, G., and W. Wadhwa. 2005. "Framing the Engineering Outsourcing Debate: Placing the United States on a Level Playing Field with China and India." Master of Engineering and Management Program, Duke University.

Gereffi, Gary, and Miguel Korzeniewicz, eds. 1993. *Commodity Chains and Global Capitalism.* Westport, Conn.: Greenwood.

Global Insight. 2005. "U.S. Truck Driver Shortage: Analysis and Forecasts," May. Available online at http://advancedmaritimetechnology.aticorp.org/short-sea-shipping/ATADriverShortageStudy05.pdf. Accessed March 7, 2010

Ginsborg, Paul. 2005. *Silvio Berlusconi: Television, Power and Patrimony.* London: Verso.

Gmelch, George. 2003. *Behind the Smile: the Working Lives of Caribbean Tourism.* Bloomington: Indiana University Press.

Goldfield, Michael. 1987. *The Decline of Organized Labor in the United States.* Chicago: University of Chicago Press.

Gonzalez, Gilbert. 2006. *Guest Workers or Colonized Labor? Mexican Labor Migration to the U.S.* Boulder, Colo.: Paradigm.

Gordon, Jennifer. 2005. *Suburban Sweatshops: The Fight for Immigrant Rights.* Cambridge, Mass.: Harvard University Press.

———. 2007. "Transnational Labor Citizenship," 80. *University of Southern California Law Review.*

Gray, John. 2000. *False Dawn: The Delusions of Global Capitalism.* New York: The New Press.

Gray, Obika. 2004. *Demeaned but Empowered: The Social Power of the Urban Poor in Jamaica.* Mona, Jamaica: University of the West Indies Press.

Greater Hyderabad Municipal Corporation. 2010. *Hyderabad: City Development Plan.* Hyderabad, India.

Greenhouse, Steven. 2004. "North Carolina Growers' Group Signs Union Contract for Mexican Workers." *New York Times,* September 17.

Grubacic, Andrej, and Staughton Lynd. 2010. *From Here to There: The Staughton Lynd Reader.* Oakland, Calif.: PM Press.

Gurney's Inn. Brochure. Available online at http://www.gurneysinn.com/Accommodations/Brochure.pdf. Accessed March 6, 2010.

Guskin, Jane, and David L. Wilson. 2007. *The Politics of Immigration: Questions and Answers.* New York: Monthly Review Press.

Hafner, Katie, and Daniel Preysman. 2003. "Special Visa's Use for Tech Workers Is Challenged." *New York Times,* June 1.

Hahamovitch, Cindy. 2001. "In America Life is Given Away: Jamaican Farmworkers and the Making of Agricultural Immigration Policy," in Catherine McNicol Stock and Robert D. Johnson, ed., *The Countryside in the Age of the Modern State: Political Histories of Rural America.* Ithaca, N.Y.: Cornell University Press, 134–60.

Hanson, Victor Davis. 2007. *Mexifornia: A State of Becoming.* San Francisco: Encounter Books.

Harvey, David. 2006. *A Brief History of Neoliberalism.* Oxford: Oxford University Press.

Haus, Leah. 2002. *Unions, Immigration, and Internationalization: New Challenges and Changing Coalitions in the U.S. and France.* New York: Palgrave Macmillan.

———. 2007. "Transnational Labor Citizenship." *Southern California Law Review,* vol. 80.

Hayworth, J. D. 2006. *Whatever It Takes: Illegal Immigration, Border Security and the War on Terror.* Washington, D.C.: Regnery.

Helgerson, John L. 2002. "Speech: The National Security Implications of Global Demographic Change." National Intelligence Council. Available online at www.cia.gov/nic/speeches_demochange.htm.

Helps, Horace. 2010. "Jamaican Police Quell Prison Riot, 45 Injured." *Reuters,* February 9. Available online at http://www.reuters.com/article/idUSN09242544. Accessed March 10, 2010.

Hill, Jennifer. 2008. "Binational Guestworker Unions: Moving Guestworkers into the House of Labor." *Fordham Urban Law Journal* 35, 307–48.

The Hindu. 2008. "Hospital to Treat Dental Patients from U.S." January 31. Available online at http://www.hinduonnet.com/2008/01/31/stories/2008013158900300.htm. Accessed August 6, 2010.

Hirsch, Barry, and David Macpherson. 2010. Union Membership and Coverage Database from the CPS (documentation). Available online at www.unionstats.com. Accessed February 24, 2010.

Hobsbawm, Eric. 2010. "Interview: World Distempers." *New Left Review* 61, January–February, 133–50.

Hoffa, James P. 2006. "Teamsters Call Senate Immigration Compromise Bill 'Shortsighted." *Freight Teamsters.* April 7. Available online at http://freightteamsters.blogspot.com/2006/04/teamsters-call-senate-immigration.html. Accessed February 1, 2010.

Hoffa, Jim. 2006. "Immigration Bill Passed by Senate Leaves Workers Behind." Official Statement of Teamsters General President. May 31. Available online at www.teamster.org/content/immigration-bill-passed-senate-leaves-workers-behind. Accessed August 6, 2010.

Hondagneu-Sotelo, Pierrette. 2001. *Doméstica: Immigrant Workers Cleaning and Caring in the Shadows of Affluence.* Berkeley: University of California Press.

Hunger, Uwe. 2002. *The "Brain Gain" Hypothesis: Third-World Elites in Industrialized Countries and Socioeconomic Development in their Home Country.* San Diego: Center for Comparative Immigration Studies. January. Working Paper 47.

Hyde, Alan. 2003. *Working in Silicon Valley: Economic and Legal Analysis of a High-Velocity Labor Market.* Armonk, N.Y.: M.E. Sharpe.

Indian Workers Solidarity Congress. 2008. *International Labour Trafficking from India to U.S.: Signal Workers on Hunger Strike for Justice.* New Delhi: Society for Labour & Development.

Industrial Workers of the World. 1905. *Industrial Union Manifesto.* Chicago: Conference of Industrial Unionists, January 2–4.

International Organization for Migration. 2005. *World Migration 2005: Costs and Benefits of International Migration.* Geneva: International Organization for Migration.

———. 2008. *World Migration, 2008: Managing Labour Mobility in the Evolving Economy.* Geneva: International Organization for Migration.

Isard, Peter. 2005. *Globalization and the International Financial System: What's Wrong and What Can be Done.* Cambridge, U.K.: Cambridge University Press.

Jacoby, Tamar. 2005a. "Speech: Immigration Reform: Politics and Prospects." Washington, D.C., American Enterprise Institute. January 10.

———. 2005b. Testimony of Tamar Jacoby before the U.S. Senate Committee on the Judiciary. Washington, D.C.: Government Printing Office, July 26.

———. 2006. "'Guest Workers' Won't Work': A Path to Permanent Citizenship Would Benefit Everyone." *Washington Post,* March 26.

Jamaica Information Service. 2007. "Jamaica's Agriculture Stands to Benefit from Spanish Tourism Investment—Ambassador Silva." Available online at www.jis .gov.jm. Accessed August 9, 2010.

———. 2010. "PSRA Setting Standards for Private Security Industry." Kingston: Ministry of National Security, January 26.

Jha, Raghbendra, ed. 2008. *The Indian Economy Sixty Years after Independence.* Houndmills, Basingstoke, Hampshire, U.K.: Palgrave Macmillan.

Joshi, Chitra. 2005. *Lost Worlds: Indian Labour and its Forgotten Histories.* London: Anthem Press.

Kabeer, Naila. 2004. "Globalization, Labor Standards, and Women's Rights: Dilemmas of Collective (In)Action in an Interdependent World." *Feminist Economics* 10, no. 1 (March): 3–35.

Kalleberg, Arne. 2003. "Flexible Firms and Labor Market Segmentation: Effects of Workplace Restructuring on Jobs and Workers," *Jobs and Occupations* 30, no. 2, 154–75.

Kalleberg, Arne L., Barbara F. Reskin, and Ken Hudson. 2000. "Bad Jobs in America: Standard and Nonstandard Employment Relations and Job Quality in the United States," *American Sociological Review* A, no. 2 (April): 256–78.

Kalleberg, Arne L., Edith Rasell, Naomi Cassirer, Barbara F. Reskin, Ken Hudson, David Webster, Eileen Applebaum, and Roberta M. Spalter-Roth. 1997. *Nonstan-*

dard Work, Substandard Jobs. Flexible Work Arrangements in the U.S. Washington, D.C.: Economic Policy Institute.

Kanstroom, Daniel. 2007. *Deportation Nation: Outsiders in American History*. Cambridge, Mass.: Harvard University Press.

Kasinitz, Philip. 1992. *Caribbean New York: Black Immigrants and the Politics of Race*. Ithaca, N.Y.: Cornell University Press.

Key, Sydney J. 2003. *The Doha Round and Financial Services Negotiations*. Washington, D.C.: AEI Press.

Khadria, Binod, ed. 2009. *India Migration Report 2009: Past, Present and the Future Outlook*. New Delhi: International Migration and Diaspora Studies Project.

Kumar, Ravi. 2008. "Against Neoliberal Assault on Education in India: A Counternarrative of Resistance." *Journal of Critical Education Policy Studies* 6, no. 1, May. Available online at www.jceps.com/index.php?pageID=articleGarticleID=112.

Kumar, V. Anil. 2005. *Farmers' Suicides in Andhra Pradesh: The Response of Political Institutions*. Hyderabad, India: Centre for Economic and Social Studies, May.

Kwong, Peter. 1999. *Forbidden Workers: Illegal Chinese Immigrants and American Labor*. New York: The New Press.

Kyōkai, Nihon Rōdō. 2003. *Migration and the Labour Market in Asia: Recent Trends and Policies*. Paris: OECD.

Lafer, Gordon. 2002. *The Job Training Charade*. Ithaca, N.Y.: Cornell University Press.

LeMay, Michael C. 2003. *U.S. Immigration: A Reference Handbook*. Santa Barbara, Calif.: ABC-CLIO.

Levesque, Karen, Doug Lauen, Peter Teitelbaum, Martha Alt, and Sally Librera. 2000. MPR Associates. *Vocational Education in the United States: Toward the Year 2000*. Washington, D.C. National Center for Education Statistics. U.S. Department of Education, Office of Educational Research and Improvement NCES 2000-029. February.

Levy, Frank, and Richard J. Murnane. 2004. *The New Division of Labor: How Computers Are Creating the Next Job Market*. Princeton, N.J.: Princeton University Press.

Lieten, G. K., and Alakh N. Sharma. 2007. *Globalization and Social Exclusion*. New Delhi: Institute for Human Development.

Lynd, Staughton. 1992. *Solidarity Unionism: Rebuilding the Labor Movement from Below*. Chicago: Charles H. Kerr.

———. 2008. "Commentary: Another World is Possible." *Working USA: The Journal of Labor and Society* 11, no. 1, March.

Maharidge, Dale. 2005. *Denison, Iowa: Searching for the Soul of America through the Secrets of a Midwest Town*. New York: The Free Press.

Maimbo, Samuel Munzele, and Ratha Dilip. 2005. *Remittances: Development Impact and Future Prospects*. Washington: The World Bank.

Mandel, Ernest. 1991. "Introduction." In Karl Marx, *Capital: A Critique of Political Economy, Volume III*. London: Penguin Books.

Mandel, Ernest. 1995. *Long Waves of Capitalist Development: A Marxist Interpretation*. Rev. ed. London: Verso.

Martin, Philip L. 2009. *Importing Poverty? Immigration and the Changing Face of Rural America.* New Haven, Conn.: Yale University Press.

Martin, Philip, Manolo Abella, and Christiane Kuptsch. 2006. *Managing Labor Migration in the Twenty-first Century.* New Haven, Conn.: Yale University Press.

Marx, Karl. 1867/1915. *Capital: A Critique of Political Economy, Volume I,* 443–44. Chicago: Charles H. Kerr.

Massey, Douglas S. 2003. *Beyond Smoke and Mirrors: Mexican Immigration in an Era of Economic Integration.* New York: Russell Sage Foundation.

Massey, Douglas S., Joaquin Arango, Graeme Hugo, Ali Kouaouci, Adela Pelligrino, and J. Edward Taylor. 1993. "Theories of International Migration: A Review and Appraisal." *Population and Development Review* 19, no. 3 (September): 431–66.

Matloff, Norman. 2002. "Debunking the Myth of a Desperate Software Labor Shortage." Testimony to the U.S. House Judiciary Committee, Subcommittee on Immigration, April 21, 1998 (updated December 9, 2002).

Mattoo, A., and A. G. Carzaniga, eds. 2003. *Moving People to Deliver Services.* Washington, D.C.: The World Bank and Oxford University Press.

McCarthy, J. C. 2004. *Near-Term Growth of Offshoring Accelerating: Resizing U.S. Services Jobs Going Offshore.* Cambridge, Mass.: Forrester Research.

Meetings Net. 2001. "Industry in Crisis: A State of the Industry Post 9/11." Available online at http://meetingsnet.com/news/meetings_industry_crisis_state/index .html. Accessed November 6, 2001.

Middlehurst, Robin, and Steve Woodfield. 2004. *Summary Report: The Role of Transnational, Private, and For-Profit Provision in Meeting Global Demand for Tertiary Education: Mapping, Regulation and Impact—Case Study Jamaica.* Vancouver: Commonwealth of Learning/UNESCO.

Migration Policy Institute. 1999. "INS: Fewer Workplace Raids." *Migration News,* April, 6:4.

Milkman, Ruth. 2006. *L.A. Story: Immigrant Workers and the Future of the U.S. Labor Movement.* New York: Russell Sage Foundation.

Milkman, Ruth, ed. 2000. *Organizing Immigrants: The Challenge for Unions in Contemporary California.* Ithaca, N.Y.: Cornell University Press.

Mink, Gwendolyn. 1990. *Old Labor and New Immigrants in American Political Development: Union, Party and State 1875–1920.* Ithaca, N.Y.: Cornell University Press.

Mishra, Pankaj. 2006. "The Myth of the New India." *New York Times.* July 6.

Mississippi Immigrant Rights Alliance. 2007. Available online at http://www .yourmira.org/. Accessed September 2, 2007.

Munck, Ronaldo. 2005. *Globalization and Social Exclusion: a Transformationalist Perspective.* Bloomfield, Conn.: Kumarian Press.

Morstead, Stuart, and Greg Blount. 2003. *Offshore Ready: Strategies to Plan & Profit from Offshore IT-Enabled Services.* Flower Mound, Tex.: ISANI Press.

NASSCOM. 2010. Available online at http://www.nasscom.in/ Accessed March 8, 2010.

National Research Council. 2001. *Building a Workforce for the Information Economy.* Washington, D.C.: National Academy Press.

National Sample Survey Organisation, Ministry of Statistics and Programme Implementation, Government of India. 2006. "Press Note on Level and Pattern of Consumption Expenditure, 2004–05," Report No. 508, December 27.

National Workers Union. 2010. "A New Union with Old Values: Organise the Unorganised, Workers of the World Unite." Available online at http://www .workersunion.org.tt/system/app/pages/search?q=temporary+workers&scope =search-site. Accessed July 28, 2010.

Nayyar, Rohini, and Alakh N. Sharma. 2005. *Rural Transformation in India: The Role of Non-farm Sector.* New Delhi: Institute for Human Development.

Ness, Immanuel. 2005. *Immigrants Unions and the New U.S. Labor Market.* Philadelphia: Temple University Press.

Nevins, Joseph. 2001. *Operation Gatekeeper: The Rise of the "Illegal Alien" and the Remaking of the U.S.–Mexico Boundary.* New York: Routledge.

Neumark, David, ed. 2000. *On the Job: Is Long-Term Employment a Thing of the Past?* New York: Russell Sage Foundation.

Ngai, Mae M. 2005. *Impossible Subjects: Illegal Aliens and the Making of Modern America.* Princeton, N.J.: Princeton University Press.

Nilekani, Nandan. 2009. *Imagining India: The Idea of a Renewed Nation.* New York: Penguin Press.

NOSTOPS: National Organization for Software and Technology Professionals. "Real Jobs, Real People: Identifying the Good Apples, Promoting the Best and Brightest." Available online at http://www.nostops.org/. Accessed September 2, 2007.

Obama, Barack. 2008. *The Audacity of Hope: Thoughts on Reclaiming the American Dream.* New York: Random House.

OECD. 2001. *International Mobility and the Highly Skilled.* Paris: Organization for Economic Co-Operation and Development.

———. 2009. *OECD.Stat Extracts: Demography and Population, Migration Statistics.* Database on Immigrants in OECD Countries. Available online at http://stats.oecd .org/Index.aspx?DataSetCode=MIG#.

OMCAP. Office of Trade and Industry Information, Manufacturing and Services. 2006. National Trade Data. International Trade Administration, U.S. Department of Commerce: Washington, D.C. Available online at http://tse.export.gov/ NTDMapPP.aspx?UniqueURL=dtkj5ranxj1s414xtb1m045-2006-4-21-2006.

Orren, Karen. 1991. *Belated Feudalism: Labor, the Law and Liberal Development in the United States.* New York: Cambridge University Press.

Papademetriou, Demetrios G., and Stephen Yale-Loehr. 1996. *Balancing Interests: Rethinking U.S. Selection of Skilled Immigrants.* New York: International Migration Policy Program of the Carnegie Endowment for International Peace.

Papadopoulos, Dimitris, Niamh Stephenson, and Vassilis Tsianos. 2009. *Escape Routes: Control and Subversion in the Twenty-first Century.* London: Pluto Press.

Pattullo, Polly. 2005. *The Cost of Tourism in the Caribbean.* New York: Monthly Review Press.

Peet, Richard. 2003. *Unholy Trinity: The IMF, World Bank, and WTO.* London: Zed Books.

Pellow, David N., and Lisa Sun Hee Park. 2002. *The Silicon Valley of Dreams: Environmental Injustice, Immigrant Workers and the High-Tech Global Economy.* New York: New York University Press.

Phillips, Kate. 2006. "Business Lobbyists Call for Action on Immigration." *New York Times,* April 15.

Phillips, Nicola. 2009. "Migration as Development Strategy? The New Political Economy of Dispossession and Inequality in the Americas." *Review of International Political Economy* 16, no. 2, 231–59.

Piven, Frances Fox, and Richard Cloward. 1993. *Regulating the Poor: The Functions of Public Welfare.* New York: Vintage.

Piven, Frances Fox, and Richard A. Cloward. 2000. "Power Repertoires and Globalization." *Politics & Society* 28, no. 3, 413–30.

Portes, Alejandro, and Rubén G. Rumbaut. 2006. *Immigrant America: A Portrait.* Berkeley: University of California Press.

Preston, Peter Wallace, and Jürgen Haacke. 2003. *Contemporary China: The Dynamics of Change at the Start of the New Millennium.* London: Routledge.

Puri, Shivani, and Tineke Ritzema. 1999. *Migrant Worker Remittances, Micro-finance and the Informal Economy: Prospects and Issues.* Geneva: International Labour Organization, Working Paper Number 21.

Purkayashtha, Debapratim. 2008. "Labor Unrest at Signal International." Hyderabad, India: ICFAI Center for Management Research, 2008, 2.

Rajan, Ramkishen S. 2009. *Monetary Investment and Trade Issues in India.* New York: Oxford University Press.

Rajeev, M. 2007. "Fresh Way of Hope for Trained Truckers." *The Hindu,* May 6. Available online at http://www.thehindu.com/2007/05/06/stories/2007050617000100.htm. Accessed August 20, 2007.

Ratha, Dilip. 2008. "As the economic crisis deepens, migration and remittances has become even more important for development." *blogs.worldbank.org.* December 18. Available online at http://blogs.worldbank.org/peoplemove/as-the-economic-crisis-deepens.

Regional Labour Board. 2004. *Exporting Labour in the 21st Century—Strategic Outreach Plan for the Expansion of the H-2B Programme.* Kingston: Ministry of Labour & Social Security.

Reynolds, Marylee. 2008. "The War on Drugs, Prison Building, and Globalization: Catalysts for the Global Incarceration of Women." *NWSA Journal* 20, no. 2 (Summer): 72–95.

Richardson, Bonham C. 1986. *Panama Money in Barbados, 1900–1920.* Knoxville: University of Tennessee Press.

Rodriguez, Arturo S. 2006. Statement by Arturo S. Rodriguez Announcing UFW Contract with Global Horizons. Seattle, April 11.

Rodriguez, Robyn Margalit. 2010. *Migrants for Export: How the Philippine State Brokers Labor to the World*. Minneapolis: University of Minnesota Press.

Sakthivel, S., and Pinaki Joddar. 2006. "Unorganized Sector Workforce in India: Trends Patterns and Social Security Coverage." *Economic and Political Weekly*, May 27.

Samuelson, Paul A. 2004. "Where Ricardo and Mill Rebut and Confirm Arguments of Mainstream Economists Supporting Globalization." *Journal of Economic Perspectives* 18, no. 3 (Summer): 135–46.

Sassen, Saskia. 1991. *The Global City: New York, London, Tokyo*. Princeton, N.J.: Princeton University Press.

———. 2006. *Territory, Authority, Rights: From Medieval to Global Assemblages*. Princeton, N.J.: Princeton University Press.

Saxenian, Anna Lee. 2006. *The New Argonauts: Regional Advantage in a Global Economy*. Cambridge, Mass.: Harvard University Press.

Seminara, David. 2010. *Dirty Work: In-Sourcing American Jobs with H-2B Guestworkers*. Washington, D.C.: Center for Immigration Studies.

Sen, Sukomal. 1997. *Working Class India: History of Emergence and Movement 1830–1990*. 2nd ed. Calcutta: K.P. Bagchi.

Shailor, Barbara 2007. "International Trafficking in Persons: Taking Action to Eliminate Modern Day Slavery." House Committee on Foreign Affairs, Washington, D.C., October 18.

Sharma, Alakh N, Rajeev Sharma, and Nikhil Raj. Undated. *Child Labor in Carpet Industry: Impact of Social Labelling in India*. New Delhi: Institute for Human Development.

Sheshabalaya, Ashutosh. 2005. *Rising Elephant: The Growing Clash With India Over White-Collar Jobs and its Challenge to America and the World*. Monroe, Maine: Common Courage Press.

Shrinivasan, Rukmini. 2010. "55% of India's Population Poor: Report." *The Times of India*, July 15, 2010. Available online at http://timesofindia.indiatimes.com/india/55-of-Indias-population-poor-Report/articleshow/6169549.cms. Accessed July 26, 2010.

Shulman, Robin. 2007. "Immigration Raid Rips Families: Illegal Workers in Massachusetts Separated from Children." *Washington Post*, March 18. Available online at http://www.washingtonpost.com/wp-dyn/content/article/2007/03/17/AR2007031701113.html. Accessed February 16, 2010.

Sinclair, Upton. 2004 [1906]. *The Jungle*. New York: Simon & Schuster.

Smith, Michael Peter. 2000. *Transnational Urbanism: Locating Globalism*. Oxford: Blackwell.

Smith, Robert Courtney. 2006. *Mexican New York: Transnational Lives of New Immigrants*. Berkeley: University of California Press.

Smith-Nonini, Sandy. 2009. "H2A Guest Workers and the State of North Carolina: From Transnational Production to Transnational Organizing," in Fran Ansley and Jon Shefner, ed., *Global Connections and Local Receptions: New Latino Immigration to the Southeastern United States*. Knoxville: University of Tennessee Press.

Southern Poverty Law Center. 2007. "Close to Slavery: Guestworker Programs in the United States." Available online at http://www.splcenter.org/index.jsp. Accessed April 8, 2009.

Spirit Cultural Exchange. 2006. "H2B America — Participants." Available online at http://spiritexchange.com/programs/prog_part_h2b.html. Accessed March 23, 2006.

Srinivas, Alam. 2008. *The Indian Consumer: One Billion Myths, One Billion Realities*. Singapore: John Wiley & Sons.

Srinivasulu, K, V. Anil Kumar, and K.S. Vijaya Sekhar. 2004. *Crisis in Handloom Sector in Andhra Pradesh: The Ways Forward*. Hyderabad, India: Centre for Economic and Social Studies, September.

Staudt, Kathleen, and Irasema Coronado. 2002. *Fronteras No Mas: Toward Social Justice at the U.S.-Mexico Border*. New York: Palgrave Macmillan.

Steinberg, Stephen. 2006. "Immigration, African Americans, and Race Discourse," in Marable Manning, Immanuel Ness, and Joseph Wilson, ed., *Race and Labor Matters in the New U.S. Economy*. Lanham, Md.: Rowman and Littlefield.

Sullivan, Abby. 2008–09. "On Thin ICE: Cracking Down on the Racial Profiling of Immigrants and Implementing a Compassionate Enforcement Policy." *Hastings Race & Poverty Law Journal* 6, no. 1, 101.

Swarns, Rachel L. 2006. "Immigrants Rally in Scores of Cities for Legal Status." *New York Times*, April 11.

Sweeney, John J. 2004. "Statement by AFL-CIO President John J. Sweeney on President Bush's Principles for Immigration Reform." Washington, D.C., AFL-CIO press release, January 8.

Supreme Court of the United States. 2002. *Hoffman Plastic Compounds, Inc. v. National Labor Relations Board*. Certiorari to the United States Court of Appeals for the District of Columbia Circuit. No. 00-1595.

Tancredo, Tom. 2006. *In Mortal Danger: The Battle for America's Border and Security*. Nashville, Tenn.: Cumberland House.

Taylor, Marcia, and Dori Finley. 2008. "Communication Training for Foreign Guest Workers in Seasonal Resorts." *Business Communication Quarterly* 71, no. 2, 246–50.
———. 2009. "Three Views of 'guest workers' in the United States." *International Journal of Contemporary Hospitality Management* 2 1/2, 191–200.

Thaindian News. 2008. "U.S. job racket agents' licenses suspended," March 2008, p. 11. Available online at http://www.thaindian.com/newsportal/uncategorized/us-job-racket-agents-licences-suspended_10026348.html. Accessed August 13, 2009.

Thakur, Atul. 2007. "A Myth Called the Indian Middle Class." *The Times of India* (Kolkata edition), September 17, p. 9.

Thakurta, Paranjoy Gura. 2010. *The 2009 General Elections in India: An Analysis.* Singapore: Institute of South Asian Studies. Number 70. July 3.

Thatchenkery, Tojo Joseph, and Roger Stough. 2005. *Information Communication Technology and Economic Development: Learning from the Indian Experience.* Cheltenham, U.K.: Edward Elgar.

Thomas, Deborah. 2003. "Seasonal Labor, Global Vision; Jamaica Woman & the U.S. Hospitality Industry." Available online at www.yorku.ca/cerlac/migration/documents.htm.

Thomas, Norman. 2005. "Probe into Jamaican Prison Riot Underway." Caribbean Net News, April 4. Available online at http://www.caribbeannetnews.com/2005/04/02/prison.shtml.

TimesOnline. 2007. "Gordon Brown's Vow to Send Foreign Inmates Home is Questioned," October 25. Available online at www.timesonline.co.uk/tol/news/politics/article/2733663/ece.

Uchitelle, Louis. 2007. *The Disposable American: Layoffs and their Consequences.* New York: Vintage Books.

United Nations. 2002. Press Release POP/844, United Nations, October 28.

———. 2005. The Population Division of the Department of Economic and Social Affairs. *Trends in Total Migrant Stock: The 2003 Revision.* New York: United Nations Press Office.

———. 2006a. Department of Economic and Social Affairs, Population Division. "International Migration and Development." Thirty-Ninth Session, April 3–7. Available online at http://www.un.org/esa/population/cpd/comm2006.htm.

———. 2006b. Commission on Population and Development, *United Nations Economic and Social Council.* Commission on Population and Development, April 3, 39th session, 2nd Meeting, United Nations: New York.

———. 2008. *Trends in Migrant Stock: The 2008 Revision.* Data in digital form. New York: United Nations.

UNFPA. 2005. *State of the World Population 2005.* New York: United Nations Population Fund.

U.S. Census Bureau. 2007. "State Rankings—Statistical Abstract of the United States: Personal Income Per Capita in Current Dollars, 2007." Available online at http://www.census.gov/compendia/statab/2010/ranks/rank29.html. Accessed March 7, 2010.

U.S. Department of Labor, Bureau of Labor Statistics. 2006a. "Union Members in 2005." Available online at ftp:/ftp.bls.gov/pub/news.release/union2.txt.

———. 2006b. "Labor Force Statistics from the Current Population Survey: Series LNU04032237." Available online at http://data.bls.gov/servlet/SurveyOutputServlet?&series_id=LNU04032237. Accessed February 26, 2006.

———. 2007. "Labor Force Statistics from the Current Population Survey." Available online at http://www.bls.gov/cps/cpslutabs.htm. Accessed August 4, 2010.

————. 2010. *Occupational Outlook Handbook*. Washington, D.C.: U.S. Department of Labor.

U.S. Department of State. 2008. *Foreign Affairs Manual, Volume 9—Visas*. Available online at http://www.state.gov/documents/organization/87232.pdf. Accessed December 22, 2009.

U.S. House of Representatives. 1999. *Congressional Record*. Washington, D.C.: Government Printing Office. November.

U.S. Immigration and Customs Enforcement. 2009. "Enforcement and Removal Operations." Available online at http://www.ice.gov/pi/news/factsheets/worksite .htm. Accessed August 2, 2010.

U.S. Trade Representative. 2005. "U.S. Submits Revised Services Offer to the WTO." Press release. Available online at www.ustr.gov/Docuent_Library/Press_ Releases/2005/MayU.S. Submits_Revised_Services_offer_to_the_WTO.

USCIS. 2004a. "USCIS to Implement L-1 Reform Act of 2004: New Law Changes Aspects of the Temporary Work Program." Washington, D.C., U.S. Department of Homeland Security Press Office. December 8.

————. 2004b. Immigration and Nationality Act: INA 203: Allocation of Immigration Visas. Sec 203 [8 USC. 1153]. Washington, D.C., Department of Homeland Security. Available online at http://uscis.gov/lpBin/lpext.dll/inserts/slb/slb-1/slb -21/slb-1261?f=templates&fn=document-frame.htm#slb-act203.

————. 2005. "USCIS to Implement H-1B Visa Reform Act of 2004." Washington, D.C., U.S. Department of Homeland Security Press Office, March 8.

————. 2010a. Immigration Reform and Control Act of 1986 (IRCA). Available online at http://www.uscis.gov/portal/site/uscis/menuitem.5af9bb95919f35e66 f614176543f6d1a/?vgnextchannel=b328194d3e88d010VgnVCM10000048f3d6 a1RCRD&vgnextoid=04a295c4f635f010VgnVCM1000000ecd190aRCRD, Accessed March 5, 2010.

————. 2010b. Immigration Act of 1990. Available online at http://www.uscis.gov/ portal/site/uscis/menuitem.5af9bb95919f35e66f614176543f6d1a/?vgnextoid=84ff9 5c4f635f010VgnVCM1000000ecd190aRCRD&vgnextchannel=b328194d3e88d010 VgnVCM10000048f3d6a1RCRD. Accessed August 2, 2010.

Van der Linden, Marcel. 1999. "Transnationalizing American Labor." *Journal of American History* 86, no. 3 (December): 1078–92.

Velazquez, Baldemar. 2007. Statement, Baldemar Velazquez, President Farm Laborers Organizing Committee (FLOC), AFL-CIO to U.S. House of Representatives, Committee on Education and Labor. "Protecting U.S. and Guest Workers: the Recruitment and Employment of Foreign Labor," June 7. Available online at http:// edlabor.house.gov/testimony/060707BaldemarVelasquezTestimony.pdf.

Vogel, Richard D. 2007. "Transient Servitude: The U.S. Guest Worker Program for Exploiting Mexican and Central American Workers." *Monthly Review* 58, no. 7 (January): 1–23.

Waldinger, Roger. 1999. *Still the Promised City? African-Americans and New Immigrants in Postindustrial New York.* Cambridge, Mass.: Harvard University Press.

Waldinger, Roger, and Michael I. Lichter. 2003. *How the Other Half Works: Immigration and the Social Organization of Labor.* Berkeley: University of California Press.

Waldman, Amy. 2005. "Mile by Mile, India Paves a Smoother Road to its Future." *New York Times,* December 4.

Wall Street Journal. 2006. "Immigration and the GOP: Is it Still the Party of Reagan, or of Tom Tancredo?" March 31. Available online at www.opinionjournal.com/editorial/feature.html?id=110008164REVIEW & OUTLOOK.

Wang, Jing. 2008. *Brand New China: Advertising, Media, and Commercial Culture.* Cambridge, Mass.: Harvard University Press.

The White House. 2006. "Comprehensive Immigration Reform: Securing Our Border." Washington, D.C., April 24. Available online at www.whitehouse.gov/infocus/immigration.

Wilson, Michael J. 2007. "Testimony on Behalf of the United Food and Commercial Workers Union (UFCW) Before the House Subcommittee on Immigration, Citizenship, Refugees, Border Security and International Law of the Committee on the Judiciary: Labor Movement Perspectives on Comprehensive Immigration Reform," Washington, D.C., May 24.

The World Bank. 2005. *World Development Indicators Database.* Washington, D.C.: The World Bank Group. Available online at http://web.worldbank.org/WBSITE/EXTERNAL/COUNTRIES EASTASIAPACIFICEXT/CHINAEXTN/0,menuPK:318956~pagePK:141159~piPK:141110~theSite PK:318950,00.html. Accessed March 19, 2006.

———. 2006. *Global Economic Prospects: Economic Implications of Remittances and Migration: 2006.* Washington, D.C.: The World Bank.

———. 2009a. *Regional Cooperation & Integration—Energy: Opportunity for Trade.* Available online at http://web.worldbank.org/WBSITE/EXTERNAL/COUNTRIES/SOUTHASIAEXT/0,contentMDK:21510953~pagePK:146736~piPK:146830~theSitePK:223547,00.html. Accessed April 8, 2009.

———. 2009b *New Global Poverty Estimates: What it Means for India.* Available online at http://www.worldbank.org.in/WBSITE/EXTERNAL/COUNTRIES/SOUTHASIAEXT/INDIAEXTN/0,contentMDK:21880725~pagePK:141137~piPK:141127~theSitePK:295584,00.html. Accessed April 8, 2009.

World Bank Group. 2008. *World Development Report 2009: Reshaping Economic Geography.* Washington, D.C.: World Bank Publications.

Worthen, B. 2003. "The Radicalization of Mike Emmons." *CIO Magazine,* September 1.

Xiang Biao. 2006. *Global 'Body Shopping': An Indian Labor System in the Information Technology Industry.* Princeton, N.J.: Princeton University Press.

Zakaria, Fareed. 2008. *The Post-American World.* New York: W.W. Norton.

Zavodny, Madeline. 2003. "The H-1B Program and Its Effects on Information Technology Workers." *Economic Review,* Federal Reserve Bank of Atlanta, third quarter.
Zhu, Ming M. 2010. The Page Act of 1875: In the Name of Morality (March 23, 2010). Available online at SSRN: http://ssrn.com/abstract=1577213. Accessed August 4, 2010.
Zolberg, Aristede R. 2006. *Nation by Design: Immigration Policy in the Fashioning of America.* Cambridge, Mass.: Harvard University Press.

Interviews

WORKERS

John Bauman, Engineer, president, TORAW, Queens, New York, August 10, 2004
Mike Blain, IT worker, organizer, Washtech/CWA, Seattle, Washington, July 6, 2004
Mike Emmons, IT worker, Lake Mary, Florida, August 20, 2005 (telephone)
Rob Sanchez, Web site administrator, www.zazona.com, June 9, 2005 (telephone, from Arizona)
Sona Shah, IT worker, New Jersey, March 18, 2005 (telephone)

ANONYMOUS WORKER INTERVIEWS

Five anonymous high-technology and business service workers, October 9, 2005, Mumbai, India
Twenty-two anonymous workers applying for or enrolled in H-2B Guest Worker Program, Kingston Jamaica, February 14–17, 2006
Six anonymous interviews, returning H-2B guest workers and J1 students, Kingston, Jamaica, February 14–15, 2006
Seven anonymous Jamaican workers employed as H-2B workers in the United States, from March 12, 2006, Brooklyn, New York, and Nantucket, Massachusetts, August 2008
Thirty-eight anonymous workers, Hyderabad/Telangana, November 2006–February 2007, assisted by Dr. Arun Kumar, Centre for Economic and Social Studies, Hyderabad, Andhra Pradesh

OTHER INTERVIEWS

Amiya Kumar Bagchi, Kolkata, Kolkata, West Bengal, India, December 18, 2008
Debdas Banerjee, Kolkata, West Bengal, India, October 5, 2005, and December 18, 2008
Ken Barger, Farm Laborers Organizing Committee, AFL-CIO, September 18, 2005
Anannya Bhattacharya, secretary, Society for Labour and Development, New Delhi, India, December 15, 2008
Charles Calvert, University of South Carolina, Beaufort, Department of Hospitality Management, January 20, 2006
Guduras Dasgupta, All-India Trade Union Congress, New Delhi, India, December 19, 2008

Donna S. Dewitt, president, South Carolina AFL-CIO, St. Helena Island, South Carolina, September 20, 2008

Alex Julca, economic affairs officer, United Nations, January 11, 2010

Gregory Junemann, president, International Federation of Professional and Technical Engineers (IFPTE), September 17, 2005 (telephone)

Arun Kumar, Centre for Economic and Social Studies, Hyderabad, Andhra Pradesh, December 16–17, 2008

Kevin Gusscott, researcher/graduate student, Kingston, Jamaica, February 15, 2008

Vincent Morrison, president, Jamaica National Workers Union (JNWU), February 20, 2006

M. K. Pandhe, vice president, Centre of Indian Trade Unions (CITU), New Delhi, India, December 18, 2008.

Arun Patnaik, Central University of Hyderabad, Andhra Pradesh, October 7, 2005; December 17, 2008

Shri Aseem Prakash, senior fellow, Institute for Human Development, New Delhi, September 29, 2005

Prakash C. Sarangi, Central University of Hyderabad, Andhra Pradesh, October 6, 2005

Tapan Sen, general secretary, Centre of Indian Trade Unions (CITU), New Delhi, India, December 10, 2008

Alakh N. Sharma, director, Institute for Human Development, Lucknow, India, December 9, 2008

Karin Astrid Siegmann, Institute for Social Studies, Rotterdam, The Netherlands, New York, June 29, 2009

Index

IMMANUEL NESS is a professor of political science at Brooklyn College, City University of New York. He is the author of *Real World Labor* and *Immigrants, Unions, and the U.S. Labor Market.*

The University of Illinois Press
is a founding member of the
Association of American University Presses.

Composed in 10.5/13 Minion Pro
with Meta Medium display
by Celia Shapland
at the University of Illinois Press
Manufactured by Sheridan Books, Inc.

University of Illinois Press
1325 South Oak Street
Champaign, IL 61820-6903
www.press.u illinois.edu